The Death of Jesus in Luke–Acts

The Death of
JESUS
in Luke–Acts

BY JOSEPH B. TYSON

UNIVERSITY OF SOUTH CAROLINA PRESS

Tyson, Joseph B.
  The death of Jesus in Luke–Acts.

  Bibliography: p.
  Includes index.
  1. Jesus Christ—Trial. 2. Jesus Christ—Crucifixion.
3. Bible. N.T. Luke—Criticism, interpretation, etc.
4. Bible. N.T. Acts—Criticism, interpretation, etc.
I. Title.
BT431.T97 1986   226'.406   85–32288
ISBN 0–87249–461–6

TO PEGGY

CONTENTS

The discipline of New Testament studies has witnessed an amazing methodological proliferation during the last quarter-century. New ways of studying these ancient texts have been vigorously proposed and aggressively pursued. Among the most promising developments have been those that apply methods from other disciplines, such as the social sciences and literary criticism. These developments promise to deepen and broaden our understanding of the NT texts and of the world in which they were produced.

This book is an attempt to deepen the understanding of one NT author—Luke—through the application of literary-critical methods. In order to sharpen the focus it treats one principal issue. This issue is, however, the most dramatic segment of the gospel of Luke and the central event in Luke–Acts, the death of Jesus.

The key questions that are treated focus on the meaning of the text in its original context rather than on its historical accuracy or its relevance for contemporary theology. Attention is thus given to the intention of the author and the understanding of the first readers of Luke–Acts.

All books begin with assumptions, and this one is no exception. I assume that both the gospel of Luke and the book of Acts were written in Greek by the same person and that they appeared in the last quarter of the first century. Further, I assume that the two books were intended to be read consecutively and that they tell a

single story that begins with Zechariah in Jerusalem and ends with
Paul in Rome. Finally, I assume that the author was acquainted
with at least some of the ways of writing narratives and that he
made use of literary techniques that were available in the Hellenistic world of the first century.

It is normal to think of the Lukan passion narrative when one
thinks of Luke's treatment of the death of Jesus. This narrative has
been treasured and loved for many centuries, and it has received its
share of critical attention. In fact, however, Luke's treatment of the
death of Jesus is not confined to the passion narrative; nor is it confined to his gospel. The earlier parts of the gospel build toward it
and anticipate it, and the book of Acts recalls it and reflects on its
implications. Thus, all sections of Luke–Acts contribute to the
forging of a particular understanding of the forces that brought
about Jesus' death. For these reasons, we will range through both
the gospel of Luke and the book of Acts.

There are significant problems with treating Luke–Acts or any
other early Christian documents as literature, and there are per-
plexing questions about the ways in which one does literary criticism. These problems will be discussed in chapter 1. In chapters 2–5
we will examine the ways in which the Lukan Jesus and his followers engaged in conflict, who the opponents were, and what were
the circumstances that led to the crucifixion. In chapter 6, we examine the question of the distinctiveness of Luke by comparing his
treatment of the death of Jesus with that in Matthew and Mark. Finally we summarize the conclusions and make some suggestions
about the coherence of Luke's treatment and about his community.

Portions of chapter 2 have been revised from material that originally appeared in my article "The Jewish Public in Luke–Acts,"
New Testament Studies 30 (1984): 574–83. I am grateful to *New
Testament Studies* and Cambridge University Press for their permission to use this material.

Portions of chapter 3 originally appeared, in a different form, in
my article "Conflict as a Literary Theme in the Gospel of Luke," in
New Synoptic Studies, edited by William R. Farmer (Mercer University Press, 1983), pp. 303–27.

Transliteration of Greek follows the guidelines of the Society of
Biblical Literature's *Member Handbook* (1980), except that I have

consistently used the letter *u* for the Greek upsilon. Abbreviations of Biblical books also follow the guidelines of the Society of Biblical Literature.

I am indebted to a number of people for their helpful comments on this work as it has progressed. I particularly wish to thank Professors Donald L. Jones of the University of South Carolina; David P. Moessner, Columbia Theological Seminary; and Franklin W. Young, Duke University, who read the entire manuscript in an earlier version. David B. Peabody and Eugene H. Lovering, Jr., provided invaluable aid as research assistants. Although none of the above bears any responsibility for the final shape of the book, their suggestions and comments have helped to make it clearer and more accurate than it would have been otherwise. I am also grateful to the administration of Southern Methodist University for providing me valuable time for a research leave at a critical stage in the preparation of the manuscript.

ONE

Luke–Acts and Literary Criticism

The death of Jesus is of central importance in all four NT gospels. All contain anticipations of it and signs that point to its meaning. The attentive reader of any of these gospels is led to expect a narrative about Jesus' death at the climactic point. The scenes that immediately precede the death, including Jesus' last supper with his disciples and the various trial narratives, constitute a large portion of the gospels, considering quantity alone. Martin Kähler's description of the gospels as "passion narratives with extended introductions"[1] is widely accepted and points to the significance of the death of Jesus in the gospel tradition.

The attention which the evangelists paid to Jesus' death is a measure of its importance in the Christian community as a whole. Although there are early documents that do not contain narratives about the crucifixion or even allusions to it, there still is evidence of a preponderant interest in it in the early church. It appears to be both a problem and a promise. It was a problem for belief in Jesus as Messiah, for contemporary Jewish expectation provided little or no basis for belief in a Messiah who had died. But it was also perceived as a promise, because resurrection narratives were coupled with passion narratives and thus Jesus' death could be presented as the means for his elevation to a new form of existence. Moreover, in view of the association of Jesus' death with expectations of redemption, early Christians tended to focus a great deal of attention on the crucifixion.

3

The death of Jesus has received a great deal of attention also in the history of NT scholarship. Perhaps most of the interest, on the part of critical scholarship, has been in investigating the historical aspects of the crucifixion. When did it occur? Who was responsible for it? What was the legal process which led to it? What charges were brought against Jesus? These and similar questions have governed many if not most critical approaches to the death of Jesus.[2]

But some scholars have devoted attention to a different aspect of Jesus' death and have inquired about the various ways in which it was interpreted in the early Christian communities. Clearly, the letters of Paul lend themselves more easily to this kind of study than to the investigation of the historical events associated with the crucifixion. But the gospels also have been searched for theological meaning as well as for historical information. Mark especially has been studied extensively in this regard, but the others have not been neglected.[3]

The purpose of the present study is to investigate the meaning that the death of Jesus has in the two-volume work, Luke–Acts. In this study the writings will be approached holistically. The assumption that one person wrote the two books, a judgment on which both ancient and modern scholars concur, will be taken seriously. This is not to suggest that an individual named Luke composed his books without benefit of previous traditions or sources, but it is to affirm that one person is responsible for Luke–Acts in its final written form. The way in which this narrative is organized, the treatment of recurrent themes, the various characterizations, though probably influenced by tradition or source, were finally the results of the literary activity of an individual. It is thus to be expected that one will gain insight into the theological thought of this person by paying special attention to his written work in its final form.

The prologue to Acts (1:1–3) suggests that the author expected the reader, Theophilus by name, to read the two books consecutively, if not one immediately after the other. But modern critical scholars have not, it seems, taken this suggestion seriously.[4] Although there are investigations of the crucifixion in Luke and studies of the theology of the death of Jesus in Acts, there has not been, to my knowledge, a study that examines the meaning of this central phenomenon in the two writings together. Except in commentaries there have been few efforts to work through the gospel of Luke holistically, until quite recently.[5] For a variety of reasons there has been a greater tendency to study the synoptic gospels in fragments than as wholes. Although the Acts of the Apostles has not often been studied in the same fragmenting way that the gospel of Luke has, the lack of a holistic treatment of one volume means the lack of treatment of the whole.

To concentrate on a writing in holistic fashion is to emphasize an aspect of the literary character of that writing. Thus, this exercise will be a form of literary criticism; i.e., it will be based on the assumption that Luke–Acts is a literary composition, although it is one that is set within the context of a developing religious tradition and makes use of earlier sources.

Developments in two areas of NT scholarship have prepared the way for literary-critical work on the gospels and Acts and have made it potentially fruitful to read these books holistically. These developments have occurred primarily in areas relating to the study of the synoptic gospels. Although they appear to have less immediate relevance for the study of Acts, they necessarily affect our treatment of Luke–Acts as a whole. The developments to be considered have occurred in redaction criticism and source criticism.

REDACTION CRITICISM

Redaction criticism has been most useful in the study of the synoptic gospels. On the assumption that there is a particular documentary relationship among these gospels, redaction critics have attempted to identify the actual editorial work that each of the evangelists did. It is assumed that each writer possessed written and perhaps oral sources and that his task was to edit these materials in order to produce a coherent writing that would give expression not only to the tradition but also to his own particular theological concepts. The editorial work would be most visible in chronological and geographical notes, scene-setting devices, transitional sections, and interpretative glosses. But it would also be seen in the arrangement of the material and the structure of the gospel as a whole. Moreover, in cases where it seems reasonable to say that one of the synoptic writers used another gospel as a source, the changes that the later evangelist made are identifiable and serve as signs of his redactional activity.[6]

Norman R. Petersen has recently shown that redaction criticism has implicitly brought NT scholarship to the threshold of literary criticism.[7] It has done so, says Petersen, by questioning, again implicitly, the historical model on which previous critical studies were based. He explains that NT form criticism made use of an evolutionary model of history, in which the events of Jesus' life were thought to have been transmitted by means of oral traditions, which in time were collected and became sources, written and oral, for the earliest Christian gospels.[8] In other words, the traditions evolved into the gospels. In this model it is appropriate to think of the gospels as products of the community that preserved and transmitted the traditions and to think of the evangelists as, for the most part, compilers of traditions. Thus, the gospels are not literary documents, since no individual authors composed them.

But Petersen claims that redaction criticism has brought about the collapse of this evolutionary model, because it actually treats the gospels as literary documents. Redaction critics do not eliminate the role that tradition played in the formation of the gospels, but neither do they look upon the evangelists as quasi-passive collectors of these traditions. Rather, they regard them as persons who gave shape and organization to the traditions they received, adapted and altered traditional material, and perhaps even composed some narratives and sayings. Thus, redaction criticism concentrates on the work of those individuals who produced the gospels in their final form and attempts to understand their ideology, theology, and literary style. Petersen therefore claims that, in its concentration on the editorial and authorial work of the evangelists, redaction criticism has taken gospel studies to the threshold of literary criticism. It has made it essential to ask literary questions, but it has provided no means to answer them.[9]

SOURCE CRITICISM

Developments in the source-critical study of the synoptic gospels have also encouraged NT scholars to raise new questions and use different critical methods. The two-document hypothesis, which claims that Mark and Q were sources for Matthew and Luke, is accepted and used by most students of the gospels.[10] There has, however, been an erosion of confidence in this hypothesis as the correct solution to the synoptic problem. Since B. C. Butler, in 1951, claimed that Matthew was prior to Mark and questioned the reasons that B. H. Streeter and others had cited in support of Markan priority, the synoptic problem has become a problem indeed.[11] A number of writers, in important articles and monographs, have contributed to the discussion of the problem, but probably the most important has been William R. Farmer, especially in his book *The Synoptic Problem*, first published in 1964.[12] There Farmer was able to show that, in the history of research on the question, theological factors played a major role in the development of a scholarly consensus about the two-document hypothesis and in the consequent abandonment of other theories, including the views of the eighteenth-century scholar J. J. Griesbach. Farmer's survey of the history of research was intended to raise doubts about the accuracy of the two-document hypothesis, and it succeeded in influencing several scholars to reconsider Griesbach's views. Farmer himself now feels that Griesbach was basically correct and that the literary phenomena in the synoptic gospels are best explained by the "two-gospel" hypothesis: i.e., the theory that the order of the gospels is Matthew, Luke, Mark; that Luke used Matthew; and that Mark used both Matthew and Luke.[13] But that is not all. Several new theories have been proposed, some that are strictly documentary and others that require a number of hypothetical written and oral sources. Almost every conceivable alternative has been put forward.[14]

It would be inaccurate to claim that recent studies of the synoptic problem have revolutionized critical approaches to the Christian gospels. Such is not the case, since most scholars continue to express confidence in the two-document hypothesis. But it would also be inaccurate to say that such confidence is as high as it once was. More and more it becomes necessary for an author to state what source hypothesis is being used. We are also beginning to see the publication of books and articles in which hypotheses other than the two-document are being tested.[15] Sometimes redaction criticism is done on the basis of an alternate hypothesis.[16] Clearly, confidence in the two-document hypothesis is waning, and it can no longer be claimed that we have an assured solution to the synoptic problem.

Thus it is that a major problem now occurs at the intersection of redaction criticism and source criticism. Up to now, reliance on the two-document hypothesis has facilitated the task of redaction criticism. This has been especially notable in respect to the gospel of Luke, for here one has been able to isolate the work of the third evangelist partly by comparing it with the supposed source documents. If we can be certain, for example, that Luke used Mark in a particular section, it then becomes possible to see what alterations he made in his Markan source material and to draw conclusions about his redactional activity. If, however, one takes seriously the various challenges to the two-document hypothesis and if one is sensitive to the waning confidence in that hypothesis, it becomes necessary to raise questions about the dependence of redaction criticism on the two-document hypothesis.

The present situation in source criticism may, indeed, open several alternative possibilities. It may be thought desirable to suspend redaction-critical work on the synoptic gospels until the source problem has been successfully solved, or at least until there is greater confidence in some solution. Surely investigation of the synoptic problem will and should continue, but it is difficult to foresee a time when the scholarly community will reunite behind any one solution to it. Alternatively, it may be fruitful to admit that this is an age of pluralism in respect to studies of the synoptic gospels. This means that we may expect redaction-critical work to be done on the basis of several different paradigms. Instead of a nearly universal dependence on the two-document hypothesis, we may expect the Griesbach and other theories to serve as bases for some redaction-critical work. One may then compare the ideology of each of the synoptic gospels as determined in the various schools of thought. We could, for example, see what difference it would make to regard Luke as using Mark and Q or as using Matthew. The fruitfulness of this pluralistic approach is, however, limited by the lack of controls, for it is theoretically possible to paint a credible picture of Luke on the basis of almost any source hypothesis. But a credible picture is not necessarily an accurate picture, and criteria are lacking for making judgments about the superior merit of a particular result. Nor is it likely that the proponents of one source theory will persuade the supporters of another simply by displaying the results of their redaction-critical work.

A more feasible alternative, perhaps the only viable alternative, would seem to be to bracket the source question as, for the present, unresolved. As a result we would be able to read each synoptic gospel holistically, although not without attention to the similarities and differences among them. Redaction criticism has called attention to the possibility of studies that make use of literary-critical methods. The present situation in source criticism seems to make such studies necessary.

Before we can move on to a discussion of the appropriate literary-critical principles that may be applied to Luke–Acts, it is necessary to face the question of the literary character and genre of these writings.

THE LITERARY CHARACTER AND THE GENRE OF THE GOSPELS (AND ACTS)

The problems of the literary character and the genre of the gospels and Acts have been perceived to be formidable barriers to their literary-critical study. It has been thought either that these writings are not literary or that they do not fit into any generic category; hence, one cannot utilize literary-critical principles in studying them.

Early in this century it was customary to refer to the Christian gospels as popular or folk literature. C. W. Votaw in 1915 distinguished between popular and historical biography and put the gospels in the former category.[17] In 1923 Karl Ludwig Schmidt claimed that the gospels should be classified as folk literature (*Kleinliteratur*).[18] He called attention to the lack of authorial consciousness and sense of structure, vague chronology, and indefinite connections.[19] The inference is that, since the gospels and Acts are lacking in literary character, it is inappropriate to utilize literary-critical methods in studying them.

The discussion of the literary character of the gospels and Acts should be informed by developments in contemporary literary criticism. Indeed, the question involves the very definition of literature, a problem of notorious difficulty among literary critics.

Writing in 1949, René Wellek and Austin Warren claimed that there is a relationship between aesthetic qualities and literary documents.[20] They recognized three kinds of writing: scientific, everyday, and literary. Scientific writing has a form that is clearly defined, a diction that is characterized by leanness, and a vocabulary made up of denotative symbols. Everyday writing includes a number of kinds, such as essays, letters, reports, pamphlets, and sermons. It is chiefly recognized by its function; i.e., its function is an immediate and pragmatic one. Everyday writings are intended to affect policy or morals, to provide information, or to bring about some change. Literature, however, is that body of writing in which "the aesthetic function is dominant." Admitting that there are overlapping areas in these classifications, Wellek and Warren say:

> It seems, however, best to consider as literature only works in which the aesthetic function is dominant, while we can recognize that there are aesthetic elements, such as style and composition, in works which have a completely different, non-aesthetic purpose, such as scientific treatises, philosophical dissertations, political pamphlets, sermons.[21]

This definition is not without problems. The acknowledged presence of aesthetic elements in nonliterary works requires one to make an evaluative judgment. In making such a judgment about a piece of writing, one must examine the aesthetic elements and determine if the text in question exhibits a dominant aesthetic function. One would ask if the text comes across to readers in such a way that its stylistic qualities are perceived to be more impressive than its concepts. An answer to this question would involve highly controversial matters.

In contrast to Wellek and Warren some literary theorists, such as John M. Ellis, have made a serious attempt to dissociate definition from the qualities that are reputed to reside in a piece of writing. In 1974 Ellis published a forceful attempt to redefine literature. He rejected those definitions of literature which identify certain characteristics as belonging to or associated with a literary text. Among the definitions Ellis rejected are those which identify "(a) specific 'literary' ingredients in the texts, (b) specifically 'literary' organization of ordinary linguistic material of the texts, (c) the authorship of the texts by specifically 'literary' authors, i.e. poets."[22] As an analogy he called attention to the definition of a weed. A weed cannot be defined by any properties inherent in the plant itself, for all such properties can be found in nonweeds: color, shape, size, etc. What defines a weed as a weed is the attitude taken toward it. It is a plant that is *regarded* as useless, unwanted, and to be eradicated.. The weed is the plant that the gardener does not want in the garden. Ellis recommends that the person who questions this definition should send a small child out into a garden with the instruction: "Pull out the weeds and only the weeds." When the child returns with the demonstrated need for clarification, the difficulty of definition will also become clear.

Ellis claims that literature can be defined only in terms of the ways in which certain texts are regarded. More specifically, "literary texts are defined as those that are used by the society in such a way that *the text is not taken as specifically relevant to the immediate context of its origin.*"[23] On the evaluation of literary texts Ellis says, "It is essential to begin by saying that great works of literature are those that are particularly successful in performing as works of literature, rather than by assuming that they have a quality called aesthetic value, which we must then try to locate."[24]

It is quite clear that, while the gospels and Acts may or may not qualify as literature on the basis of the definition by Wellek and Warren, they surely do if we accept Ellis' definition. These writings have clearly outlived their original context, and they have functioned in multifarious historical contexts since the time of their origin. We may say, therefore, that according to important schools of contemporary literary theory, the gospels and Acts may be regarded as literature.

In light of Ellis' definition of literature the question of genre becomes of secondary importance, for genre may be regarded as one of those aesthetic aspects that do not belong to the definition of literature. Nevertheless, readers tend to expect the books they read to belong to certain known categories, and they are puzzled by writings that appear to stand outside them. Moreover, recent studies of the genre of the gospels have carried with them a reassessment of their literary character. Some modern scholars have emphasized similarities between the Christian gospels and certain types of Greco-Roman literature. Moses Hadas and Morton Smith classify them as aretalogies. An aretalogy is defined as "a formal account of the remarkable career of an impressive teacher that was used as a basis for moral instruction."[25] Still more recently Charles Talbert has argued that the gospels are biographies, in the sense in which that genre was understood among Hellenistic writers.[26] Philip Shuler classifies them as *encomia,* or laudatory biographies.[27] Alongside these developments there is, nevertheless, a formidable school of thought that insists on the generic uniqueness of the gospels. This school is represented by, among others, Rudolf Bultmann, Norman Perrin, and Helmut Koester.[28] M. Jack Suggs says that this is the consensus position among NT scholars, but he adds that "recent developments have put the consensus in doubt and have led to a renewed investigation of the genre issue."[29]

Although the identification of the Christian gospels in terms of genres of contemporary literature remains an unresolved problem, it is possible to see elements in them that are similar to certain features in classical and Hellenistic literature. In this respect one of the more significant recent studies is Gilbert Bilezikian's comparison of the gospel of Mark with Greek tragedy. Bilezikian stops short of classifying Mark as a traditional Greek tragedy, but he finds a number of comparable elements. He says that the major element in tragedy is the immutable moral structure, and he approvingly quotes Northrop Frye's definition of tragedy as "an affirmation of the inviolability of moral law."[30] Bilezikian also finds similarities in plot structure and in several dramatic features. It will be fruitful to examine his suggestions about tragedy and to discuss their implications for Lukan studies.

Bilezikian draws heavily on Aristotle's treatment of tragedy. In his *Poetics,* Aristotle defined tragedy as the dramatic imitation of an action that involves persons who are ethically superior to and more noble than contemporary people. He complains about "episodic" tragedies, i.e., those consisting of episodes that "do not follow each other probably or inevitably." "Tragedy represents not only a complete action but also incidents that cause fear and pity, and this happens most of all when the incidents are unexpected and yet one is a consequence of the other."[31] Tragedy is characterized by sudden reversals. In the best tragedies, said Aristotle, there is a change in the hero's fortune from good to ill, or the hero undergoes a change from happiness to misery. The cause of the change lies in some error on the part of the hero. Aristotle analyzed the structure of tragic drama in three major parts: *dēsis,* or complication, in which the plot becomes increasingly tangled; *metabasis,* the crisis or change; and *lusis,* the resolution or, as Bilezikian calls it, the denouement. The *metabasis,* or crisis in the plot, is the turning point, that episode in which the reversal begins to take place. It may consist of a recognition scene, or some other device may be used in which the hero suddenly realizes that his fortune has changed. The *dēsis* is that section of the narrative that leads up to the crisis, and, as the term implies, the movement in the plot is from the simple to the complex. The Greek term *dēsis* suggests a progressive knotting or tying. As the *dēsis* progresses, more and more the events pile up; more and more the situation builds toward the inevitable climax. Foreshadowings are frequently used in this part of the plot. The Greek word *lusis* means the act of untying or loosing, and so it is used here to express the working out of the crisis. Here things move toward a resolution, thus the movement is from complex to simple. Throughout the drama in its entirety there is a motif of inevitability. The audience at a performance of Sophocles' *Oedipus Rex,* for example, becomes convinced that Oedipus must undergo some kind of punishment and atone for his errors before the play is over.

Bilezikian believes that in several respects the gospel of Mark conforms to the Aristotelian analysis of tragedy. Jesus, the protagonist, is better than other humans; there is a sudden reversal; and the plot structure follows Aristotle's three-part analysis. Bilezikian maintains that the crisis (*metabasis*) in Mark is Peter's confession at Caesarea Philippi (Mark 8:27–30), which he labels as a recognition scene.[32] He designates all the rest of Mark, including Jesus' resurrection, as denouement. In this last section of the gospel the program that began with Peter's confession works itself out, and it does so in the terms foreshadowed in Jesus' response to Peter's recognition (Mark 8:31). Thus in summary, Bilezikian is able to say, "The flawless development of the plot from complication to denouement conforms to Aristotle's requirements for Greek tragedy."[33]

Many of the comparisons that Bilezikian makes between the gospel of Mark and Greek tragedy are impressive. Mark does indeed present the reader with a protagonist who is better than other humans and whose passion evokes pity and fear. Moreover, it may be possible to outline Mark's gospel by using Aristotle's three-part scheme. But Bilezikian is right to stop short of claiming that Mark is a traditional Greek tragedy. Although Jesus is a tragic hero in the sense that he is superior to other humans, he has no "fatal flaw," and he commits no error that leads to his downfall.[34] Nor is there a change in Mark's characterization of Jesus. Although, after the confession of Peter, Jesus tends to confine his attention to the disciples and to avoid the crowds, his character remains the same. A Sophoclean Oedipus may undergo a dramatic change after he discovers that he is an incestuous murderer, but no real change comes over the Markan Jesus.

Moreover, the discovery of Jesus' empty tomb in Mark (16:1–8) constitutes a problem for interpreting this gospel as tragedy. Bilezikian does not acknowledge it as a problem but attempts to designate it as part of Mark's *lusis,* or denouement. He maintains that it is the final working out of the messianic program that began when Peter confessed Jesus to be the Messiah. But the implied resurrection is better understood as a sudden reversal. Indeed, it is more obviously a reversal than is Peter's confession, for there is nothing more elemental than the change from death to life. But it is precisely the kind of reversal that Aristotle wanted to rule out of tragedy. "The change," said the philosopher, "must be not to good fortune from bad but, on the contrary, from good to bad fortune."[35] Surely the change from death to life is an extreme form of a change from bad fortune to good.

For these reasons it would be misleading to speak of Mark, or any of the gospels, as tragedy. Dan O. Via may be closer to the target in applying the generic label of tragicomedy.[36] But Northrop Frye seems to be most helpful in what he says about the U-shaped narrative.[37] Frye maintains that the plot of the Christian Bible as a whole is constituted of "a series of ups and downs in which God's people periodically fall into bondage and are then rescued by a leader, while the great heathen empires rise and fall in the opposite rhythm."[38] One of these U-shaped narratives is the death and resurrection of Jesus. This narrative is the one "around which the New Testament revolves."[39] Frye refuses to use any classical literary term to describe these narratives.

Thus, although it is probably inaccurate to describe Mark, or any of the Christian gospels, as tragedy, Bilezikian has performed an important service in pointing out a number of tragic elements in Mark. Much of what he observed in respect to Mark may be applied equally well to Luke. The Lukan Jesus is similar to the tragic hero in terms of his status and virtue. The passion narrative in Luke (as well as in the other synoptic gospels) comes close to fitting Aristotle's description of tragedy as consisting of a plot that evokes pity and fear. Although one may correctly use the term "episodic" to describe large sections of Luke–Acts, the passion narrative (Luke 22:47–24:53) is, for the most part, a series of related incidents; one incident follows as a consequence of another. Moreover, Jesus' death may be seen as an extreme form of a change from good fortune to ill. The sense of inevitability probably comes in for greater stress in Luke than in Mark. Luke frequently uses the Greek verb *dei* to express divine necessity. "The Son of man *must* suffer many things" (Luke 9:22). "But first he [the Son of man] *must* suffer many things and be rejected by this generation" (Luke 17:25). "The Son of man *must* be delivered into the hands of sinful men" (Luke 24:7; cf. 13:33; 21:9; 24:26,44; Acts 1:16; 17:3; 23:11; 27:24).

Despite the characterization of Jesus, the use of certain elements of tragic plot, and the stress on inevitability, Luke is no more a traditional Greek tragedy than is Mark. The resurrection cannot be made to square with tragic plots, and Jesus has no fatal flaw.

The same is true for Acts, which also has tragic elements. Although Paul emerges as the hero of the book after chapter 12, much attention is also given to Peter, Philip, and Stephen. In particular, the ending of Acts is a difficulty. Although it is not possible to be certain whether the present ending was the one that the author intended, whether Luke planned to write another volume, or whether it is an accidental result of textual transmission, the ending as it now stands is not characteristic of traditional Greek tragedy. There is no description of a disastrous outcome for Paul. Despite the trials he is preaching "openly and unhindered" at the end (Acts 28:31), and there is a hint of continued work even after the two years in Rome

(Acts 28:28). There is also a hint of Paul's martyrdom in the words addressed to him in Acts 23:11, "You must bear witness [*marturēsai*] also at Rome." But since the projected testimony at Rome is compared with that in Jerusalem, where Paul was tried but not killed, it is not certain that Luke meant to refer to Paul's death in this passage. Perhaps he meant Acts 28:31 to suggest a reversal for Paul, from ill to good fortune. In this way the reader would be reminded of the ending of the gospel of Luke, in which Jesus' death is turned to life. In any event, a sense of the inevitability of Paul's imminent death is not strong, and the optimistic note at the end of Acts is not a suitable ending for a tragedy.

We may, therefore, speak of tragic elements in Luke–Acts, but we should avoid classifying the work generically as tragedy.

Although no firm conclusions have been reached about the precise generic classification of the gospels, the study of genre has contributed to the possibility of examining them in ways that compare with methods generally used in literary criticism.[40] So long as it was necessary to think of the gospels as folk literature or as unique, questions about their literary shape did not seem very important. But if these writings in fact fall under the definition of literature, and if it is plausible to think of them as, at least in some respects, comparable to other Greco-Roman writings that have been studied as literature, the situation is different. It now seems appropriate to talk about the evangelists as authors, even if disagreement remains about the specific literary genre of the gospels and Acts.

SOME PRINCIPLES OF LITERARY CRITICISM

The application of literary-critical principles to writings such as the Christian gospels has already produced some noteworthy studies. But NT scholars have not yet come to an agreement on precisely what methods are appropriate. Structural studies seem to be aimed at the analysis of a cognitive or precognitive level below the semantic, or meaning, level.[41] Other studies concentrate on literary aspects of individual sections of a book or on the component parts of a gospel, parts that may have had an independent pregospel existence, such as collections of parables and conflict stories.[42] In view of these signs of a lack of consensus, it seems appropriate to examine here some fundamental principles and issues that have emerged in recent literary-critical studies and that may be applicable in the present case.

One principle has already been mentioned. It is that we should respect the integrity of the text under examination. Holistic interpretation is a fundamental aspect of literary criticism, but it has not had a long history in gospel studies. Form criticism tends to focus attention on the small units of tradition. Source criticism calls upon us to look for the strata underlying the gospels, rather than at the gospels themselves. Redaction criticism frequently concentrates on the seams and other editorial sections. Literary criticism now asks us to look at a gospel holistically, as the product of an author who consciously brought it into being.

A second principle is that we should respect the world of the text. The world of the text is that world that the text assumes and describes. As readers we cannot assume that the world of a particular text is identical to the one we commonly experience. It may, in fact, be quite different from this world. In a given text we may be introduced to a world in which animals talk or only one person is of a normal human size. We may see the difference between the world as commonly experienced—i.e., the "real world"—and the world of the text by taking note of the treatment of time. In a narrative time does not pass as it does in real life. Wellek and Warren refer to this as narrative time, "which is controlled, of course, by the novelist, who passes over years in a few sentences but gives two long chapters to a dance or tea-party."[43]

Respecting the world of the text also means that the interpretation of character is limited by the text. In reading Luke–Acts, for example, Jesus is to be understood as a character to whom we have access only in this text. To be sure, there is also a Jesus who is available in the other gospels and perhaps through the application of certain historical-critical methods, but these other Jesuses are not primary concerns in literary criticism. It may be said that a literary-critical study of Luke–Acts requires a total immersion in this text, with only an occasional resurfacing to look at other worlds.

A third principle requires somewhat more extended treatment and raises critical questions about traditional exegetical procedures used in NT studies. NT critical scholarship has generally insisted that a fundamental goal of exegesis is to understand the intention of the author. Thus, emphasis has been put on the historical conditions under which the various NT documents were written. It seemed necessary to determine, insofar as possible, the identity of the author, the date, the place, and the occasion of a document in order to understand it. In addition, the author's purpose in writing has been of special importance. NT scholars have attempted to separate the intention of the author from the various interpretations of subsequent readers. Thus, the location of a document in time and place has been used in order to determine the possibilities and limits of meaning in a text.

Some contemporary literary theory raises serious questions about the possibility of determining the intention of an author. Indeed, the questions are often raised precisely by those who define literature as does John Ellis. Ellis' definition emphasizes the evaluation of a text by societies subsequent to the time of its writing. Hence he dissociates the text from its original context and, indeed, from its author. The only candidates for literary texts are those that have outlived the contexts in which they originated. Thus, if a text is judged to be literary on the basis of the regard in which it is held in modern society, the relationship of the text to its original setting is peculiarly irrelevant. Ellis states the point bluntly:

> These [literary] texts are defined as those that outgrow the original context of their utterance, and which function in the community at large. They do not function in that original context, are not dependent on that context for meaning, and are not judged according to their appropriateness or success in achieving what was to be achieved there. Therefore, when we decide to treat a piece of language as literature, that decision is in itself a decision not to refer the text to its originator nor to treat it as a communication from him.[44]

Ellis insists that literary criticism has no concern with the author of a literary text. The author belongs to the past and is part of the original culture, acquaintance with which has no place in literary criticism. Ellis observes that, since people do not always say what they mean, there is no inevitable correspondence between a written

text and whatever intention the author had in writing it. The function of literary criticism, therefore, is to describe the meaning of a
piece of language. To illustrate the dissociation of text from authorial intent, Ellis cites the fate of Edward Gibbon's *Decline and Fall
of the Roman Empire,* which was intended to be a historical study
but which now is regarded as literature. The consequences are in-
structive for gospel studies:

> For, when we begin to regard Gibbon as literature, we
> characteristically stop worrying about the facts of Ro-
> man history; we cease to regard the book primarily as
> historical information, neither do we relate it to the con-
> text of the remaining evidence for what actually hap-
> pened in Rome. Truth or falsity relevant to the specific
> historical context is no longer the main point, for Gib-
> bon's is no longer the book for that purpose; we now
> read it as a narrative with its own kind of rationale.[45]

Some literary critics have, however, recently questioned the dissociation of author and text. Probably the most persuasive among
them is E. D. Hirsch, Jr. Hirsch is interested in the question of validity in interpretation, and he distinguishes two norms for interpreting texts. One he calls the reader-based norm, which concentrates on the response of the reader to a text, on the ground that
"after a text has been around a long time it is impossible for a modern reader to have all of the cultural and linguistic knowledge that
the original author assumed his original readers would have."[46]
The other is called the author-based norm, which "assumes that the
recovery of original meaning is not inherently impossible, and may
have been achieved by some of those who read the text before."[47]
Hirsch reminds us that all ancient texts have been established by
critics who followed the author-based model: "Reader-based theories overlook the inconvenient truth that the older texts being interpreted were invariably established by scholars who believed that
the authors' intentions could be known and agreed upon. In fact
without the norm of authorial intention we could not establish de-
finitive texts."[48]

Hirsch claims that only the author-based norm can provide a valid
interpretation of a text. He maintains that if one does not speak

about the author's meaning as conveyed in a text, there is nothing to go on except responses of readers, which can and do vary. There is no ground, he claims, for identifying a particular reader's response with the meaning of the text. A response is simply a response and not meaning. A valid interpretation, one which is to be identified with the meaning of the text, can only be the meaning that was intended by the person who brought the text into being. Hirsch is aware that an author's meaning may not be known with certainty, but he claims that is it not totally inaccessible. There may be some texts for which the author's meaning is not available, but this is not the case with all, not even with all texts from the distant past. So Hirsch can say, "All valid interpretation of every sort is founded on re-cognition of what an author meant."[49] Moreover, "to banish the original author as the determiner of meaning was to reject the only compelling normative principle that could lend validity to an interpretation."[50]

Paradoxically, the case that Hirsch makes for an author-based norm of interpretation is not opposed to Ellis' definition of literature. If a literary text is one that a community finds to be literary, using Ellis' definition, it would seem to follow that any concern with the author is a retreat from acceptance of a text as literary. Ellis would, in fact, say that concern with the author's intention is an act of turning a literary text into a nonliterary text.[51] He regards such activity as inappropriate but not impossible. This means that in asking historical questions about the origin of a text, we are not treating that text as literature. But if the definition of a literary text is not dependent on any kind of inherent qualities in the text but is something that is granted by the community, historical inquiries do not turn the text into something it is not. Rather, they approach the text from a perspective that is not that of the community at large. To take Ellis' analogy of the weed, some people may regard certain plants as desirable and may nurture them, even if the community at large regards them as weeds. Their refusal to treat these plants the same way everybody else does may mean that such people are thought to be deviant, but their attitude is neither impossible nor inappropriate to the plant itself. To the extent to which one dissociates the definition of literature from inherent characteristics, to that degree must there be a recognition of a diversity of approach and judgment.

This discussion of literary theory has not been introduced in the attempt to solve problems in that controversial field. It has, however, been necessary to look over the fence into the field of literary theory and criticism in order to position the present study of two NT documents. The inquiry that follows should be understood as one that will ask about the literary function and meaning of the theme of Jesus' death in Luke–Acts. It is a holistic study, i.e., one that respects the integrity of the text under consideration. It intends to accept the world that is presumed in the text. Cautioned by the reminder that our knowledge about the author and his context is extremely limited, we shall nevertheless use Hirsch's model of the author-based norm and attempt to determine the meaning that the author intended to convey to his readers.

AN OUTLINE OF LUKE–ACTS

The final preliminary matter that needs to be considered is that of the organization of Luke–Acts. Although some scholars, such as Karl Ludwig Schmidt, have been impressed with the lack of a sense of structure in the Christian gospels, recent scholarship has reversed that judgment. Many now call attention to the structural elements in all the gospels.[52]

Convenience alone demands that an attempt should be made to outline Luke–Acts, for such an outline will be helpful in the subsequent discussions. The outline that follows should be regarded only as a tool to aid the task of exegesis, not as a claim to represent the mind of the author of Luke–Acts. But even so, an outline should be as free of bias as possible. It is possible to take a thematic approach to the problem of discovering Luke's organizing principles and to trace the development of one or more themes in the two books. It is also possible to find rhetorical or literary patterns, the recognition of which might guide the interpretation of the texts. But there are problems with both these ways of understanding the structure of a book in which the author does not explicitly call attention to his methods of organization. In the case of the present study, in which we are attempting to understand the ways in which certain themes and literary devices are used, it seems hazardous to adopt a thematic approach to the matter of organization. An outline that, for the most part, depends on a geographical analysis of the text would appear to be the least theory-dependent. Since there are geographical references in the text, there is no danger that the interpreter will import something alien. Moreover, in the case of Luke–Acts such references seem to be significant. In particular, the city of Jerusalem appears to be pivotal to the writing as a whole. The gospel begins and ends there, and it is the setting for the first seven chapters of Acts. An effort will be made to explore the meaning of Jerusalem in chapter 4, but the centrality of the city in Luke's narrative seems sufficiently clear even at the outset. Thus, the outline that follows is primarily dependent on a geographical analysis of the text. At a few points, however, it seems best to use topical rather than geographical designations. For example, although Luke 1:5–2:52 takes place mainly in Jerusalem, it would be misleading to abandon the traditional topical title for these chapters, namely, infancy narratives.

LUKE
  A. Prologue, 1:1–4
  B. Infancy narratives, 1:5–2:52
  C. Narratives about John, Jesus' baptism and temptation, 3:1–4:13
  D. Jesus' activity outside Jerusalem, 4:14–19:44
      1. Jesus in Galilee, 4:14–9:50
      2. Jesus in transit, 9:51–19:44[53]
  E. Jesus' activity in Jerusalem, 19:45–22:46
  F. Jesus' trial, death, and resurrection, 22:47–24:53

ACTS
  A. Prologue, 1:1–3
  B. Christianity in Jerusalem, 1:4–8:3
  C. Christianity outside Jerusalem, 8:4–12:25
  D. Paul's activity outside Jerusalem, 13:1–21:16
  E. Paul's activity in Jerusalem, 21:17–22:29
  F. Paul's trials, 22:30–26:32
  G. Paul's trip to Rome, 27:1–28:31

The study that follows is largely a conversation with Luke–Acts in which we will inquire about the literary function and meaning of the theme of Jesus' death. In the process we will examine several aspects of the Lukan narrative and ask about their bearing on the theme of Jesus' death. We will look first at those groups that may play roles as opponents of Jesus—the Jewish public in chapter 2 and the Jewish leaders in chapter 3. In chapter 4, we will look at some issues that, according to Luke, produced hostility between Jesus and some of his opponents, and in chapter 5 there will be a detailed analysis of Jesus' trial. The distinctiveness of Luke's perspective will be examined vis-à-vis Matthew and Mark in chapter 6, and the final chapter will contain our conclusions about the meaning of Jesus' death for Luke.

NOTES

1. Martin Kähler, *The So-Called Historical Jesus and the Historic Biblical Christ,* trans. Carl E. Braaten (Philadelphia: Fortress Press, 1964), p. 80, n. 11. The translation is from a German edition published in 1896.
2. See, e.g., Ernst Bammel, ed., *The Trial of Jesus* (Naperville, Ill.: Allenson, 1970); S. G. F. Brandon, *The Trial of Jesus of Nazareth* (New York: Stein and Day, 1968); David R. Catchpole, *The Trial of Jesus* (Leiden: E. J. Brill, 1971); Haim H. Cohn, *Jewish Law in Ancient and Modern Israel* (New York: KTAV, 1971), pp. 83–130; Paul Winter, *On the Trial of Jesus* (Berlin: Walter de Gruyter, 1961); Solomon Zeitlin, *Who Crucified Jesus?* (New York: Harper and Bros., 1942).
3. See, e.g., A. E. Harvey, *Jesus on Trial: A Study in the Fourth Gospel* (Atlanta: John Knox Press, 1976); Robert J. Karris, *Luke: Artist and Theologian: Luke's Passion Account as Literature* (New York: Paulist Press, 1985); Werner H. Kelber, ed., *The Passion in Mark* (Philadelphia: Fortress Press, 1976); Eta Linnemann, *Studien zur Passiongeschichte* (Göttingen: Vandenhoeck und Ruprecht, 1970); Gerhard Schneider, *Verleugnung, Verspottung, und Verhör Jesu nach Lukas 22, 54–71* (Munich: Kösel Verlag, 1969); idem., *Die Passion Jesu nach den drei Älteren Evangelien* (Munich: Kösel Verlag, 1973); Vincent Taylor, *The Passion Narrative of St. Luke,* ed. Owen E. Evans (Cambridge: Cambridge University Press, 1972).
4. But see Henry J. Cadbury, *The Making of Luke–Acts,* 2nd ed. (London: SPCK, 1958); Helmut Flender, *St. Luke: Theologian of Redemptive History,* trans. R. H. and Ilse Fuller (Philadelphia: Fortress Press, 1967); Robert Maddox, *The Purpose of Luke–Acts* (Edinburgh: T. and T. Clark, 1982); Charles H. Talbert, *Literary Patterns, Theological Themes and the Genre of Luke–Acts* (Missoula, Mont.: Scholars Press, 1974). In addition, some scholars have traced

themes in Luke–Acts other than those relating to the death of Jesus. See, e.g., Schuyler Brown, *Apostasy and Perseverance in the Theology of Luke* (Rome: Pontifical Biblical Institute, 1969); Luke T. Johnson, *The Literary Function of Possessions in Luke–Acts* (Missoula: Scholars Press, 1977); Donald Juel, *Luke–Acts: The Promise of History* (Atlanta: John Knox Press, 1983); David L. Tiede, *Prophecy and History in Luke–Acts* (Philadelphia: Fortress Press, 1980).

5. E.g., Robert F. O'Toole, *The Unity of Luke's Theology* (Wilmington, Del.: Michael Glazier, 1984); Charles H. Talbert, *Reading Luke: A Literary and Theological Commentary on the Third Gospel* (New York: Crossroad Books, 1982).

6. Perhaps the best comprehensive redaction-critical study of Luke–Acts to date is that of Hans Conzelmann, *The Theology of St. Luke*, trans. Geoffrey Buswell (New York: Harper and Bros., 1960). See also William C. Robinson, *Der Weg des Herrn* (Hamburg: Herbert Reich, 1964). For redaction-critical studies of portions of the Lukan passion narrative see Gerhard Schneider, *Verleugnung;* Anton Büchele, *Der Tod Jesu im Lukasevangelium: Eine redaktionsgeschichtliche Untersuchung zu Lk 23* (Frankfurt am Main: Josef Knecht, 1978).

7. Norman R. Petersen, *Literary Criticism for New Testament Critics* (Philadelphia: Fortress Press, 1978).

8. Form criticism is the name given to the study of pregospel oral traditions. Consideration is given to the shape of the individual sayings and stories and to the alterations that occurred in the process of transmission. See Rudolf Bultmann, *The History of the Synoptic Tradition,* trans. John Marsh (New York: Harper and Row, 1963); Martin Dibelius, *From Tradition to Gospel,* trans. Bertram L. Woolf (New York: Charles Scribner's Sons, 1935); Vincent Taylor, *The Formation of the Gospel Tradition,* 2nd ed. (London: Macmillan and Co., 1935).

9. See Petersen, *Literary Criticism,* pp. 17–20. Ernst Haenchen may have anticipated this move when, in referring to the work of Willi Marxsen, he expressed a preference for the term *Kompositionsgeschichte* to *Redaktionsgeschichte.* See his *Der Weg Jesu: Eine Erklärung des Markus-Evangeliums und der kanonischen Parallelen,* 2nd ed. (Berlin: Walter de Gruyter, 1968), p. 24.

10. The symbol Q is used to designate the source for material that is found in Matthew and Luke but not in Mark.

11. B. C. Butler, *The Originality of St. Matthew* (Cambridge: Cambridge University Press, 1951); B. H. Streeter, *The Four Gospels* (London: Macmillan and Co., 1924).

12. William R. Farmer, *The Synoptic Problem,* 2nd ed. (Macon, Ga.: Mercer University Press, 1976).

13. William R. Farmer, "Modern Developments of Griesbach's Hypothesis," *New Testament Studies* 23 (1977): 275–95; Reginald H. Fuller, E. P. Sanders, and Thomas R. W. Longstaff, "The Synoptic Problem: After Ten Years," *Perkins Journal* 28 (1975): 63–74.

14. For a critical review of the various hypotheses as they affect the gospel of Luke see my article "Source Criticism of the Gospel of Luke," in *Perspectives on Luke–Acts,* ed. Charles H. Talbert (Macon, Ga.: Mercer University Press, 1978), pp. 24–39.

15. See e.g., Charles H. Talbert and Edgar V. McKnight, "Can the Griesbach Hypothesis Be Falsified?" *Journal of Biblical Literature* 91 (1972): 338–68; George W. Buchanan, "Has the Griesbach Hypothesis Been Falsified?" *Journal of Biblical Literature* 93 (1974): 550–72; William R. Farmer, ed., *New Synoptic Studies* (Macon, Ga.: Mercer University Press, 1983).

16. Bernard Orchard, *Matthew, Luke and Mark* (Manchester, Eng.: Koinonia Press, 1976); also Orchard, ed., *A Synopsis of the Four Gospels in a New Translation Arranged According to the Two-Gospel Hypothesis* (Macon, Ga.: Mercer University Press, 1982). See Jack Dean Kingsbury, "The Theology of St. Matthew's Gospel According to the Griesbach Hypothesis," in *New Synoptic Studies,* pp. 331–61; J. G. F. Collison, "Eschatology in the Gospel of Luke," ibid., pp. 363–71; Thomas R. W. Longstaff, "Crisis and Christology: The Theology of Mark," ibid., pp. 373–92; Orchard, "The 'Common Step' Phenomenon in the Synoptic Pericopes," ibid., pp. 393–407.

17. Clyde W. Votaw, "The Gospels and Contemporary Biographies," *American Journal of Theology* 19 (1915): 45–73; 217–49.

18. Karl Ludwig Schmidt, "Die Stellung der Evangelien in der allgemeinen Literaturgeschichte," in *Eucharisterion,* ed. Hans Schmidt (Göttingen: Vandenhoeck und Ruprecht, 1923), part 2, pp. 50–134.

19. Despite the tendency to think of the gospels as nonliterary documents, some early twentieth-century scholars, notably H. J. Cadbury and Martin Dibelius, paid serious attention to certain literary aspects of Luke's work. Cadbury subscribed to the view that Mark was a source for Luke in the gospel, and he analyzed the changes that Luke made in this source. But he also gave significant attention to Luke's vocabulary and concluded that "the vocabulary of Luke, while it has its natural affiliations with the Greek of the Bible, is not so far removed from the literary style of the Atticists as to be beyond comparison with them" (*The Style and Literary Method of Luke* [Cambridge, Mass.: Harvard University Press, 1920], p. 38). He judged Luke to be "a gentleman of ability and breadth of interest." "His vocabulary no purist could wholly commend, but no ignorant man could entirely equal it, though he could always understand it" (*The Making of Luke-Acts,* p. 220). In terms of genre, Cadbury thought of Luke chiefly as a transmitter of popular tradition, who attempted to impose a literary form on the traditions that he received. He wrote: "His [Luke's] efforts at literary form only bring into sharper outline the incurably unliterary character of his materials" (ibid., p. 134). See also Cadbury's contributions to *The Acts of the Apostles,* ed. F. J. Foakes-Jackson and Kirsopp Lake, 5 vols. (repr.; Grand Rapids: Baker Book House, 1979). Dibelius generally agreed with Cadbury about the gospel of Luke, but he claimed that the literary merit of Acts was far higher. He thought that Luke exercised greater authorial freedom in the second book than in the first. He found, e.g., that Luke composed speeches for his heroes in much the same way that other historians did. He did not hesitate to call Luke the first Christian historian, although he based that judgment only on the writing of Acts, not the gospel. See his *Studies in the Acts of the Apostles,* ed. Heinrich Greeven (New York: Charles Scribner's Sons, 1956).

20. René Wellek and Austin Warren, *Theory of Literature* (New York: Harcourt, Brace, 1949).

21. Ibid., p. 15.

22. John M. Ellis, *The Theory of Literary Criticism* (Berkeley: University of California Press, 1974), pp. 26–27.

23. Ibid., p. 44; italics Ellis's.

24. Ibid., p. 88.

25. Moses Hadas and Morton Smith, *Heroes and Gods* (New York: Harper and Row, 1965), p. 3.

26. Charles H. Talbert, *What Is a Gospel?* (Philadelphia: Fortress Press, 1977). Talbert has also analyzed certain literary patterns in Luke–Acts; cf. his *Literary Patterns,* where he calls attention to what he calls the architecture of the writing and the principle of balance that is found throughout the Hellenistic world. He claims that this principle guided Luke as he organized his materials in the two volumes. The trials of Jesus in the gospel, for example, are balanced by the trials of Paul in Acts. Thus, Talbert finds parallels between the two volumes and within each volume. He compares the architecture of Luke–Acts with similar patterns in Homer, Herodotus, and Vergil.

27. Philip L. Shuler, *A Genre for the Gospels* (Philadelphia: Fortress Press, 1982).

28. See Rudolf Bultmann, "The Gospels (Form)," in *Twentieth Century Theology in the Making,* ed. Jaroslav Pelikan (New York: Harper and Row, 1969), 1:86–92; Norman Perrin, "The Literary *Gattung* 'Gospel'—Some Observations," *Expository Times* 82 (1970): 4–7; Helmut Koester, "One Jesus and Four Primitive Gospels," in *Trajectories Through Early Christianity,* ed. James M. Robinson and Helmut Koester (Philadelphia: Fortress Press, 1971), pp. 158–204.

29. M. Jack Suggs, "Gospel, Genre," *Interpreter's Dictionary of the Bible Supplementary Volume* (Nashville: Abingdon Press, 1976), p. 370.

30 Gilbert G. Bilezikian, *The Liberated Gospel: A Comparison of the Gospel of Mark and Greek Tragedy* (Grand Rapids: Baker Book House, 1977), p. 27.

31. Aristotle, *The Poetics,* IX, 11, trans. W. Hamilton Fyfe in the Loeb Classical Library (Cambridge, Mass.: Harvard University Press, 1932).

32. Bilezikian, *The Liberated Gospel,* p. 55.

33. Ibid., p. 100.

34. Perhaps the choice of Judas as a disciple may be regarded as an error on Jesus' part, but Bilezikian does not consider this possibility.

35. Aristotle, *Poetics,* XIII, 6.

36. Dan O. Via, Jr., *Kerygma and Comedy in the New Testament* (Philadelphia: Fortress Press, 1975).

37. Northrop Frye, *The Great Code: The Bible and Literature* (New York: Harcourt Brace Jovanovich, 1981), pp. 169–98.

38. Ibid., p. 192.

39. Ibid., p. 171.

40. See e.g., Talbert, *Literary Patterns* and *Reading Luke;* O'Toole, *The Unity of Luke's Theology.* See also Eckhard Plümacher, *Lukas als hellenistischer Schriftsteller* (Göttingen: Vandenhoeck und Ruprecht, 1972), a study of Acts. For studies of literary themes see Johnson, *The Literary Function of Possessions;* Tiede, *Prophecy and History in Luke–Acts.*

41. E.g., Daniel Patte, *What Is Structural Exegesis?* (Philadelphia: Fortress Press, 1976); Daniel and Aline Patte, *Structural Exegesis: From Theory to Practice* (Philadelphia: Fortress Press, 1978).

42. On Mark see Joanna Dewey, *Markan Public Debate* (Chico, Calif.: Scholars Press, 1980); on conflict stories see Arland J. Hultgren, *Jesus and His Adversaries: The Form and Function of the Conflict Stories in the Synoptic Tradition* (Minneapolis: Augsburg Publishing House, 1979); on parables see Dan O. Via, Jr., *The Parables* (Philadelphia: Fortress Press, 1967); Madeleine Boucher, *The Mysterious Parable: A Literary Study* (Washington: Catholic Biblical Association of America, 1977). See also Büchele, *Der Tod Jesu im Lukasevangelium;* Karris, *Luke: Artist and Theologian.*

43. Wellek and Warren, *Theory of Literature,* p. 226.

44. Ellis, *Theory of Literary Criticism,* pp. 111–12.

45. Ibid., p. 48. Ellis' position at this point is not entirely clear, however. His points about Gibbon's book do not seem to be directed at the intention that Gibbon had in mind in writing. Rather, Ellis seems to be making comparisons between the world that is assumed in Gibbon and the real world—i.e., what actually happened in Rome during the period covered by Gibbon.

From a different perspective Paul Ricoeur claims that a written text should not be regarded as a communication from author to reader ("What Is a Text? Explanation and Interpretation," in *Mythic-Symbolic Language and Philosophical Anthropology,* ed. David M. Rasmussen [The Hague: Martinus Nijhoff, 1971], pp. 135–50). He calls attention to the differences between speaking and writing and claims that speech is a fuller kind of discourse, because, in speech, dialogue can take place and because both speaker and listener share the same perceptual surroundings and cultural background. In writing and reading there is no dialogue; there is no "situation of discourse"; and the cultural background may not be the same. Ricoeur writes: "Rather, the book introduces a shift between the act of writing and the act of reading, between which two acts there is no communication: the reader is absent from the writing of the book, the writer is absent from its reading" (p. 136).

46. E. D. Hirsch, Jr., "Carnal Knowledge," *The New York Review of Books,* June 14, 1979, p. 18. The article is a review of Frank Kermode, *The Genesis of Secrecy: On the Interpretation of Narrative* (Cambridge, Mass.: Harvard University Press, 1979).

47. "Carnal Knowledge," p. 18.

48. Ibid.

49. E. D. Hirsch, Jr., *Validity in Interpretation,* (New Haven: Yale University Press, 1967), p. 126.

50. Ibid., p. 5. For a critique of Hirsch see Monroe E. Beardsley, "Textual Meaning and Authorial Meaning," *Genre* 1 (1968): 169–81. Beardsley allows a place for the study of authorial meaning but does not want to identify it exclusively with textual meaning.

51. Ellis says: "Literary texts can be converted into nonliterary texts quite simply: since the use made of the one is quite different from the use made of the other and, since it is this use (not properties of the texts) which is defining, we can make a

poem not a poem by so treating it. We can treat a poem of Goethe as a letter from him to Friederike Brion. It may well have functioned that way in its context of origin; and there is nothing logically wrong in doing this. But we must be clear about our aim in doing so: it is not the aim of literary study" (*Theory of Literary Criticism*, p. 112).

52. See, e.g., Jack Dean Kingsbury, *Matthew: Structure, Christology, Kingdom* (Philadelphia: Fortress Press, 1975); Patte, *What Is Structural Exegesis?*

53. Although it has become customary to mark this section to end at Luke 18:14, our own geographical outline requires its extension to 19:44. Luke 9:51–18:14 appears significant as a meaningful section of Luke only if one thinks that Luke used Mark. It then becomes a section in which Luke departed from Mark. But if one treats Luke without respect to a source theory and observes the geographical references, it will be clear that the section does not end until 19:44, just before Jesus arrives in Jerusalem. It is important to note that, in contrast to the parallels in Matthew and Mark, Jesus does not enter Jerusalem in the narrative of Luke 19:28–40. Indeed, he is still outside the city in Luke 19:41–44, and he enters the temple in 19:45. For this reason the section "Jesus in transit" ends at Luke 19:44.

The character of this section as a travel narrative has often been questioned. See, e.g., Karl Ludwig Schmidt, *Der Rahmen der Geschichte Jesu* (Berlin: Trowitzsch und Sohn, 1919). But Hans Conzelmann (*Theology of St. Luke*, pp. 60–65) surveyed the debates and concluded that Luke intended it to be a travel narrative; and more recently David P. Moessner (*Lord of the Banquet: The Prophet Like Moses of the Lukan Travel Narrative* [University of Basel Dissertation, 1982]) has argued persuasively that there are abundant indications in the section that Jesus is on a trip to Jerusalem. Some of these indications will be cited in a later chapter.

Acceptance and Rejection: Jesus and the Jewish Public

Since Luke did not produce a piece of literature that may be readily classified in terms of the generic categories of his day, it probably is not profitable to make detailed comparisons between Luke–Acts and Greek literature. But, since there are affinities between Luke's writing and certain Greek genres, notably tragedy, some comparisons are inevitable. In view of our major concern with Luke's presentation of the death of Jesus, such comparisons are particularly significant. Since Luke did not take the option of presenting a traditionally tragic hero in the case of either Jesus or Paul, he did not trace their misfortunes to some fatal flaw in their characters. In Luke's narrative there clearly is a motif of divine inevitability about Jesus' death. Aside from this, the death of Jesus is seen as the result of a complex of events involving certain lines of opposition. The various groups that heard Jesus' message responded to him in different ways, and the rejection of him and his message by some groups is surely connected with his execution. For Luke the question of the acceptance or rejection of Jesus was far more significant than Jesus' personal happiness or fortune. So Luke did not point to a fatal flaw in Jesus but substituted for it the character of the response to him on the part of the various Jewish groups who heard him.

The question of the Jewish response to Jesus and to the early Christians is complicated by the fact that Luke portrays a mixed response. In general there is a distinction between the response of the people at large and that of the Jewish leaders. There is also a distinction between different categories of Jewish leaders, specifically between the Pharisees and the chief priests. We shall investigate this latter distinction in chapter 3, but the important thing to note here is that those Jewish leaders who rejected Jesus did so from the first. In the case of the Jewish people, however, Luke shows that initial acceptance was followed by final rejection.

The distinction between the people and the leaders is prominently treated in Luke 7:18–35. In this passage John the Baptist has sent two disciples to ask about Jesus' identity. The two emissaries ask Jesus, "Are you he who is to come, or shall we look for another?" (7:20). Luke explains that Jesus was at that time performing cures and exorcisms, and he has Jesus call attention to this activity without explicitly answering the question that was addressed to him. After the two disciples leave, Jesus speaks about John to the crowds. He identifies the Baptist as a prophet and as more than a prophet. He maintains that John is the one who was spoken of in Malachi 3:1, i.e., a messenger who prepares the way. No one, except the least in the kingdom of God, is greater than John (7:28; cf. 16:16).[1] Then in 7:29–30 we have Luke's editorial aside: "When they heard this all the people and the tax collectors justified God, having been baptized with the baptism of John; but the Pharisees and the lawyers rejected the purpose of God for themselves, not having been baptized by him."[2] Luke makes a sharp distinction between the people (*laos*) and the tax collectors on one side and Pharisees and lawyers on the other. The former justified God (or acknowledged God's justice [*edikaiōsan ton theon*]) and were baptized by John. The Pharisees and lawyers "rejected the purpose of God for themselves" and were not baptized by John. In other words, a positive response to John is a positive response to God, and it is the people, not the leaders, who make the proper response.

In Luke 7:31–32 different kinds of responses are treated in the form of a simile. The people (*anthrōpoi*) of this generation are like children who sit in the agora and refuse to respond to other children. They refuse to respond to the flute by dancing, and they refuse to respond to the sound of mourning by crying. The simile becomes literal speech in 7:33–34. John was ascetic, but he was thought to be a demoniac. Jesus was not ascetic, and he was charged with gluttony. In the case of both Jesus and John the responses, like those of the children in the agora, were negative.

Luke 7:35—"Yet wisdom is justified by all her children"—appears at first to be unsuited to its present context and reads more like a popular maxim. But the concept of justification connects this saying with 7:29. The children of wisdom justify wisdom as the people and the tax collectors justify God. The use of children in 7:35 (*tekna*) also connects with the use of children in 7:32 (*paidioi*).

When taken as a whole, Luke 7:29–35 expresses some clear lines of opposition between those who accept Jesus and John and those who reject them. Those who accept them are the people (*laos*) and the tax collectors, who may be described as wisdom's children. By contrast, Jesus and John are rejected by Pharisees and lawyers, who may be described as the people (*anthrōpoi*) of this generation. Behind these lines of opposition lies the distinction between the Jewish people and their leaders, a distinction that Luke frequently notes (e.g., Luke 13:17).

The people are enthusiastically supportive of Jesus throughout the first part of Luke's gospel. By the end, however, there has been a significant change; indeed, a reversal. The same is true in Acts, where the initially favorable response to the early Christians is treated in the first part. By the end of Acts, the Christian movement, as symbolized by Paul, receives sharp, even violent, public opposition.[3] These observations suggest that Luke may have made use of a particular literary pattern in order to treat the Jewish public reaction to Jesus and his successors. It is a pattern of initial acceptance followed by rejection. It appears in several individual passages as well as in the overall structure of both Luke and Acts. The use of this literary pattern must be explored in some detail.

In order to study Luke's treatment of the Jewish public, it is inevitable that we focus attention on the crowds in contexts in which it is obvious that the author is writing about masses of indeterminate and undefined Jewish people. Although this is not simply a word study, something needs to be said about the linguistic phenomena. The usual word that we should expect as a designation for the Jewish public is *ochlos,* and Luke uses this word frequently, both in the singular and the plural. But he also uses the term *laos* in a number of places. In an important article published in 1958 Nils Dahl showed that, with the exception of two references in Acts (15:14; 18:10), *laos* always signifies Israel. Dahl acknowledged that *laos* does not always have "the full theological meaning 'the people of God' in its contrast to Gentiles; in many cases Luke simply uses it as a synonym for *ochlos,* = 'people' in the collective, unspecified sense of this word." But Dahl added: "This 'vulgar' usage is only found in contexts where the people in question is a crowd of Israelites."[4] In the two exceptions in Acts, Luke is specifically calling attention to the constitution of Gentiles as now belonging to God "in the same way as Israel does, or, rather: as Israel should do."[5] It will be necessary to keep Dahl's comments in mind as we examine the use of *ochlos* and *laos*. In addition, we must explore those passages in which groups of Jews, otherwise unspecified, appear, whatever word or phrase is used to describe them.[6]

ACCEPTANCE AND REJECTION IN LUKE

A particularly important section of the gospel of Luke that deals with the response of the Jewish public to Jesus and makes use of the literary pattern of initial acceptance followed by rejection is 4:16–30, Jesus' sermon at Nazareth. This passage has often been regarded as programmatic for the gospel of Luke and even for Luke–Acts as a whole. Although it is similar in some respects to passages in Matthew and Mark, the distinctive aspects of Luke's narrative give a different meaning to his report of the incident.[7] The location of the narrative at the very beginning of Jesus' public ministry establishes the programmatic nature of the sermon. Here the Lukan Jesus announces the themes that will be developed in the rest of Luke–Acts. He asserts that his own work is to be a fulfillment of the Isaianic scripture (Isa 61:1–2), and he goes on to speak of the work of Elijah and Elisha, who passed by widows and lepers in Israel only to offer help to Gentiles. Is not one to understand that the fulfillment of Isaiah is to be accomplished by Jesus but that the benefits of the fulfillment will be enjoyed by Gentiles rather than by Jews?

The response of Jesus' audience in this passage follows the lines of initial acceptance followed by rejection. Since the setting is in a synagogue, the implied audience would be composed of Jews who have assembled for the sabbath service. It is described as an attentive audience that was initially favorable to Jesus' message. When he proclaimed himself as the fulfillment of scripture, "all spoke well of him, and wondered at the gracious words which proceeded out of his mouth" (4:22). But when Jesus began to talk about the work of Elijah and Elisha among Gentiles, the audience turned against him: "When they heard this, all in the synagogue were filled with wrath" (4:28). Jesus was thrown out of the city and almost killed. In terms of public response the pattern is clear: initial acceptance followed by rejection.[8] Luke 4:16–30 anticipates the Jewish public response that will be worked out in the rest of the gospel and Acts. It is significant that the rejection is connected with favorable treatment of Gentiles.[9]

In terms of Jewish public response to Jesus the Nazareth incident presents in miniature the pattern that shapes the Lukan narrative in the gospel as a whole. In the earlier part of the gospel the mass of Jewish people, as distinguished from the leaders, is supportive of Jesus. At the end the crowd has turned against him.

The ministry of Jesus in Galilee (Luke 4:14–9:50) is especially marked by a warm public response that is sometimes overwhelming. At times Jesus tries to escape the crowds (5:12–16), but they seek him out even in the loneliest of places (4:42–44). On one occasion the pressure of the crowd requires him to teach from a boat on the lake (5:1–3). Crowds make it difficult for the paralytic's friends to bring him to Jesus for healing (5:17–26), and they prevent Jesus' mother and brothers from approaching him (8:19–21). Large multitudes seem to accompany him wherever he goes (7:9,11; 8:40,42, 45; 9:11,37). A large crowd gathers to hear Jesus' sermon on the plain (6:17–19) and for other teaching occasions (8:4). Popular response is characterized with words such as ecstasy, fear (5:26), and astonishment (9:43). Jesus is called "a great prophet" (7:16), John the Baptist, Elijah, and one of the ancient resurrected prophets (9:19). Except for the conclusion to the Nazareth incident (4:28–29) and one negative expression following the healing of the Gerasene demoniac (the frightened people from the region asked Jesus to leave, 8:37), the popular response to Jesus in this portion of Luke's gospel is altogether positive.[10]

The same is true in the section on Jesus in transit (Luke 9:51–19:44). The presence of large supportive groups is frequently noted (11:29; 12:1,54; 14:25; 18:36). Because of the crowd the short Zacchaeus must climb a tree to see Jesus (19:3–4). The attitude of the crowd toward Jesus is no less favorable here than in the Galilean section (e.g., 13:17).

Jewish mass support continues even in the section on Jesus' activity in Jerusalem (Luke 19:45–22:46). In 19:45 he enters the temple, and the entry is followed by a long section of teaching material in chapters 20–21.[11] In this account of Jesus' teaching in the temple Luke seems to make a special effort to call attention to the relationship between Jesus and the people. In introducing the section, he says that Jesus taught the people (*laos*) in the temple (20:1), and in summarizing Jesus' activity in Jerusalem he says that all the people (*laos*) got up early in the morning to hear him teach in the temple (21:38). As he is engaged in teaching, it is the people (*laos*) who protect him from the Jewish leaders. Jesus' popular support thwarts the intentions of his opponents (19:48; 20:26), who are afraid of the people (20:19; 22:2). Popular support for the Baptist means that Jesus' opponents are unable to answer his questions (20:6). Jesus delivers the parable of the vintner as a criticism of the scribes and chief priests, and he does so in the presence of the people (20:9). He condemns the scribes "in the hearing of all the people" (20:45). In Luke 1:1–22:46, Jewish public response is overwhelmingly positive.

But when we come to the scenes of Jesus' trial, death, and resurrection (Luke 22:47–24:53), we find that, although Jesus is not without some popular support, the crowd as a whole is lined up with his opponents, who are led by the chief priests. With them, they insist before Pilate on Jesus' guilt (23:4–5, 13–14), call for the release of Barabbas (23:18), call for Jesus' crucifixion (23:21,23), and stand around watching it (23:35).[12]

The treatment of crowds is exceedingly complex in Luke's trial narrative. We should observe that two distinct groups appear to be present at various stages of the proceedings. One group consists of people who are loyal to Jesus. The other is the crowd, and it is this latter group that represents the Jewish public response to Jesus.

Jesus' supporters are mentioned several times in the narratives of the trial and the crucifixion. In 23:27 Luke reports that "a great multitude of the people [*polu plēthos tou laou*]" followed Jesus to the place of crucifixion. He also notes that there were women "who bewailed and lamented him." Jesus addresses this mourning group directly as "daughters of Jerusalem" in 23:28, a verse that suggests that the women, if not the entire multitude, were Jerusalemites. Moreover, in 23:49 Luke draws attention to the presence of some of Jesus' acquaintances and some Galilean women at the site of the crucifixion. These people are situated at some distance from the crowd that witnessed the crucifixion (23:35). In 23:55 he reports that the Galilean women inspected Jesus' tomb. Presumably they are the ones who will discover the tomb to be empty on Easter morning. This group is physically distant and morally distinct from the crowd as a whole. They, together with the multitude mentioned in 23:27, represent Jesus' loyal remnant, a beleaguered group of disciples and sympathizers whose support is totally ineffective when put up against the rejection of the crowd, but whose presence in the narrative as witnesses is absolutely necessary.

The second group present at the trial and crucifixion is composed of those who condemned Jesus before Pilate (Luke 23:4–5, 13–14), called for the release of Barabbas (23:18), joined the chief priests in calling for Jesus' execution (23:21,23), witnessed the crucifixion (23:35), and returned home beating their breasts (23:48). The dominance of this group is indicated by its connection with the Jewish leaders and by the successful implementation of its demands.

In some respects both of these groups resemble a Greek chorus. In many tragic dramas the author has composed speeches for a chorus in order to express judgments on an action, to draw out the implications of an action, or to provide an emotional response to a certain event or situation. Choruses frequently provide musical relief after tense emotional scenes. The chorus most often represents the social group within which the dramatic action takes place. Dramatically, it frequently guides the audience to make the response that the author thought to be appropriate. It seldom affects the action in the play. It is a dramatic device that both links and separates the audience and the actors.

In Luke's passion narrative his supporters mourn (Luke 23:27), large masses of people watch the crucifixion (23:35) and, after Jesus' death, return home beating their breasts (23:48). It is plausible to think that in the acts of mourning and beating the breasts these groups are acting as a Greek chorus by demonstrating the proper response to Jesus' death.[13] We have already observed that, in some respects, the Lukan passion narrative fits reasonably well Aristotle's description of a good tragic drama. It is not episodic, but it is rather a narrative of a closely related series of events that evoke pity and fear. In these acts of lamentation the two groups demonstrate these emotions. The nature of drama allows the Greek dramatist to give a speaking role to the chorus, and at crucial points the chorus may exhibit the emotions which the author wishes to evoke from the audience. Consider, for example, a speech of the chorus in Sophocles' *Oedipus Rex,* given just as the blinded Oedipus appears on stage:

> This is a terrible sight for men to see!
> I never found a worse!
> Poor wretch, what madness came upon you!
> What evil spirit leaped upon your life
> to your ill-luck—a leap beyond man's strength!
> Indeed I pity you, but I cannot
> look at you, though there's much I want to ask
> and much to learn and much to see.
> I shudder at the sight of you.[14]

Fear and pity are explicitly spoken of by the Sophoclean chorus. No less effectively, the Lukan groups demonstrate the appropriate responses to Jesus' crucifixion.

Despite the resemblances the Lukan groups depart significantly from the role of the Greek chorus. This is particularly true of the dominant group in Luke, the one representing the Jewish public. While a Greek dramatist may use a chorus to express a moral or legal judgment on a character, that judgment is one that, from the author's point of view, is to be regarded as appropriate. But in calling for the execution of Jesus, the crowd in Luke 23 is acting in a way that, from the author's perspective, is entirely inappropriate. The inappropriateness of the crowd's response in Luke's narrative will

become clearer when we investigate the trial of Jesus in chapter 5.
But even without such a detailed investigation there should be little
question that Luke does not approve of the crowd's rejection of Jesus. Indeed, that point is made clear in some of the speeches in Acts
(2:23; 3:13–15; 4:10,27; 10:39; 13:27–28), where the apostles
condemn the people for Jesus' death.

Luke wants the reader to know that, although there was a group
of loyalists present at the time of Jesus' death, he was finally rejected
by the Jewish public at large. This public rejection is not a function
of a literary device in which the crowd is treated as a chorus. Rather, it
conforms to a literary pattern in which public acceptance is followed by rejection.

Thus, while we may not ignore the role of Jesus' supporters, we
may justifiably speak of a shift on the part of the Jewish public from
acceptance to rejection. A major effect of this shift is to focus attention more and more on the sole figure of Jesus. In 1:1–22:46 Luke
presented a Jesus who had been supported by his disciples and by
crowds of people. But at the arrest there was only token support—
no crowd, sleeping disciples, betrayal by one of the twelve, and a
futile effort at resistance. After that we have the denial of Peter and
only the ineffective presence of indefinite acquaintances and women
from Jerusalem and Galilee. The rest of the disciples seem to be ig-
nored by Luke and are probably to be thought of as absent. Above
all, the motif of diminishing support inevitably focuses attention on
Jesus himself, who virtually meets his opponents in total solitude.

The change in the role of the Jewish public seems to occur specifically at the scene of Jesus' arrest (Luke 22:47–53). In connection
with the arrangements that Judas had made with the chief priests
and scribes, Luke said that Judas "sought an opportunity to betray
him to them in the absence of the multitude" (*ater ochlou,* 22:6).[15]
Luke seems to be very deliberate in describing these arrangements.
In the apocalyptic discourse that immediately preceded, readers
have been told about the danger of betrayals (21:16–17). They
have also been told, in 6:16, that Judas would be the traitor, and
now in 22:3 they are reminded that Judas was "of the number of the
twelve." After Jesus' temptation the devil had withdrawn "until an
opportune time" (4:13), but now he returns and enters Judas
(22:3).[16] Luke had emphasized the protection that the people af-

forded Jesus throughout the period of his teaching in the temple (19:45–21:38). Therefore, it is appropriate for Judas to look for an opportunity to betray him without this protection. For Judas to be successful it will be necessary for him to isolate Jesus from the crowd, and this is what he intends to do.

As Luke describes the arrest of Jesus (Luke 22:47–53), Judas is completely successful. Just prior to this scene Jesus and the disciples had gone to the Mount of Olives (22:39). It is evidently night (cf. Luke 22:39 with 21:37), and there is no crowd present—only Jesus with a handful of sleeping disciples. Moreover, the crowd (*ochlos*) now forms part of the arresting party, along with Judas, the chief priests, elders, and *stratēgoi* (22:47, 52).[17] The crowd has deserted Jesus, and from now on it is part of the opposition.

Although Luke did not write a tragedy with a hero who had a fatal flaw, it is possible to regard his treatment of the Jewish public in the gospel as an adaptation of the traditional tragic plot. The hero does not move on to his dreaded fate because he has committed an error, but he does undergo something that inspires fear and pity. The fault for this is not in himself but in the public response to him, and this response has the character of a sudden reversal. Despite all of the plot complications that mount up in Luke 1:1–22:46, including the encounters with the Jewish leaders and the foreshadowings of death, Jesus is protected as long as he has public support. The betrayal and the arrest, however, constitute a turning point, and thereafter the lack of support allows the narrative to come to its inevitable resolution in Jesus' death. In this light the resurrection constitutes a surprise ending, which stands outside the traditional plot line.

ACCEPTANCE AND REJECTION IN ACTS

The treatment of the Jewish public is more complex in Acts than in the gospel. Acts contains several reflections of material in the gospel, and the reader may be assumed to know about the reversal in the public response to Jesus. One reflection from the gospel appears in Acts 4:24–30, liturgical material that contains a quotation from Psalm 2 and an exegesis that identifies the people of Israel, together with Herod, Pontius Pilate, and Gentiles, as the opponents of Jesus. It is worth noting that this exegesis reflects the trial scenes in Luke, and only in Luke among the synoptic gospels.

Despite the increased complexity, the pattern of initial acceptance followed by rejection is clearly present in Acts, both in several individual sections and in the book as a whole. The pattern is found in several narratives that describe Paul's missionary activity. Indeed, it is virtually a formula: Paul enters a city and preaches or teaches in a synagogue. At first there is a positive response, but later the unconverted Jews turn the masses against Paul, and he then goes out to address Gentiles. Sometimes Jews stir up non-Jews, and as a result Paul is forced to go on to another city, leaving a believing group behind. The pattern appears to be Luke's major means of shaping his narratives about Paul's activity in Pisidian Antioch (Acts 13:13–52), Iconium (14:1–7), Thessalonica (17:1–9), Beroea (17:10–15), and Ephesus (19:8–10).

The narrative about Paul at Pisidian Antioch (Acts 13:13–52) is a particularly good illustration of Lukan literary usage. It may, in fact, serve as a programmatic introduction to Paul's ministry as Luke 4:16–30 served for Jesus' ministry, although the Antioch narrative is longer and more detailed. When Paul and company arrived in Antioch, they attended synagogue on the sabbath, and "after the reading of the law and the prophets" (13:15) they were invited to speak. Paul responded by telling of Jesus' coming, his death, and his resurrection, fortifying the narrative by the use of a number of OT references. Paul ended his speech with an offer of salvation. Luke suggests that Paul's message was quite acceptable, for he reports that "many Jews and devout converts to Judaism followed Paul and Barnabas" (13:43) and that the missionaries were invited to return on the next sabbath. But when they did arrive, they were met with hostility from the Jews. As a result Paul and Barnabas announced, for the first of three times, the decision to go to Gentiles: "It was necessary that the word of God should be spoken first to you. Since you thrust it from you, and judge yourselves unworthy of eternal life, behold, we turn to the Gentiles" (13:46; see 18:6; 28:28). Just as in Jesus' sermon at Nazareth, initial acceptance by Jews had turned into rejection, and the issue is connected with the movement of the Christian gospel from Jews to Gentiles. On this passage Robert Tannehill appropriately comments, "By means of these words Luke alludes to and interprets the rejection of the gospel by the Jews of Antioch and the turning of the mission to the Gentiles before they take place."[18]

Luke also makes use of this literary pattern in the overall structure of Acts. In the early chapters he gives the reader the impression that the apostolic successors of Jesus are enjoying remarkable success, just as Jesus did in the early chapters of the gospel. Especially in the section on Christianity in Jerusalem (Acts 1:4–8:3) the reader learns that the believing community is growing by leaps and bounds. It grows numerically, starting with a mere handful (1:13–14), adding 120 (1:15) and 3,000 (2:41), and finally totaling around 5,000 (4:4). The mass response among Jews in Jerusalem is summarized by James and the elders in 21:20, when they say to Paul, "You see, brother, how many thousands [muriades] there are among the Jews of those who have believed; they are all zealous for the law."[19] Not only does Luke call attention to the growth of the believing community; he also emphasizes the esteem, even veneration, in which the early Christians were held. The believers had favor among all the people (2:47). The people honored them highly, even if they did not convert (5:13). It was believed that the apostles, even Peter's shadow, had curative power (5:15–16). As in the gospel, most of the Jewish leaders were opposed to the Christian community, but mass support protected the believers. These leaders were unable to punish Peter and John "because of the people; for all men praised God for what had happened" (4:21). At one point, although the officials arrested the apostles, they did so without violence, "for they were afraid of being stoned by the people" (5:26).

But near the end of Acts the situation changes drastically. On Paul's last visit to Jerusalem the Jewish mob turned against him, and we have scenes of plots, riots, and violence (Acts 21:27–22:29). Roman soldiers were required to protect him from the mob violence that broke out near the temple. Although he was allowed to address the people in Hebrew and although they listened up to a point, they finally shouted, "Away with such a fellow from the earth! For he ought not to live" (22:22).[20] Then follow the trials of Paul, when the Jewish leaders, now with popular support, accused Paul of teaching against the law, the temple, and the people. Perhaps in 25:24 Luke wished to emphasize the total rejection of Paul.

Here Festus addresses Agrippa: "King Agrippa and all who are present with us, you see this man about whom the whole Jewish people petitioned me, both at Jerusalem and here, shouting that he ought not to live any longer." Paul now stands without popular support, just as Jesus had done at his trial.

It is difficult to find a precise *metabasis,* or turning point, in Acts, but it surely comes near Paul's return to Jerusalem in 21:17. There are foreshadowings of the coming misfortune in Paul's speech to the elders at Miletus (20:17–35) and in the warning of Agabus (21:10–11). Paul and company arrive in Jerusalem in Acts 21:17 and meet with James and the elders of the Jerusalem church. The latter report that the Christian movement in Jerusalem includes "myriads" of Jews, who "are all zealous for the law and they have been told about you [Paul], that you teach all the Jews who are among the Gentiles to forsake Moses, telling them not to circumcise their children or observe the customs" (21:20–21). Then comes the suggestion that Paul should pay the expenses of four Jewish men who are under a vow. Paul follows the suggestion, but he is nevertheless met with hostility from Asian Jews.[21] From the time of Paul's arrival in Jerusalem up to his departure for Rome, the Jewish mob stands against him. In respect, then, to the attitude of the Jewish public, Paul's arrival in Jerusalem in Acts 21:17 seems to be the crisis. The crisis point does not stand out so clearly as one might wish, because Paul has experienced a number of similar minicrises already. But in terms of the overall structure of Acts, Paul's misfortune among the Jews (and hence the ill fortune of Christians generally) begins with his arrival in Jerusalem.

It is notable that not even the Christians in Jerusalem are pictured as supportive of Paul. It is this group that he attempts to pacify by following the suggestion of James and the elders. The Jewish Christians in Jerusalem are disturbed by what they have heard about Paul's preaching among diaspora Jews. Apparently his action in the temple is meant to neutralize this disturbance and to demonstrate that he is not so radical as he is thought to be. The question of Gentile believers seems not to be an issue at this point. James and the elders simply remind Paul of the decision that was made in Acts 15:19–20: "We have sent a letter with our judgment that they should abstain from what has been sacrificed to idols and from blood and from what is strangled and from unchastity" (21:25).[22] How did the "myriads" of Jewish Christians in Jerusalem respond to Paul's action in the temple? We are not told. After the narrative about this episode, the focus of attention shifts in 21:27 to the opposition from multitudes of Jews and then to Paul's trials. In none of these narratives do the believers figure. They have disappeared in the same way that Jesus' popular support (and his disciples) effectively evaporated in Luke's gospel. To be sure, Luke does not clearly group the believers with Paul's enemies, but neither does he count them among the supporters. The only supporters are those implied by the use of the pronoun "we," which ceases just after the arrival in Jerusalem (21:17) and does not begin again until the departure for Rome (27:1).

It appears, therefore, that a controlling literary pattern in the composition of both Luke and Acts was used to demonstrate the change in the Jewish public response from acceptance to rejection. In the early sections of both books the Jewish public warmly accepts the heroes. In both, however, there are foreshadowings of misfortune to come. In both, the crisis point occurs in Jerusalem. In both, the Jewish crowd finally rejects the hero; and in both, the hero faces a series of trials.

CONCLUSION

The strength of this literary pattern may be seen in the fact that its use involves certain logical inconsistencies. In reading the two books consecutively we find that the same public that finally rejected Jesus initially accepted his successors. This logical inconsistency is created by the use of the same literary pattern first in the gospel and then again in Acts.

Another inconsistency has frequently been observed. There are three Pauline statements that announce the end of his mission to the Jews (Acts 13:46; 18:6; 28:28). But after the first two of these, Paul returns to speak in synagogues to Jewish people. One may explain the apparent inconsistency by saying that it was necessary to give notice to different Jewish localities or regions—Asia, Greece, and Italy.[23] Or it may be useful to compare these announcements with the passion predictions in the gospel (Luke 9:22,44; 17:25;

18:31–34) and to suggest that, in both cases, they serve to fore-shadow the events to come. But it seems most useful to refer to the way in which Luke has written about Paul's missionary activity and to conclude that the repeated use of a particular literary pattern has produced a logical inconsistency. The Lukan Paul rejects any further mission to Jews, but he must resume it because the literary pattern demands it.

These considerations lead to the question: Does Luke mean to suggest that the Jewish rejection of Jesus, the Christian gospel, and Paul is final? The probable answer is yes. Although there are myriads of believers in Jerusalem, they are suspicious of Luke's hero, and they seem to drop out of the picture before Paul's trials. Thus, in the closing narratives virtually the entire Jewish population in Judea is set over against the gospel, i.e., against Paul as its representative (Acts 25:24). In most literary works the end of the book is the most impressive part.[24] Endings not only conclude stories, but they also resolve tensions that were developed in the body. They tell how the story turned out. Although Acts may imply a continuation of the story, with Paul in Rome, the ending nevertheless functions in the usual way. Despite the bright happiness of the early chapters, the end of the story is the more impressive part in respect to Jewish public response. The final words are likely to constitute an expression of the author's controlling concept. In Acts the final words are ironic and negative. The quotation from Isa 6:9–10 is ironic: "You shall indeed hear but never understand, and you shall indeed see but never perceive" (28:26). In association with the quotation and in reference to the Jewish public, Paul's last words are negative: "Let it be known to you then that this salvation of God has been sent to the Gentiles; they will listen" (28:28). The Jewish acceptance of Jesus and the early Christians previously described has finally been either neglected or suppressed. In this way Luke claims that the Jewish public has heard but rejected the gospel. Thus, the failed mission to the Jews is terminated in favor of the successful mission to the Gentiles.[25]

Authors almost never explain their use of literary patterns, so it is fruitless to look to Luke for an explanation of this one. Why the Jewish public suddenly changed from acceptance to rejection is not a question that Luke wished to answer in any explicit way. But if we look at the ways in which this pattern of acceptance and rejection has been used at various points in Luke–Acts, it becomes possible to draw certain inferences.

In the programmatic narrative of Jesus at Nazareth (Luke 4:16–30) the change from public acceptance to rejection occurred when Jesus, in his sermon, pointed out that Elijah and Elisha neglected Israelite widows and lepers but granted help to Gentiles. In the mission to Pisidian Antioch (Acts 13:13–52) Jewish rejection led to the first Pauline announcement of the Gentile mission, which meant the end of the Jewish mission (13:46). After Paul returned to Jerusalem, the Jewish crowd turned against him when it was thought that he had taken the Gentile Trophimus into the temple (Acts 21:27–29). The charge they leveled against Paul is ironic; it is, within the Lukan account, literally false but metaphorically true. The Lukan Paul did not take Trophimus into the temple, but he preached that the benefits that had been promised to Jews were now available to Gentiles. In a similar way the various narratives that tell of Paul's missionary visits make a connection between the rejection of Paul and his Gentile mission. It is the Jewish rejection that paved the way for Paul's presentation of the gospel to Gentiles.

It is significant to observe that the use of the pattern of initial acceptance and final rejection reveals something about Luke's view of the Jewish people, which should be described as ambivalent. First, the initial acceptance is looked on favorably, and it means that the Christian message could be accepted by Jews. Second, the rejection by the Jews, since it is final, is more significant than the acceptance. Jewish rejection has opened the way to the Gentile mission, but it has also revealed the irony of the Jewish response. Third, there is the character of divine necessity. It was necessary for the gospel to be preached first to Jews.

It seems reasonable to assume that Luke's use of the pattern of acceptance and rejection has a relationship to his presentation of the death of Jesus. Although it is an overstatement to say that the Lukan Jesus was killed because there was a change in the public response to him, it is nevertheless clear that the withdrawal of popular support had an effect. Once Jesus had been isolated from the crowd, he could be arrested. The leaders no longer hesitated to make their move against him, and both leaders and public called for his conviction and execution. The use of this literary pattern suggests that there was, in Luke's mind, a relationship between the response of the Jewish public, the initiation of the Gentile mission, and the death of Jesus. In ironic fashion the Jewish rejection of Jesus, which played a role in his execution, is seen both as a rejection of the Christian mission to the Gentiles and as a way of facilitating that very mission. These relationships should be kept in mind as we continue to explore Luke's narrative.

NOTES

1. For Hans Conzelmann, Luke 16:16 is pivotal. He claims that, for Luke, John the Baptist marks the conclusion of the period of Israel. See his *The Theology of St. Luke,* trans. Geoffrey Buswell (New York: Harper and Bros., 1960).
2. The RSV prints Luke 7:29–30 in parentheses.
3. Charles H. Talbert called attention to a number of parallels between Luke and Acts, although he did not mention the literary pattern we are investigating here. See his *Literary Patterns, Theological Themes and the Genre of Luke–Acts* (Missoula, Mont.: Scholars Press, 1974).
4. Nils A. Dahl, "A People for His Name, (Acts xv. 14)," *New Testament Studies* 4 (1958): 324.
5. Ibid., p. 326.
6. *Plēthos* sometimes is used to designate a Jewish group, but in several cases it also designates Christians, either Jewish or Greek (e.g., Acts 4:32; 5:14; 6:2,5; 14:1; 15:12,30; 17:4). *Dēmos,* used only in Acts in the NT, usually has a political connotation, i.e., citizens (Acts 12:22; 17:5; 19:30,33). Of course, the plural *Ioudaioi* is frequently found. The plural *Israēlitai* is used only in combination with *andres,* as a form of address (Acts 2:22; 3:12; 5:35; 13:16; 21:28).
7. See Matt 13:54–58; Mark 6:1–6; chapter 6 below.
8. In his commentary on Luke 4:16–30, I. Howard Marshall discounts the initially favorable response to Jesus; see his *The Gospel of Luke: A Commentary on the Greek Text* (Grand Rapids: Eerdmans, 1978), pp. 177–90. In his Anchor Bible Commentary, Joseph A. Fitzmyer recognizes the initially favorable response but calls attention to a lack of literary unity in the passage; see *The Gospel According to Luke (I–IX)* (Garden City, N.Y.: Doubleday, 1981), pp. 525–40. Neither Marshall nor Fitzmyer believes that a literary pattern has affected the composition of Luke 4:16–30.
9. See Robert C. Tannehill, "The Mission of Jesus According to Luke IV: 16–30," in *Jesus in Nazareth,* ed. E. Grässer et al. (Berlin: Walter de Gruyter, 1972), pp.

51–75. Tannehill says that verses 25–27 "were inserted here by Luke in order to suggest the connection between the rejection of Jesus and his turning to others which occurs at Nazareth and the rejection of the gospel by the Jews and turning of the missionaries to the Gentiles which Luke will trace in Acts" (p. 59).

10. Luke explicitly locates the narrative of 8:26–39 outside Galilee. He probably means to designate a city in the Decapolis, and thus this narrative is the only one in Luke in which Jesus goes outside predominantly Jewish territory. The reference to swine in 8:32–33 may reinforce the impression that Jesus is outside Jewish territory. On the basis of these considerations we may understand that the negative response in 8:37 comes from Gentiles. On the other hand, these indications may have been too subtle for Luke's first readers. They would be required to have acquaintance with local Palestinian geography and with Jewish practices, and nothing of this sort has been explained in Luke's book. We probably should not emphasize the Gentile setting of this narrative or classify the response in 8:37 as Gentile.

11. This section is dealt with further in chapter 4.

12. In Luke 23:18,21,23 the subject is an indefinite third person plural, but the reference is to the chief priests and the people (*laos*) in 23:13.

13. The suggestion that the act of beating the breast is to be understood as a symbol of Jewish corporate repentance is unsuitable to the Lukan context and literary structure. Marshall rejects the idea that the crowd is here expressing repentance and prefers to say that it is expressing grief (*The Gospel of Luke,* pp. 876–77). If Luke has been influenced by the use of the chorus in Greek drama, he might well have used the crowd to express grief.

14. "Oedipus the King," trans. David Grene, in *An Anthology of Greek Drama,* 1st series, ed. C. A. Robinson, Jr. (New York: Holt, Rinehart and Winston, 1949), p. 94.

15. The parallels in Matthew and Mark do not have the words *ater ochlou* or anything similar (Matt 26:16; Mark 14:11). See chapter 6.

16. Conzelmann (*The Theology of St. Luke*) emphasizes the ministry of Jesus as a time when the devil has no effect. This devil-free period extends from Luke 4:13 to 22:3.

17. On the meaning of *stratēgos,* see below, p. 76.

18. Tannehill, "The Mission of Jesus According to Luke IV: 16–30," p. 63.

19. Some texts read "in Judea" instead of "among the Jews" in Acts 21:20.

20 The speakers in Acts 22:22 are indefinite, but the third person plural refers to the people who were being addressed, last mentioned in Acts 21:40. Thus, in 22:22 Luke means to signify that the assembled Jewish people demanded the death of Paul.

21. In Acts 21:27 (cf. 24:18) Luke says that the riot at the temple was incited by Jews from Asia, but he does not consistently indicate that the actions of diaspora Jews were different from those of Palestinian Jews. For example, the plot against Paul that is described in 23:12–22 is probably to be understood as devised by Palestinian Jews.

22. Cf. Acts 15:19–20,29; note should be taken of the textual problems in the so-called apostolic decree. For an excellent discussion of the various interpretations

of the decree see S. G. Wilson, *Luke and the Law* (Cambridge: Cambridge University Press, 1983), pp. 68–103.

23. Ernst Haenchen and others have made this observation; see his *The Acts of the Apostles,* trans. Bernard Noble et al. (Oxford: Basil Blackwell, 1971), p. 724.

24. See Aristotle, *The Poetics,* VII, 5: "An end on the contrary is that which is inevitably or, as a rule, the natural result of something else but from which nothing else follows" (trans. W. Hamilton Fyfe in the Loeb Classical Library [Cambridge, Mass.: Harvard University Press, 1932]).

25. For an opposing view see Jacob Jervell, *Luke and the People of God* (Minneapolis: Augsburg Publishing House, 1972), esp. pp. 41–74.

Conflict: Jesus and the Jewish Leaders

I
n Luke's story the response of the Jewish public to Jesus clearly has some bearing on his death. But as we
examined this public response, it became clear that
this alone did not have the power to bring about the death of Jesus.
Even a dramatic shift in public opinion, such as Luke pictures, was
not of itself an efficient cause. The crucifixion came about only
when the crowd joined the leaders in demanding it, and so the Lukan portrayal of those whose positions gave them the requisite
power has a major bearing on our problem. Thus, we come in this
chapter to examine Luke's treatment of one sector of power—the
leading groups of Jews. The sector represented by certain powerful
individuals will be included in the discussion of the trial of Jesus in
chapter 5.

It is generally recognized that in Acts, Luke took special pains to
show that responsible Roman officials saw no offense in the Christian movement and indeed regarded Christians as law-abiding citizens. The problems Christians encountered were with Jewish leaders. Festus' verdict about Paul in Acts 25:25 seems to represent the
way in which Luke wanted his readers to understand the Roman attitude in general, namely, that Christians have committed no cap-
ital crimes against Roman law and do not stand in opposition to
those who uphold Roman justice. By contrast, Paul and the other
Christians in Acts are perennially on the verge of conflict with Jewish leaders. The same is true with Jesus. The gospel of Luke is filled

with scenes of conflict between Jesus and various groups. The conflicts would seem to be designed to prepare the reader to understand the nature of the opposition to Jesus and to assess the forces that brought about his death.

Since, in the gospel and Acts, Luke was writing a narrative (*diēgēsis*, Luke 1:1), elements of plot would have been important to him as a literary artist. A fundamental element that makes a narrative move is the way in which an author deals with conflict. It is, in fact, difficult to conceive of a story without conflict. Some form of opposition appears essential, for at its base a story is the working out of some task against certain odds and despite opposing forces. Many folktales tell of conflict between a hero and a villain. Many complex stories have opposing forces or groups. Psychological narratives call attention to oppositions within an individual or to more subtle forms of conflict. In all these story types conflict is an essential ingredient.

As a writer of narrative Luke knows how to provide conflict situations in which his hero or heroes meet various threats. Indeed, this author does not minimize the role of conflict. He appears to be sensitive to the effects of such conflict narration on readers. The importance of conflict in Luke–Acts has not often been recognized, however, perhaps because most scholars have been impressed with the irenic character of much of the material in these documents. But conflict is present in Luke's writing, and it is necessary to analyze his general use of it before moving on to the treatment of the Jewish leaders.

CONFLICT IN LUKE–ACTS

The general use of conflict as a literary device may be seen in the various ways Luke presents situations of conflict, as well as anticipations and allusions to it.

Luke includes anticipations of conflict in the infancy narratives (Luke 1:5–2:52). The overall literary function of these narratives appears to be to alert the reader to the significance of the events that are about to be presented. As such, they prepare the reader to expect events of cosmic significance, occurrences of a miraculous nature, and events that have been predetermined by divine action.

Heavenly announcements, marvelous recognitions, and scenes from a precocious childhood were frequently used in Hellenistic biography, and partial parallels may be found in birth stories of Plato, Alexander the Great, Apollonius of Tyana, and others.[1]

Luke's infancy narrative is distinct from the others, however, in its inclusion of two birth stories—that of John and of Jesus. Moreover, there are clear similarities between the two accounts: in each there is an angelic announcement, a miraculous birth, an account of circumcision and naming, hymns of expectation and hope, and statements of growth.[2]

The dominant tone of Luke's infancy narratives is one of joyful expectation, but there are, nevertheless, signals of conflict to come. Some of the signals are compatible with tragic patterns, for they alert the reader to expect sudden reversals in fortune or circumstances. In the infancy narratives and elsewhere Luke uses a motif that we shall refer to as the *motif of transposition*. This is a literary device in which positions are changed—the rich become poor, the powerful become powerless, the first become last, or vice versa.

In the infancy narratives the births of John and Jesus portend a transposition of present social conditions, which are viewed from the perspective of the unfortunate or oppressed. A transposition of social conditions implies conflict, and conflict language is present in the infancy narratives. The Magnificat of Mary speaks rather directly of class conflict:

> He has put down powerful people from thrones
> And lifted up lowly ones.
> The hungry he has filled with good things,
> And the rich he has sent away empty.
> He has come to the aid of Israel his child,
> To remember mercy (Luke 1:52–54, author's translation).

The lines of opposition in these verses pit the powerful and the rich against the lowly and the hungry. The expectation of aid for Israel implies the activity of some enemy that intends harm for God's child. The hope that is expressed in these verses is that which proceeds from the lowly, the hungry, and the Israelites. But the expectation is wrapped up in anticipated conflict, in which positions are changed: the powerful and the powerless exchange places, as do the hungry and the rich, and Israel and its enemies.[3]

In the same way Zechariah's speech after the birth of John seems to elaborate the concept of aid for Israel. He expresses the hope of redemption and salvation for Israel in Luke 1:68–69. Although salvation, according to 1:77, includes forgiveness of sins, the chief emphasis in Zechariah's speech is on the rescue of Israel from its enemies. In 1:71 Zechariah defines the rescue expressly as being "saved from our enemies, and from the hand of all who hate us," and in 1:74 he speaks of deliverance from the hand of enemies. Here the language is that of the oppressed Jew looking for national relief. Only when relief comes is Israel able to serve God in piety and righteousness (1:75).[4]

The conclusion of Simeon's speech (Luke 2:34–35) contrasts with the earlier portion (2:29–32) and with the dominant tone of joyful expectation in the infancy narratives. Simeon says that Jesus is to be a person about whom people will take sides. He will be a controversial sign, i.e., a source of conflict. The word that Jesus "is set for the fall and rising of many in Israel" (2:34) reminds us of the transpositions in 1:52–54. The shocking words in 2:35 ("And a sword will pierce through your own soul also") add a personal quality to the theme of conflict, which has become explicit in Simeon's speech.

The language of conflict is not dominant in the infancy narratives, but readers are given a sufficient signal. They should understand that the births of John and Jesus constitute the beginning of a divine work in which there will be social revolution. The powerful and the powerless will change places; there will be controversy and division caused by Jesus; and there will be a release of Israel from its enemies.

Not only does Luke weave anticipations of conflict into the otherwise joyful infancy narratives, he also includes specific predictions of conflict and persecution at several significant points in the gospel and Acts. There are four specific predictions by Jesus of his own persecution.[5] In Luke 9:22 he speaks of suffering, rejection, death, and resurrection. In 9:44 he foretells betrayal, and in 17:25, suffering and rejection. Luke 18:31–34 is the most specific of the passion predictions, and it identifies Jerusalem as the place of betrayal, ridicule, insult, punishment, death, and resurrection. These four predictions also include indications of the identity of the persecuting groups. Although 18:31–34 is the only one of the four to name Jerusalem as the place of Jesus' execution, the prediction about the city comes as no surprise to the alert reader. As early as 9:31 that signal is given, as Moses and Elijah speak with the transfigured Jesus "of his departure [*exodos*], which he was to accomplish at Jerusalem." The ominous character of the city is portrayed in Luke 9:51–19:44, the section on Jesus in transit, where Jesus' approach to Jerusalem is traced (note especially 13:22; 17:11; 18:31; 19:11). In 13:34–35 Jerusalem is said to be the place where prophets are killed.[6]

There are also predictions that Jesus' disciples will be persecuted. In Luke 9:23–27, immediately following the first prediction of his own death, Jesus lays down the conditions for discipleship, and these words make it clear that the disciple must expect opposition and persecution. He must take up a cross, deny himself, and lose his life. Denial of Jesus under these circumstances carries the most severe ultimate penalties, for when the Son of man comes, he will be ashamed of the person who is ashamed of Jesus. Luke 9:27 is usually taken to be a prediction about the time of the coming of the kingdom, and so it may be. But in the context of the previous verses, which speak of suffering and death both for Jesus (9:22) and the disciples (9:23–26), this verse takes on a different meaning. It reads more like a concession than a promise: *some* will not die, but death and the kingdom go together for most. The general rule is that discipleship to Jesus carries with it the necessity of conflict, even to the point of death. In Luke 12:4–7, 11–12 Jesus' disciples are told how to prepare for persecution, and in 12:8–10 they are told again of the importance of confession and the danger of apostasy. They are told to fear God rather than the political authorities, who are presented here as having awesome power and as posing a serious threat to the community.

In a few places future conflict is spoken of as *peirasmos,* temptation. In 4:13 Luke had described Jesus' conflict with the devil as a *peirasmos,* and he had said that at the end of it the devil withdrew for a time. That sentence serves as a signal to the reader that the devil will return and that ultimate conflict is yet to come. In the interpretation of the parable of the sower, the seed that fell on rock is said to stand for persons who initially accept the word but desert at the time of *peirasmos* (8:13). In the Lord's Prayer the disciples are taught to say, "Do not lead us into *peirasmos* (11:4). The anticipation of a coming *peirasmos* is picked up again in 22:28,40,46.

In Luke 19:41–44 Jesus speaks of disastrous conflicts that the citizens of Jerusalem will experience. As he weeps, he says to the city, "Would that even today you knew the things that make for peace!" In the Lukan apocalyptic discourse (21:5–36) the nature of these conflicts becomes explicit. Predictions of conflict pervade the apocalyptic discourse in such obvious ways that we may simply note them. Here Jesus says that the temple will be demolished (21:6), there will be battles and disorders (21:9), nation will go against nation and kingdom against kingdom (21:10), and there will be natural and cosmic catastrophes (21:11). Luke 21:12–19 seems to be directed to the disciples, and these verses form a parallel to 12:11–12.[7] The disciples are told to expect persecution. They will be turned over to synagogues and prisons and led to kings and governors "for my name's sake" (21:12). They are told not to prepare a defense beforehand, because Jesus himself will give to them "a mouth and wisdom, which none of your adversaries will be able to withstand or contradict" (21:15).[8] The apocalyptic discourse contains predictions of betrayal by friends and relatives and predictions of universal hatred, but it also has a promise that "not a hair of your head will perish" (21:18). Luke 21:20–22 reminds one of 19:43–44 and speaks of the siege and destruction of Jerusalem and the flight of refugees. Then follow words about great distress and anger (21:23), death by the sword, imprisonment, and the trampling of Jerusalem by Gentiles (or nations, 21:24). The apocalyptic discourse closes with warnings that the disciples should stay awake so that they may escape the difficulties to come (21:34–36).

The narrative of the last supper (Luke 22:7–38) gives Luke a final opportunity to face the reader with predictions of conflict involving Jesus. It is a change of scene, for the previous setting had been in the temple. Now Jesus is in the city with the disciples, in a large furnished upstairs room, which serves as a dining room for the Passover meal. At the meal Jesus lets his disciples know that it is his last and uses bread and wine to symbolize his approaching death. He foretells his betrayal and condemns the betrayer (22:21–23). Jesus' words about the betrayer lead to questions about who the guilty one may be and to internal controversy about who is the greatest of the disciples (22:23–27; cf. 9:46). Jesus attempts to settle the dispute by insisting that the leader must be the servant, by conferring on the disciples a kingdom, and by promising them places in his own kingdom (22:28–30). The connection is apparently suggested by the reference to the kings of the Gentiles in verse 25. The disciples are not to model themselves on those kings; nevertheless they are to be kings, sitting on thrones and "judging the twelve tribes of Israel" (22:30). The role of the disciples as kings is consonant with the theme of social revolution that Luke pictured as beginning with the birth of Jesus. The reason cited for the disciples' reward is that they remained with Jesus during his trials. But in Luke 22:31–34 Jesus reminds the disciples that no one is invulnerable to Satan. And although Peter insists that he is ready to go with Jesus to prison and death, Jesus foretells his apostasy before morning. In the final verses of the supper narrative (22:35–38) he requires the disciples to obtain not only a purse and a bag, but also a sword. There is an explicit contrast with Luke 9:3; 10:4, and the requirement of the sword suggests violent conflict to come (see 22:49–51).

After the narratives of the crucifixion and resurrection Luke reminds the reader that Jesus' conflicts had been predicted (Luke 24:26,46). The theme of predicted suffering appears in a number of speeches in Acts: in speeches of Peter (2:23; 3:18); in Philip's reply to the Ethiopian eunuch (8:32–35); and in speeches of Paul (17:2–3; 26:22–23). Luke thus shows that Jesus' persecution was predicted by Jesus himself, and then, after describing the persecution, he shows that it was predicted in the Hebrew scriptures.

As Jesus' fate is anticipated in the gospel, so is Paul's in Acts. In two important passages the reader is warned about Paul's impending fate in Jerusalem. In the first, Paul explains things to the Ephesian elders and shows them that he expects imprisonment and trials in Jerusalem (Acts 20:17–38). In the second, the prophet Agabus announces that Paul will be captured and turned over to Gentiles (21:10–14). But Paul's fate was not finally determined in Jerusalem, so there are two more announcements about trials in Rome (23:11; 27:24).

In addition to the anticipations of conflict, Luke uses images and similes to suggest it. In Luke 5:36–39, for example, Jesus calls attention to the contrast between old and new wineskins and old and new wine, contrasts that suggest the opposition of old and new ideas, movements, times, or forces. In the parable of the sower (Luke 8:4–8) it is to be expected that some seed will fall in inhospitable places, along the road, on rocky ground, and among thorns. In the interpretation of this parable (8:11–15) the theme of opposition is one key, for it is made clear that the word of God meets opposition from the devil, from deserters, and from those who prefer wealth and pleasure. All is not hopeless, however, for some seed falls on good ground and bears fruit. In his charge to the seventy missionaries Jesus says that they will be like lambs in the midst of wolves (Luke 10:3), and the charge assumes a widespread rejection of the missionaries. The imagery of light and darkness in Luke 11:33–36 and the figures of accusers, rulers, judges, and bailiffs in 12:58–59 fit the concept of conflict. Even the brutality of the saying about the millstone in Luke 17:1–2 does not appear to be inconsistent with the other figures. In Luke 12:49–51, fire is used as a metaphor for the work of Jesus: "I came to cast fire upon the earth; and would that it were already kindled! I have a baptism to be baptized with; and how I am constrained until it is accomplished! Do you think that I have come to give peace on earth? No, I tell you, but rather division."

The words "fire" and "baptism" point back to John's statement about the task of the "stronger one"; namely, to baptize with Holy Spirit and fire and to separate the useful from the useless (3:15–18). The parable of the barren fig tree in 13:6–9 also reminds us of John's words about unfruitful trees in 3:9, although in the parable some patience is called for. Similarly, Jesus rebukes the disciples for their suggestion about bringing down fire on the Samaritan village (9:54–55).

Some of Jesus' language is more direct. There is reference in Luke 6:27–30 to enemies and to persons who hate, curse, abuse, assault, and steal. Clearly the force of these statements is to recommend love and nonretaliation as the proper responses to those who are enemies, but that there are lines of opposition here is equally clear. Similarly, the ideas of judgment and division are to be found in direct statements, such as Luke 12:51–53 and 14:25–27, where it is said that the divisions will even be within families. Jesus' condemnatory statements about Chorazin, Bethsaida, and Capernaum in Luke 10:13–16 seem to represent his denunciation of places that had rejected him. The word to Capernaum reflects the motif of transposition: its exalted position is to be lost (10:15).

The beatitudes and woes in Luke 6:20–26 also present the motif of transposition. Here Jesus says that the kingdom belongs to the poor, the hungry will be filled, mourners will laugh, and the persecuted will be rewarded. The situation of the rich, the satiated, the happy, and the highly regarded will be exactly reversed. Similar ideas appear in Luke 10:15; 13:30; 14:11; 16:15; 18:14; and Acts 4:11 (cf. Luke 20:17). The motif is most forcefully used in the parable of Lazarus and the rich man in Luke 16:19–31, and the opposition between God and wealth is clearly stated in 14:33; 16:13; 18:24–25. Luke seems to be demonstrating that wealth is totally opposed to the forces of good. The motif of transposition may help us to understand the puzzling statement in 16:16: "The Torah and the prophets were until John. From then on, the kingdom of God is being announced, and everybody is entering it forcibly" (author's translation).[9] The saying contrasts old and new and shows Jesus to be the one who comes after John, announces the kingdom, and begins the process in which the poor and the oppressed achieve power. The idea of force should not be unexpected, since we have been told that Jesus' preaching means divisions, conflicts, and transpositions.

Many of the pericopes[10] in Luke's gospel take the form of the controversy dialogue. Form critics have maintained that this type of apophthegm, or pronouncement story, was one of the major forms for the transmission of Jesus' teaching during the pregospel oral period. The discipline of form criticism intends to identify the earliest forms in which the various pericopes were transmitted. Although Luke's literary activity would have included the use of traditional material, the study of the primitive form of that material does not constitute the primary focus of the present study. Nevertheless, it seems useful to observe that at least one of the forms that the critics have isolated was used to report situations of controversy. This means that Luke probably found this form congenial and adapted it to his own theme of conflict.[11]

Rudolf Bultmann described the controversy dialogue as having a starting point in "some action or attitude which is seized on by the opponent and used in an attack by accusation or by question."[12] The question or accusation is then met by a reply which "follows more or less a set form, with special preference for the counterquestion or the metaphor, or even both together. Nevertheless—like the attack—it can also consist of a scripture quotation."[13] Bultmann found the *Sitz im Leben* for the controversy dialogues in the early church rather than the life of Jesus, but it is not necessary to settle that question in order to observe the use that Luke has made of this form. As a form for presenting controversy it fits the basic theme of conflict in Luke's narrative. So we see that Luke has used this form to show who opposed Jesus and, in some cases, what the issues were.

Luke also sets conflict in a cosmic dimension. The first conflict story involving Jesus is the temptation story in Luke 4:1–13. Here the combatants are the devil and God's son, and the imagery suggests cosmic conflict. Not only is this the first conflict story involving Jesus; it is the first story in which Jesus is the principal actor. The infancy narratives had featured Zechariah, Elizabeth, Mary, Simeon, Anna, Gabriel, and other angels. In Luke 3 John the Baptist was the featured performer. Only in Luke 3:21–22 does Jesus move toward center stage, but even here he is acted upon. He has been baptized (*baptisthentos*); the Spirit-dove descended on him, but he did not act or speak. In 4:1–2 we have both active and passive verbs: he returned (*hupestrepsen*) from the Jordan, was led (*ēgeto*) by the Spirit into the desert, and was tempted (*peirazomenos*) by the devil. His entry into the desert is both an active movement on his own part and a passive response to the Spirit. The description of Jesus as full of the Spirit and being led by the Spirit serves to anticipate the cosmic, spiritual nature of the contest to come. But as the story progresses, Jesus himself begins to speak for the first time since 2:49, his reply, at the age of twelve, to his parents. The scene, likewise, has been carefully set in the desert. Jesus has been at the Jordan, and now he goes to the desert, in a reversal of the movements of John the Baptist in 3:2–3. In the case of both Jesus and John there is contact with a nonhuman reality in the desert: John received the word of God there, and Jesus is in contact with the devil there. The forty-day period in the desert would remind Jewish readers of Israel's forty-year nomadic period.[14]

Luke has carefully placed the story of the temptation so that it connects both with John's prediction about the "stronger one" in 3:16–17 and with the baptism in 3:21–22. Jesus must prove that he is indeed the "stronger one" predicted by John, by standing up against the forces of evil. In 3:21 the Spirit descended on Jesus, so that he became full of the Spirit and under its leadership in 4:1. Above all, the heavenly voice had announced to Jesus after the baptism, "Thou art my beloved Son" (3:22). So in the contest with the devil that proposition has to be tested. Twice the devil sets the condition: "If you are the Son of God" (4:3,9). The content of the three temptations adds significance to the narrative as a whole, which constitutes a description of a conflict of cosmic proportions. It is a decisive victory for Jesus. The story concludes with the words, "And when the devil had ended every temptation [*panta peirasmon*], he departed from him until an opportune time" (4:13). The significance of this incident for Luke is plain: the narrative that Luke is about to tell is one in which the hero is in conflict with opposing forces. In the first battle he has stood up against all that his chief opponent has been able to throw at him. But this is only the beginning, for the devil will return, and there will be another temptation.[15]

The story of Jesus in conflict with the devil sets the stage for additional conflicts on the nonhuman level. Since Jesus as God's son has won a victory over the devil, he has power over all those nonhuman forces that plague people. These include demons, diseases, and destructive forces of nature. Thus Luke shows Jesus in conflict with these forces in the narratives of exorcisms, healings, and nature miracles.

The exorcisms demonstrate Jesus' power in a special way. In the first one (Luke 4:31–37) the demon addresses Jesus with the question, "Have you come to destroy us?" The violence that accompanies the exorcism suggests that the destruction of demons is indeed Jesus' purpose. Another exorcism (8:26–39) takes place in the region of the Gerasenes.[16] Here too the demon pleads with Jesus, "I beseech you, do not torment me." Images of violence fill this narrative: the demoniac had to be tied up; the demons entered a large herd of swine, and they "rushed down the steep bank into the lake and were drowned"; the response of the herdsmen is terror and rejection of Jesus. As an aspect of the theme of conflict the case of the strange exorcist in Luke 9:49–50 is very interesting. Here is a person who is not a follower of Jesus but who is able to practice exorcism in his name. Jesus' comment on this situation suggests that battle lines have been drawn: "He that is not against you is for you."

Probably the most important discussion of exorcisms occurs in Luke 11:14–26. In these verses Jesus is charged with using the power of Beelzebul, the prince of demons, to cast out demons. In answering the charge Jesus shows (1) that his use of the power of Beelzebul would, if true, be a sign of a divided kingdom, which then could not endure; (2) that other exorcists must use the same power as he; (3) that it is God's power that he uses; (4) that this is a signal that God's kingdom is being established; and (5) that the exorcist is stronger than the entire kingdom of demons. Two kingdoms are pitted against each other: the kingdom of demons, Beelzebul, and Satan is opposed to that of the exorcists, Jesus, and God. Neither kingdom is divided against itself, but the kingdom of God is stronger than the kingdom of Satan, with which it is in conflict, especially as demonstrated in the work of Jesus. The verses about the return of the evil spirit (11:24–26) seem to form a kind of commentary on the Beelzebul controversy. In Luke 11:21–22 the conflict between the two kingdoms has been represented in the figures of a strongly equipped householder and an even stronger conqueror. Now in 11:24–26 we are told that the initial conquest may not be sufficient, but rather the conquering kingdom must maintain its power, or else the defeated one will reoccupy the territory. Whatever view of demonic power may lie behind these verses, the theme of conflict in a cosmic dimension is being used.[17] The words of Jesus in 11:23 are thematic: "He who is not with me is against me, and he who does not gather with me scatters."[18]

In addition to the exorcisms there are narratives of healings and resuscitations, all of which may be understood as Jesus' conflicts in a cosmic dimension. Such would surely be the case with the manifestation of Jesus' power over death in the story of the widow's son at Nain (Luke 7:11–17). The response of the crowd in 7:16 is fear, glorification of God, and acceptance of Jesus as prophet. In Luke 5:17–26 there is a direct association of healing with forgiveness of sin. In 5:21 the scribes and Pharisees accuse Jesus of blasphemy on the grounds that only God has the power to forgive sins. In other words, God alone can prevail in the conflict with evil. But the reader knows that Jesus, who has already prevailed in conflict with the devil, has this power. Thus conflict with evil and conflict with disease form two sides of the same coin, and Jesus can ask, "Which is easier, to say, 'Your sins are forgiven you,' or to say, 'Rise and walk'?" (5:23). So Luke presents Jesus not only in conflict with the devil and sin but also with associated evils: death (7:11–17; 8:40–42, 49–56); near death (7:1–10); fever (4:38–39); leprosy (5:12–16; 17:11–19); paralysis (5:17–26; 6:6–11; 13:10–17); chronic hemorrhage (8:43–48); epilepsy (9:37–43); dropsy (14:1–6); and blindness (18:35–43).

Three other miracle stories support the theme of cosmic conflict by showing the power of Jesus over nature. In the calming of the storm in Luke 8:22–25 Jesus is in conflict with a destructive natural force. The fishing story (Luke 5:1–11) probably has additional symbolic significance, but it certainly shows Jesus in conflict with the sea.[19] The feeding of the five thousand (9:10b–17) likewise is not exhausted by understanding it as a conflict story, but it is a demonstration of Jesus' ability to overcome hunger, and it is consistent with the motif of transposition in 1:53; 3:4–6; 4:18; 6:21.[20]

In addition to the narratives of exorcisms, resuscitations, healings, and other miracles, there are some general Lukan summaries (4:40–41; 6:17–19; 8:1–3; 9:11) and comments by Jesus (9:1–6; 10:17–20). The general summaries tell us that Jesus performed many such exorcisms and healings in addition to those that are narrated. Jesus' comments are of greater interest from our point of view. In 9:1–6 he grants the power of exorcism and healing to the twelve. They return in 9:10 and report to Jesus. The sending out (10:1) and the return (10:17) of the seventy are formally parallel to the mission of the twelve in 9:1–2, 10.[21] In 10:9 Jesus charges the seventy to heal the sick and proclaim the kingdom in those cities that welcome them. The report of the seventy in 10:17–20 includes the statement, "The demons are subject to us in your name!" (10:17). Jesus' reply, "I saw Satan fall like lightning from heaven" (10:18), is a claim to complete victory over the forces of evil. This victory enables Jesus to give the seventy authority over "all the power of the enemy" (10:19), such as snakes and scorpions. The total victory over cosmic and nonhuman forces has been won by Jesus, and it is demonstrated by him and his successors.

Another section in which Jesus comments on healings has particular interest for us; namely, his reply to the disciples of John, a passage that was dealt with in part in chapter 2 above. In Luke 7:18–23 John sends disciples to inquire if Jesus is the "coming one." In the words of John, the coming one is to baptize with Holy Spirit and fire; he will execute judgment and destroy the unfruitful and useless. Jesus' response to John's disciples does not speak directly to the point of judgment, but rather recalls the language of transposition: the blind see, the lame walk, lepers have become unleprous, the deaf hear, the dead are raised, and the poor are evangelized. Jesus' reply in this section serves as a way to interpret the healing stories. As the "stronger one" of whom John spoke in Luke 3:16, Jesus is working radical changes and effecting transpositions, as had been expected before his birth and proclaimed in his first speeches (see 4:18; 6:20–26). That the transpositions are accompanied by conflict is confirmed by Jesus' final statement to John's disciples: "And blessed is he who takes no offense at me" (7:23).

Conflict in a cosmic dimension is also present in Acts. The power of Jesus' disciples over destructive forces was granted by Jesus in Luke 9 and 10. Thus, the apostles and Paul are able to cure people of lameness (Acts 3:1–10; 14:8–10), paralysis (9:32–35), and disease (19:11–12; 28:7–10); they have power over magicians and other exorcists (19:13–20); and they perform exorcisms (16:18) and resurrections (9:36–43; 20:7–12).

Whatever may have been Luke's intentions in setting conflict in a cosmic dimension, the effect of his literary usage is to convince the reader that the conflicts involving Jesus are not simply human. Even the conflicts between Jesus and the Jewish leaders and Roman officials, those conflicts on a human level, are more than political, religious, or social controversy. They form part of that ultimate conflict between good and evil.

The ways in which Luke has dealt with conflict may now be summarized. First, Luke included anticipations of conflict in the infancy narratives. Second, he scattered predictions of persecution, trial, and death throughout the gospel. Third, he made abundant use of conflict imagery in recording the teachings of Jesus. Fourth, he frequently used the motif of transposition and thereby implied social conflict. Fifth, he oftentimes presented Jesus in verbal conflict with opponents. Sixth, he set the conflicts of Jesus and his successors within a cosmic dimension.

The preceding analysis has shown that conflict is an integral part of Luke's narrative. It helps us raise, in an acute way, questions about the identity and the character of Jesus' opponents, as well as questions about the issues that separated him from them.

JESUS' CONFLICTS WITH JEWISH GROUPS

The theme of conflict as it is used generally in Luke–Acts guides the reader toward an understanding of the role of the Jewish leaders in the narrative. The motif of acceptance and rejection seems to be used by Luke only in relation to the Jewish public as a whole. When he comes to relate narratives about Jesus or early Christians and their dealings with powerful Jewish groups, the situations are usually ones involving opposition and conflict. We shall see, however, that not all such groups are treated in the same way.

Since so much attention is given in Luke–Acts to Pharisees and chief priests, we shall concentrate on them. Chapter 5, on the trial of Jesus, will examine the role of certain individuals, such as Pilate and Herod, in Jesus' death; the reader will see how Luke has brought these individuals together with the opposing groups and the Jewish public in a grand alliance against Jesus.

In chapter 2, in an examination of Luke 7:18–35, we observed the contrast between positive and negative responses to Jesus. Those who responded positively are referred to as "all the listening people," tax collectors, and wisdom's children. Those who responded negatively were designated as Pharisees, lawyers, the people of this generation, and unresponsive children. The phrase "people of this generation" (Luke 7:31) might appear to be a category covering all of Jesus' contemporaries. But this cannot be taken in its obvious literal sense, since the same passage affirms that there were responsive people among Jesus' contemporaries. It would be better for us to understand the phrase as a technical term that Luke used to refer collectively to those who responded negatively to Jesus. The phraseology appears to be consistent throughout Luke–Acts. "This generation" is the object of condemnation in Luke 11:47–51. Previous generations had killed the prophets, and this one builds their tombs, but this generation is guilty of all such murders from Abel to Zechariah. In Luke 11:29–32 "this generation" is described as evil. It demands a sign but does not respond to what has been given it. The queen of the South and the men of Nineveh will judge this generation, which does not respond to "something greater than Jonah." In Luke 9:41 Jesus calls it a "faithless and perverse generation," and in 17:25 predicts that it will reject him (cf. 16:8). A similar idea is found in Luke 13:26–27, where rejected people claim that they have eaten and drunk with Jesus and that he taught in their streets. Here Jesus rejects persons who belong to this generation. Peter, in Acts 2:40, reflects the teaching of the Lukan Jesus when he warns his hearers, "Save yourselves from this crooked generation." "This generation" appears to be Luke's shorthand for all of Jesus' opponents; it does not include those contemporaries who responded to him.

But Luke is not content with such blanket generalizations as "people of this generation." In a number of places he specifically identifies those who opposed Jesus or his successors. It is true that these identifications are usually collective and that Luke names relatively few individuals, especially in the gospel. But he does speak of Pharisees, lawyers, teachers of the law, scribes, elders, Sadducees, *stratēgoi*, and chief priests as leading Jewish groups. The various groups may in turn be gathered into two larger complexes, for Luke's tendency is to divide the groups into two blocks—one whose major constituents are the Pharisees, and the other headed by the chief priests. Moreover, the priestly block is exclusively associated with the city of Jerusalem and the temple, while the Pharisaic block is primarily associated with Galilee and certain undesignated places.[22]

With Pharisees are associated lawyers, teachers of the law, and scribes.[23] Chief priests appear to be associated with scribes, elders,

Sadducees, *stratēgoi*, and first citizens.[24] Luke's treatments indicate that he thought of Pharisees and chief priests as the dominant groups and all the others as minor. Characteristics of the minor groups are never described; rarely do they appear alone, and never do they act independently. The association of scribes with both Pharisees and chief priests may appear to present a problem. But when we recognize their minor role in the narrative, the problem becomes inconsequential. It should be emphasized, however, that Luke is very careful to associate all of the other minor groups with either Pharisees or chief priests, but not with both. With the exception of the scribes, the lines that mark off the two blocks of opponents are clean.[25]

Pharisees

The block headed by the Pharisees is primarily concerned with Torah observance, and Luke thinks of Torah as law and tradition. He has Paul describe himself as one who has lived as a Pharisee, and the Pharisaic is described by Paul as "the strictest party of our religion" (Acts 26:5). Strictness seems here to express a positive judgment about the ethical and ritualistic requirements set down by the Pharisees. Thus, as Luke understands Torah and Pharisees, it is appropriate for him to think of lawyers and teachers of law as allies of the Pharisees. In addition, the issues in which Pharisees appear to be engaged are those that may be thought of as legal issues, involving the interpretation of Torah and such practices as the observance of dietary regulations and sabbath.

A close analysis of the relevant passages will show that Luke's treatment of the Pharisees and their allies is much more ambivalent than it is usually thought to be. If we examine the Pharisees within the various general components of Luke's narrative, some interesting aspects of the evangelist's attitude will emerge. In the gospel, references to Pharisees are confined to the section on Jesus' activity outside Jerusalem (Luke 4:14–19:44).

The references to Pharisees in Luke 4:14–19:44 may be divided into three groups. In the first group there are some thirteen pericopes that tell of the controversies between Jesus and the Pharisaic block of opponents. These pericopes include questions by Pharisees and replies by Jesus.[26] In the second group there is no dialogue, and Jesus is the only speaker. These pericopes consist of several sayings and one parable. The third group consists of Lukan editorial notes. The anti-Pharisaic tone is harsher in the second and third groups than in the first.

In the first group of pericopes Pharisees are usually cast in the role of Jesus' questioners and, sometimes, antagonists. It is frequently the Pharisees and their allies who are engaged with Jesus in controversy dialogues. The following pericopes retail the controversies between the Pharisaic block of opponents and Jesus:

Luke 5:17–26—The healing of the paralytic
Luke 5:29–32—Eating with tax collectors and sinners
Luke 5:33–35—On fasting
Luke 6:1–5—Plucking grain on the sabbath
Luke 6:6–11—The man with the withered hand
Luke 7:36–50—The woman with the ointment
Luke 10:25–28—The question about the great commandment
Luke 11:37–41—On cleanliness
Luke 13:31–33—The warning about Herod
Luke 14:1–6—The man with dropsy
Luke 15:1–2—Charges against Jesus
Luke 17:20–21—The coming of the kingdom of God
Luke 19:28–40—Jesus approaching Jerusalem

In Luke 17:20–21 Pharisees ask Jesus about the coming of the kingdom, and Jesus responds with words that suggest that the kingdom is already present. The pericope that follows (17:22–37) contains more eschatological words of Jesus. The Pharisees' question (which is put in indirect discourse) provides the occasion for Jesus' pronouncement, which forms the heart and the conclusion of the story.[27] No genuine interest is displayed in the Pharisees in this particular passage. Neither their question nor Jesus' response betrays any hostility.

Just what role the Pharisees play in Luke 13:31–33 is difficult to determine. The most important part of the pericope is the statement of Jesus about Herod and about his own coming death in Jerusalem. The warning of the Pharisees serves mainly to introduce Jesus' saying, and so we should not look for much emphasis on their role at this point.[28] On the other hand, the Pharisees, in warning Jesus about Herod, appear to be friendly. It may not be correct to speak of them as Jesus' supporters, but it is difficult to think of them as opponents in this pericope.

On three occasions Jesus dines with Pharisees (Luke 7:36–50; 11:37–41; 14:1–6). The motif of a meal accompanied by a controversy is unique to Luke among the synoptic gospels. The meals may have reminded some readers of Plato's *Symposium*, which, however, is an extended philosophical discussion rather than a brief controversy. In Luke 7:36–50 and 11:37–41 there are Pharisaic criticisms of Jesus' activity—for encouraging contact with a sinful woman (7:39) and for not washing before dinner (11:38). In Luke 14:1–6 there is a note of malevolence and an implied criticism of Jesus' healing of a dropsical man on the sabbath. Thus, all three meals serve Luke as occasions for presenting Jesus' teaching and contrasting it with Pharisaic traditions, as he understood them. On all three occasions the Pharisees are presented as Jesus' critical opponents.

But the motif of the meal tends to soften the character of the opposition. The act of dining together affirms a social relationship among diners.[29] Although one could not describe the relationship between Jesus and his Pharisaic hosts as one of friendship, neither is it properly termed enmity. The setting suggests that Pharisees and Jesus hold differing interpretations of the demands of God but that the opposition does not preclude normal social intercourse. Jesus' words in Luke 7:40–50, addressed to Simon by name, even establish a relationship approaching intimacy.

Most of the remaining pericopes in this group contain genuine controversies between Pharisees and Jesus. In Luke 5:17–26 scribes and Pharisees accuse him of blasphemy after he has forgiven the sins of the paralytic, and Jesus responds by healing him.[30] In Luke 5:29–32 the Pharisees and their scribes question Jesus' practice of eating with tax collectors and sinners, and Jesus responds with the words, "Those who are well have no need of a physician, but those who are sick; I have not come to call the righteous, but sinners to repentance" (5:31–32). In the passage that follows immediately (5:33–35) the same people ask him why his disciples do not practice fasting.[31] The question involves an unfavorable comparison of Jesus' disciples with those of John and those of the Pharisees. Jesus responds that there will be occasion for fasting when the bridegroom is absent. In Luke 6:1–5 some of the Pharisees ask why Jesus' disciples are allowed to violate Torah by picking, grinding, and eating grain on the sabbath day. Jesus responds to the criticism by citing the precedent of David and by claiming, "The Son of man is lord of the sabbath" (6:5). The pericope that follows (6:6–11) relates the incidents of another sabbath, and Luke introduces it by saying that the scribes and Pharisees watched Jesus, "to see whether he would heal on the sabbath, so that they might find an accusation against him" (6:7). In his response to their unspoken question Jesus performs a healing and defends it by asking if it is legal to do good and to save life on the sabbath. The concluding verse of this pericope seems to focus on the reaction of the Pharisees, who by now are very hostile to Jesus: "But they were filled with fury and discussed with one another what they might do to Jesus" (6:11). In Luke 10:25–28 a lawyer attempts to test Jesus by asking him about the requirements for eternal life.[32] Jesus' response is to ask him what Torah says, and Jesus seems to accept his response about the love of God and neighbor. Luke 15:1–2 serves to introduce the three parables of the chapter. The words reflect the Pharisaic charges in 5:29–32 about eating with sinners. The parables of the lost sheep (15:3–7), the lost coin (15:8–10), and the prodigal son (15:11–32) may be taken as Jesus' response to this criticism. In these controversial dialogues the lines between Jesus and the Pharisees are sharply drawn.

The major purpose of these controversial dialogues appears to be to acquaint the reader with Jesus' teachings about Torah observance. Luke must have felt that the teaching is clearest when contrasted with that of the Pharisees. Thus we learn what Jesus taught about the rules of clean and unclean, specifically about eating with tax collectors and sinners (Luke 5:29–32; 15:1–2). We learn what he taught about sabbath observance, specifically about preparing food (6:1–5) and healing (6:6–11). We learn what he taught about fasting and prayer (5:33–35). In addition, we learn that he claimed the authority to forgive sins (5:17–26)[33] and that he accepted the summary of Torah that called for love of God and the neighbor (10:25–28).

The last we hear of Pharisees in the gospel is in the pericope, Luke 19:28–40. Here, as Jesus comes down the road from the

Mount of Olives and approaches Jerusalem, a large group of disciples proclaims him king and announces peace. To this, some of the Pharisees object (19:39). They ask Jesus to reprimand his disciples, but he refuses. Luke must mean to suggest that Pharisaic opposition was based on their objection to the proclamation of Jesus as king.

In most of the passages examined above, Pharisees and their associates are cast in the role of Jesus' critical opponents. They accuse him of blasphemy (Luke 5:21), of ignoring fundamental dietary regulations (5:30; 15:2), and of not observing the sabbath commandment in proper ways (6:2,7). Only in 10:25–28 is there agreement between the viewpoint of Jesus and that of the lawyer, but even here Luke says that the lawyer wanted to put Jesus to the test (10:25).

Is there an emergent picture of the Pharisees in this group of pericopes? Perhaps there is no one picture that can be described; rather, we have a range of images. In some pericopes the Pharisees are characterless or neutral; in others they appear to be friendly to Jesus or at least open to usual forms of social intercourse. In most, however, they appear as stalwart guardians, who are watchful about Torah observance. In every case where a distinction is made between them and Jesus, they come down on the side of rigor and strict interpretation. Obedience to Torah is their major concern. They do not attempt to justify their concern or to ferret out reasons for the commandments. They only intend to obey, and thus they are suspicious of one whose teachings are at variance with theirs. On some occasions Jesus' teaching fills them with anger (6:11), and their suspicions lead them to search for grounds on which he might be accused (6:7). But even here there is a kind of tentativeness, a lack of a definite plan. There is no explicit suggestion about a plot to capture Jesus, to take him to court, to turn him over to the authorities, or to kill him. These pericopes do not give us an image of Pharisees as desiring to do Jesus bodily harm. In the pericopes examined here the Pharisees are shown to be suspicious and critical of Jesus, but their opposition to him remains on the verbal level and does not take a violent turn.

A very different image of Pharisees is found in the second group of pericopes, in which Jesus specifically criticizes them. The contrast in form between these and the pericopes examined above should be reasonably clear. In most of those above, it is the Pharisees who question, criticize, or verbally attack Jesus. In the ones below, Jesus takes the initiative in attacking Pharisees and their allies. The pericopes in this group are the following:

Luke 11:42–44—Discourse against Pharisees
Luke 11:45–52—Discourse against lawyers[34]
Luke 12:1—The leaven of the Pharisees
Luke 16:14–15—Condemnation of the Pharisees
Luke 18:9–14—The Pharisee and the publican

In Luke 11:42–44 we have a series of condemnations by Jesus against Pharisees and in 11:45–52 a similar attack on lawyers. Jesus condemns Pharisaic tithing practices and their habit of selecting seats of honor in synagogues. He calls them unseen tombs that cause people to commit unintentional sins. He condemns their haughtiness, their hypocrisy, and their exclusivism. He attacks lawyers for imposing burdens and not helping with them. In 12:1 Jesus again speaks of the hypocrisy of the Pharisees. In 16:14–15 he condemns the Pharisees for demonstrating righteousness publicly, and, in a sentence that uses the language of transposition, he threatens that Pharisees will be treated as abominations by God, although they have been exalted by people. Jesus' parable of the Pharisee and the publican (18:9–14) brings home the same point: the Pharisee who exalts himself will be humbled, and the humble publican will be exalted. In both 16:14–15 and 18:9–14 the motif of transposition is applied by Jesus against the Pharisees.

In the third group of pericopes we have three important editorial notes about Pharisees: Luke 7:29–30; 11:53–54; and 16:14. In 11:53–54 Luke describes the reaction of Pharisees and scribes to the denunciations just preceding. He describes their attitude as very hostile, and he says that they interrogated Jesus on many subjects, trying to catch him in something he would say.[35] In 16:14 Luke describes Pharisees as money-lovers who ridiculed Jesus. In 7:29–30, a passage already examined in chapter 2, Luke simply gives the judgment that Pharisees and lawyers rejected the purpose of God for themselves, as seen in their rejection of John's baptism.

In the verbal attacks by Jesus and in the Lukan editorial notes we have a more hostile tone than in the pericopes in the first group. Jesus' attacks are not so much against Pharisaic teaching as against their lifestyles and their attitudes. In his editorial notes Luke pictures Pharisees as avaricious and malevolent, as persons who try to trap Jesus and who reject God's purpose.

Luke, therefore, has a wide range of images of Pharisees in his gospel. When he wants to call attention to the contrast between their interpretation of Torah and that of Jesus, they appear to be critical and suspicious opponents. When the Lukan Jesus, or Luke himself, talks about Pharisaic life style and character, Pharisees appear to be far from honorable. Despite these negative images Luke does not portray Pharisees and their allies as aiming to have Jesus put to death. Their opposition to his teaching, though frequently vigorous and heated, is not connected with the trial and execution.

Pharisees are not mentioned in Luke's gospel outside the section 4:14–19:44. They are not present in those sections in which Jesus teaches in the temple, nor are they present during the trial of Jesus or the crucifixion. Their total absence from the narratives that trace events that lead to Jesus' death would seemingly suggest to the reader that, despite their role as sometime opponents of Jesus, Pharisees were not his mortal enemies. In Luke there is no ground for thinking of them as the killers of Jesus.

When compared with the hostile passages in Luke's gospel, the treatment of Pharisees in Acts is shocking. In these passages we have a basically positive view of them and their allies. Gamaliel in Acts 5:33–39, described as a Pharisee and an esteemed teacher of the law, expresses a tolerant attitude toward the Christian movement and persuades his fellows not to prosecute its leaders. If it is of human origin, he says, it will be destroyed; but if it is of divine origin, it will not be possible to destroy it. It is well known that Acts 22:3 identifies this Gamaliel as Paul's teacher.

As the apostles were saved from prosecution by a Pharisee in Acts 5:33–39, so Paul is indirectly rescued by Pharisees in Acts 23:1–10. Here Paul is on trial before the Sanhedrin, and he takes advantage of the divided makeup of this body. Luke explains that is is made up of Pharisees, who believe in the resurrection, angels, and spirits, and, on the other side, Sadducees, who reject these beliefs. Paul announces that he is a Pharisee. Note that the identification is in the present tense and signifies that Paul's Pharisaism is not a thing of the past. A riot follows when Paul claims to be on trial because of his belief in the resurrection of the dead. As a result of the controversy the Roman tribune breaks up the meeting and rescues Paul, but not before the scribes of the Pharisees announce, "We find nothing wrong in this man. What if a spirit or an angel spoke to him?" (Acts 23:9).

In his speech before Agrippa and Festus (Acts 26:2–29) Paul reiterates that he has long lived as a Pharisee, the strictest (*akribesta-tēn*) Jewish party. In an earlier public speech (22:3–21) he makes essentially the same claim. He announces that he is a Jew—note again the present tense—and explains that he was born in Tarsus and brought up in Jerusalem. Here the term "Pharisee" is not used, but Paul's reference to himself as a student of Gamaliel and his self-description as "educated according to the strict [*akribeian*] manner of the law of our fathers" (22:3) have the force of identifying Paul as a Pharisee. The mention of Gamaliel in 22:3 should remind readers of the description of him in 5:34 as a Pharisee and a teacher of the law. The characterization of Paul's education as strict (22:3) anticipates the description of the Pharisaic as the strictest Jewish party (26:5).

Luke also shows in Acts that Paul is not the only Pharisaic Christian. It is a group of Pharisaic Christians who, in 15:5, insist that Gentile believers must be circumcised and keep Torah, and it is this group that Paul and Barnabas must oppose in the important meeting in Jerusalem described in 15:6–29. Although these Pharisees are opposed to Paul, the controversy is an internal one, since the opponents are believers.[36]

The description of Pharisees in Acts is thus a complex one, but one in which hostility to the Christian movement plays no part. Luke shows that some Pharisees remained unconvinced by Christian claims but nevertheless were tolerant toward the movement, while others became believers, still retaining their insistence on the need for circumcision and Torah observance. Paul, however, seems to occupy a third position. He is a Christian believer who rejects the need for circumcision but who nevertheless can describe himself as a Pharisee right up to the end of the book. According to Luke, the real connection between Christians and Pharisees is that they both believe in the resurrection of the dead. Paul, who believes in it, is both a Christian and a Pharisee.

Despite these differences, the description of Pharisees in Acts can best be described as positive. At the very least, Pharisees are friends of the Christian movement who aid the leaders at crucial moments. They may even be Christians, and, indeed, the very hero of a large part of the book is a Pharisee.

In summary, the following observations may be made about Luke's treatment of Pharisees and their allies in Luke–Acts as a whole: First, in connection with Jesus' activities outside Jerusalem, Pharisees appear to be critical opponents of Jesus. Their interpretation of the requirements of Torah is more rigid than his, and their understanding of Torah obedience is a more rigorous one. Second, the Lukan Jesus and Luke himself are highly critical of the Pharisaic life style and condemn their haughtiness, hypocrisy, and exclusivism. Third, the Pharisees disappear as Jesus approaches Jerusalem and are totally absent from the scenes that describe his arrest, trial, and crucifixion. Fourth, Jewish Pharisees are sympathetic with the Christian movement. Finally, some Pharisees, including Paul, are Christians, and indeed Pharisaism and Christianity are understood to be compatible, since both accept the belief in the resurrection of the dead.

Chief Priests

In a few cases Luke writes of a high priest in the singular and sometimes designates a particular one by name, such as Caiaphas, Annas, or Ananias. But most frequently he speaks of chief priests in the plural.[37] It is difficult to know just what he means by using the term in the plural. He may not have been familiar with the structure of the Jewish priesthood, which technically could have only one high priest at a time. If he did know about this practice, he may have been thinking of the families from which the high priest would come. We probably should understand Luke's usage as designating the upper echelons of the Jewish priesthood. Ordinary priests show up in his narrative, but are usually not pictured in opposition to Jesus and his successors (see Luke 1:5; 5:14; 6:4; 10:31; 17:14; Acts 6:7).[38] Acts 6:7 is particularly interesting in the light of Luke's usual treatment, for here and here only we meet priests (not chief priests) who evidently have become Christians. Although ordinary priests are usually not opponents of Jesus, chief priests always are. Their allies are scribes, elders, *stratēgoi,* and first citizens. As was done in the analysis of the Pharisaic block, so here it will be useful to examine the treatment of the chief priests and their allies in the various components of Luke–Acts.

Chief priests are not mentioned in Luke's infancy narratives. The high priest Annas is mentioned in 3:2, where Luke gives his elaborate chronological setting for the appearance of John. There is only one other mention of chief priests in connection with Jesus' activity outside Jerusalem. This is in Luke 9:22, the first passion prediction, a passage that anticipates the section on Jesus in Jerusalem. Here Jesus speaks of elders, chief priests, and scribes as those who will reject and persecute him. We have seen that scribes are frequently grouped with Pharisees. In Luke 1:1–19:44 scribes appear only once in association with chief priests, namely in 9:22. Elders are mentioned only one other time in this part of Luke's gospel. In the healing of the centurion's slave in 7:1–10 they act as intermediaries and ask Jesus to help the centurion. In this passage, at least, they appear to be friendly to Jesus.

In the last sections of Luke (19:45–24:53), however, the chief priests are conspicuous. The sequence of the relevant pericopes is important for studying their role in Luke's gospel.

Luke 19:45–48: This is the pericope about Jesus' cleansing of the temple. After describing this episode, Luke notes that Jesus was teaching daily in the temple and that the chief priests, scribes, and first citizens (*prōtoi tou laou*) wanted to kill him, but they were unable to because of the people.

Luke 20:1–8: Chief priests[39] and elders ask Jesus about the source of his authority. It is implied that these groups are challenging his authority to teach in the temple. He answers their challenge by questioning them about the authority of John.

Luke 20:9–19: The parable of the vintner immediately follows the interchange about authority. At the end of the parable Luke points again (cf. 19:47) to the hostility of the chief priests and scribes and to their fear of the people. He further explains that the chief priests and scribes knew that the parable of the vintner was directed against them (20:19).

Luke 20:20–26: The opponents in this pericope are not explicitly named, but the reference is clearly to the chief priests and scribes mentioned in 20:19. So we may understand that chief priests and scribes watched Jesus and sent spies to trap him verbally and to "deliver him up to the authority and jurisdiction of the governor" (20:20). In a span of only twenty-two verses this is the fourth reference to the hostility of the chief priests, and it is interesting to note the progression in specificity. In 19:47 the imperfect verb (*ezētoun*) indicates that the desire of the chief priests is an ongoing thing, as is Jesus' daily teaching. Luke 20:1 then records one incident that occurred on one of the days on which Jesus was teaching. Then, in 20:19, the attempt was made to lay hands on Jesus at the very time that he was teaching. Finally, 20:20 gives us more detail about the tactics the chief priests intended to employ: they tried to trap him and turn him over to the governor. Thus, they asked him a question that was designed to involve him in a dangerous political situation—the question about Roman taxation. But the trap did not work, and Jesus' popularity still protected him.

Luke 22:1–2: The chief priests are not mentioned in the apocalyptic discourse in Luke 21, but they reappear as Luke prepares for the narrative of the arrest, trial, and crucifixion. Luke 22:1–2 functions as a scene-setting device that prepares the way for the narrative about the last supper and the arrest. The time is just before Passover. Once more the reader is told that the chief priests and scribes were seeking (*ezētoun*) to find ways to kill Jesus but were afraid of the people.

Luke 22:3–6: Judas confers with the chief priests and *stratēgoi* and, for a payment, agrees to look for a chance to betray Jesus without a crowd.

Luke 22:47–54: Judas fulfills his part of the bargain by conducting the arresting party to Jesus. The party consists of the chief priests, *stratēgoi,* and elders. This pericope also includes the curious story of the high priest's servant, whose ear was cut off. After the arrest Jesus is taken to the home of the high priest.

Luke 22:66–71: The session before the Sanhedrin is held the next morning, and the examiners are chief priests, elders, and scribes.

Luke 23:1–3: The same group takes Jesus to Pilate and brings charges against him.

Luke 23:4–5: Pilate proclaims Jesus to be innocent, but the chief priests and the crowd insist that he is guilty.

Luke 23:6–12: Similarly, in the session before Herod the chief priests and scribes make charges against Jesus.

Luke 23:13–16: Pilate resumes the trial by summoning the chief priests, leaders (*archontas*), and people, and he reaffirms Jesus' innocence.

Luke 23:18–23: In this crucial section the opponents of Jesus are not explicitly named, but clear references are made back to the chief priests, leaders, and people of 23:13. These groups call for the release of Barabbas (23:18) and the crucifixion of Jesus (23:21,23).

Luke 24:13–35: The postresurrection narrative of the walk to Emmaus serves as a kind of exposition and review of the life and death of Jesus. Cleopas and the unnamed disciple explain that "our chief priests and rulers delivered him up to be condemned to death, and crucified him" (24:20).

Although they do not speak of chief priests, two other passages need to be considered at this point. The first is Luke 20:27–40. Here, for the only time in the gospel, Sadducees appear, and they question Jesus about the resurrection. Luke explains that they do not believe in it. Their question about the oft-married widow is answered by Jesus, and then, surprisingly, the scribes respond, "Teacher, you have spoken well" (20:39). The apparently complimentary remark by the scribes is interpreted by Luke as their admission of defeat: "They no longer dared to ask him any question" (20:40).

That scribes are not to be thought of in a friendly way is shown by Jesus' attack on them in another passage, Luke 20:45–47. Luke 20:46 is almost a doublet of 11:43, in which Pharisees were condemned for loving the best seats in synagogues and greetings in the agoras. The charge that scribes love the places of honor at banquets is reminiscent of 14:7–11, which was set in the home of a Pharisee.[40] But 20:47 adds something new; namely, the accusation that scribes "devour widows' houses and for a pretense make long prayers." The conclusion is a variant of the motif of transposition: scribes, who have been highly regarded and rewarded with good clothing, the best seats, and greetings, will receive "the greater condemnation."

Although the modern reader is naturally interested in the specific characteristics of the various groups that Luke mentions in this section of his gospel, little is to be learned. Only in the case of Sadducees does he include a remark that distinguishes them. Indeed, their disbelief in the resurrection is also noted by Josephus.[41] But no individual characteristics are given for any of the other groups. Even without having access to specialized information about Jewish practices, a reader may surmise that chief priests are associated with Jewish religious functions and exercise leadership roles among the religious. Scribes would naturally be thought of as writers, but it is not possible to be more specific than this. *Stratēgoi* would, in view of the verbal cognates, appear to be military figures, but Luke associates them specifically with the temple in 22:52 (cf. Acts 4:1; 5:24).[42] We are probably to think of them as forming a paramilitary security force, especially for the temple. As for elders, first citizens, and leaders, nothing distinctive is to be found beyond their leadership roles.

The lack of individual characterization means that the reader comes away from the text with blurred impressions about these groups. Luke's disinterest in characterization is dramatically illustrated in 20:27–40, in which a question is asked by Sadducees (20:27) and a response to Jesus' answer is given by scribes (20:39).[43] Here one group dissolves into another. Luke's intention is probably to convey the impression of a block of opponents, the major constituent of which is a group of chief priests. If this is so, it would be contrary to the author's intention to search for distinctions among the various groups. We should simply speak of a block of priestly opponents.

This block, in contrast to the Pharisaic block, is uniformly presented in a bad light. The overall designation of these groups as violently hostile to Jesus is the same throughout Luke's gospel. There are controversies between them and Jesus, and there are attacks on them by Jesus. Their purpose is never hidden from the reader: they seek to have Jesus put to death. Their tactics are gradually revealed, but we learn that they involve sending spies, trying to trap Jesus verbally, conspiring with a traitor, isolating Jesus from the populace, and turning him over to the political authorities. Consequently they engineer his arrest, formulate charges against him, and bring the charges before Pilate and Herod. The reluctance of these two rulers to condemn Jesus finally withers away before the insistent pleadings of the priestly block of opponents, who, in the trial scenes, have the backing of the Jewish public. The chief priests are pictured as thoroughgoing villains.

The picture of the priestly block in Acts is totally congruent with that in Luke. Their hostility to the apostles is a continuation of their hostility to Jesus. Accompanied by *stratēgoi* and Sadducees, priests or chief priests [44] arrest the apostles (Acts 4:1; cf. 5:17,21), who are then questioned by Annas, the high priest, and others (4:6; cf. 5:27; see 7:1 for a similar investigation of Stephen). The persecuting activity of the pre-Christian Paul is said to have been under the direction and authority of the chief priest(s) (Acts 9:1,14,21; 22:5; 26:10,12). When the Christian Paul returns to Jerusalem after his missionary journeys, he is met with strong opposition, most of it involving chief priests (Acts 23:14; 24:1; 25:2,15). His face-to-face meeting with the high priest Ananias and the Sadducees on the Sanhedrin (23:1–10) presents Luke a chance to dramatize the conflict between his hero and the priestly block. Paul is struck on orders of Ananias, and he speaks out in harsh terms against the high priest but then apologizes, "I did not know, brethren, that he was the high priest" (23:5). Then when Paul speaks about the resurrection, a vigorous discussion arises between the Sadducees, who oppose him, and the Pharisees, who support him.

One reference is curious, namely the story of the seven sons of Sceva, described as a Jewish high priest (Acts 19:13–16). These sons attempted to practice exorcism in Jesus' name, but they failed. They were attacked by a demon-possessed man, and they fled the scene naked and wounded. Undoubtedly the story has more than one dimension, but it has given Luke an opportunity to heap ridicule upon a Jewish high priest.

Only in Acts 6:7 do we meet priests who are not hostile to the Christian movement. Indeed, here are priests who seem to have joined the movement. This verse reminds us that in the gospel of

Luke priests were sometimes presented in a good or neutral way, while chief priests were always portrayed as evil-intentioned. The priests in Acts 6:7 might remind us of those such as Zechariah, the pious priest in Luke 1.

The characteristics of chief priests are no more interesting to Luke here than they were in the gospel. Their motivation for opposing the Christian movement is not explained, as if somehow an explanation might make the reader more sympathetic to them. The result is the same as in the gospel: we have a blurred image of this block of opponents, and we are able to perceive them as opponents pure and simple. In this way Luke is able to present chief priests in the simplest, and at the same time the strongest, of terms, as villains. We might be led to conclude that chief priests oppose Jesus and his successors because it is their nature to stand against the good, or against God. The violent, unrelieved, unremitting hostility of the priestly block of opponents constitutes, in Luke–Acts, an unredeemed and probably irredeemable villainy.

CONCLUSION

In this chapter we have seen that Luke, as a good storyteller, has filled his narrative with indications of conflict and that he has portrayed his heroes in opposition to powerful Jewish groups. But he has not cast these groups in a single role. Chief priests and their allies are thoroughgoing villains and so play out that role throughout Luke–Acts. Although Pharisees and their allies occupy a position of opposition to Jesus and his teachings, their role in Luke–Acts as a whole is far more ambivalent than that of the chief priests. Indeed, Luke seems to show that there is nothing incompatible between Pharisees and Christian believers. Luke's most significant move in the treatment of Jesus' conflicts with the Jewish leaders is to exclude the Pharisees from playing a role in the scenes that lead up to Jesus' death. This move has the effect of isolating the chief priests and their allies and identifying them as the one group of Jewish leaders who stood in mortal opposition to Jesus and his successors.

If Luke presents the chief priests as the major villains among the Jewish leaders, we are led to inquire if he gives the reader any indication of the issues on which they differed with Jesus and his successors. In connection with the Pharisees, the issues between them and Jesus were those involving Torah observance. In the following chapter, by focusing on two of the main areas of priestly concern, the city of Jerusalem and the temple, we shall explore the issues that may have involved the chief priests.

NOTES

1. See, e.g., the collection of birth narratives in David R. Cartlidge and David L. Dungan, *Documents for the Study of the Gospels* (Philadelphia: Fortress Press, 1980), pp. 129–36.

2. Although there are formal similarities in the birth accounts of Jesus and John, clearly Jesus is presented as the superior one. In the two angelic announcements there are subtle differences that indicate Jesus' superiority. In speaking to Zechariah, Gabriel gives no title to John but says, "He will be great before the Lord" (Luke 1:15). At the comparable place in the announcement to Mary the words are: "He will be great, and will be called the Son of the Most High; and the Lord God will give to him the throne of his father David, and he will reign over the house of Jacob for ever; and of his kingdom there will be no end" (1:32–33). When Elizabeth meets Mary, she addresses her as "the mother of my Lord" (1:43). The idea of John as the one who prepares the way is introduced by Zechariah in an allusion to Isa 40:3 (Luke 1:76). If Luke 1:76 does not make John's subordination to Jesus clear, later references to the idea of preparation leave no doubt that John is to be regarded as inferior to Jesus (Luke 3:4,16; 7:27). For an analysis of the structure of the birth narratives see Raymond E. Brown, *The Birth of the Messiah* (Garden City, N.Y.: Doubleday, 1977), pp. 250–53; also Charles H. Talbert, *Literary Patterns, Theological Themes and the Genre of Luke–Acts* (Missoula, Mont.: Scholars Press, 1974), pp. 44–45.

3. In commenting on these verses Raymond Brown says, "The poverty and hunger of the oppressed in the Magnificat are primarily spiritual, but we should not forget the physical realities faced by early Christians" *(Birth of the Messiah,* p. 363). But Brown does not make clear why, in this passage, we should think of spiritual poverty at all.

4. In Luke 1:6 Zechariah and Elizabeth were described as righteous and obedient to God's commandments. So it would seem possible for individuals to be righteous even though Israel's relief had not yet come. But in Luke 1:75 Zechariah was speaking for the nation, not as an individual.

5. Mark has three such predictions—8:31; 9:31; and 10:32–34. Because it has been generally thought that Luke used Mark, we have usually thought of three passion predictions in Luke—9:22; 9:44; and 18:31–34. But if we treat Luke independently of Mark (and Matthew), Luke 17:25 must also be counted among the passion predictions.

6. The significance of Jerusalem for the death of Jesus will be more fully examined in chapter 4.

7. See Talbert, *Literary Patterns*. Talbert does not list Luke 12:11–12 and 21:12–19 as parallels.

8. In Luke 12:11–12, where persecution from synagogues, rulers, and authorities is predicted, it is the Holy Spirit that will teach the disciples what to say, but in 21:15 it is Jesus.

9. For Hans Conzelmann, Luke 16:16 marks the termination of the age of Israel and the beginning of the period of Jesus; see his *The Theology of St. Luke,* trans. Geoffrey Buswell (New York: Harper and Bros., 1960). The periodization of history that Conzelmann sees in Luke–Acts is not presupposed in the present study. On the other hand, nothing here conflicts with that concept, which is the result of Conzelmann's redaction-critical study.

10. I.e., small units of material, such as discourses and narratives.

11. See, e.g., Rudolf Bultmann, *The History of the Synoptic Tradition,* trans. John Marsh (New York: Harper and Row, 1963), pp. 39–54; also Martin Dibelius, *From Tradition to Gospel,* trans. Bertram L. Woolf (New York: Charles Scribner's Sons, 1935); Vincent Taylor, *The Formation of the Gospel Tradition,* 2nd ed. (London: Macmillan and Co., 1935).

12. *History of the Synoptic Tradition,* p. 39.

13. Ibid., p. 41. Vincent Taylor prefers to use the term "pronouncement story" to refer to those forms that Bultmann and Dibelius call apophthegms. He focuses attention on the statement, or pronouncement, of Jesus that concludes these stories (*Formation of the Gospel Tradition,* pp. 63–87).

14. Note, however, that the third temptation (Luke 4:9–12) is set in Jerusalem.

15. Luke 22:3–6; for Conzelmann the period between Luke 4:13 and 22:3 was intentionally described by Luke as a time when the devil was inactive. (*Theology of St. Luke,* pp. 27–29).

16. Note the textual variants to Gerasenes in Luke 8:26.

17. See Paul J. Achtemeier, "The Lukan Perspective on the Miracles of Jesus: A Preliminary Sketch," in *Perspectives on Luke–Acts,* ed. Charles H. Talbert (Macon, Ga.: Mercer University Press, 1978), pp. 153–67. Achtemeier agrees that Luke uses the concept of a battle against the devil. He says, "The way Luke phrases 11:21–22 (cf. Matt 12:29) as the interpretation of vs. 20 makes it clear that with the appearance of Jesus as the stronger one, Satan's 'goods,' i.e., those he possesses, are in fact being despoiled, a despoliation that continues in the work of the apostles (cf. Acts 16:16–18)" (p. 163). But Achtemeier adds that Luke is not "preoccupied with Jesus' battle with the demonic" (ibid.).

18. See Luke 9:50. The language of opposition—for and against—is present in both verses.

19. Talbert lists Luke 5:1–11 and 8:22–25 as literary pairs (*Literary Patterns,* p. 40).

20. The transfiguration story in Luke 9:28–36 may be regarded as a story of Jesus with cosmic dimensions, but this narrative does not involve conflict except by anticipation.

21. Talbert does not list Luke 9:1–2,10, and 10:17 as parallels. Rather, he lists Luke 22:35–38 next to 9:1–6 (*Literary Patterns*, p. 26).

22. The only narratives that associate Pharisees with Jerusalem are those in which Pharisees are portrayed as friendly to the Christian movement. See Acts 5:33–39; 23:1–10.

23. It is useful to trace the way in which Luke has grouped the various members of the Pharisaic block. In some places he writes about a single Pharisee or about Pharisees without mentioning any allies. In others he groups them with one or more of the allied groups. In two places he refers to an ally without mentioning the Pharisees. The following list displays these groupings:

A Pharisee (singular, with no reference to allies)—Luke 7:36,37,39; 11:37,38; 14:1; 18:10,11; Acts 5:34 (a reference to Gamaliel, also described as a teacher of the law).

Pharisees (plural, with no reference to allies)—Luke 6:2; 11:39,42,43; 12:1; 13:31; 16:14; 17:20; 19:39; Acts 26:5.

Pharisees and scribes—Luke 5:21,30; 6:7; 11:53; 15:2; Acts 23:9.

Pharisees and lawyers—Luke 7:30; 14:3.

Pharisees and teachers of the law—Luke 5:17.

Disciples of the Pharisees—Luke 5:33.

Pharisees and Sadducees (but not allies)—Acts 23:6,7,8.

Pharisaic party—Acts 15:5.

Lawyer(s)—Luke 10:25; 11:45,46,52.

24. Similarly, we may see the ways in which Luke has grouped the chief priests with their allies in the following list:

A high priest (singular, without reference to allies)—Acts 5:21,27; 7:1; 9:1; 19:14; 22:5; 23:2,4,5; 24:1.

Chief priests (plural, without reference to allies)—Acts 9:14,21; 22:30; 26:10,12.

Chief priest(s) and scribes—Luke 20:19; 22:2; 23:10.

Chief priest(s) and elders—Acts 4:23; 23:14; 25:15.

A high priest and Sadducees—Acts 5:17.

Chief priest(s) and *stratēgoi*—Luke 22:4; Acts 5:24.

Chief priest(s), scribes, and elders—Luke 9:22; 20:1; 22:66; 23:1.

Chief priests, scribes, and first citizens—Luke 19:47.

Chief priests, *stratēgoi*, and elders—Luke 22:52.

Chief priests and rulers—Luke 24:20.

A high priest, rulers, elders, and scribes—Acts 4:5,6.

Priests, *stratēgoi*, and Sadducees—Acts 4:1.

Chief priests and crowd—Luke 23:4.

Chief priests, leaders, and people—Luke 23:13,18,21,23.

Scribes—Luke 20:39,45–47.

Scribes, people, and elders—Acts 6:12.

Sadducees—Luke 20:27; Acts 23:6,7,8.

Rulers and elders—Acts 4:8.

Elders—Luke 7:3.

25. See my article "The Opposition to Jesus in the Gospel of Luke," *Perspectives in Religious Studies* 5 (1978): 144–50.

26. Some of these pericopes may formally be described as controversy in dialogues or pronouncement stories. Our interest here is in their function in the Lukan context.

27. Thus Luke 17:20–21 may be thought of as a pronouncement story, to use Vincent Taylor's term (*Formation of the Gospel Tradition*, pp. 63–87).

28. Although Taylor regards Luke 13:31–33 as a story about Jesus rather than a pronouncement story, it has the basic features of the latter (ibid., p. 75).

29. For an analysis of dining patterns in first-century Palestine as reflected in Luke 7:36–50 see Kenneth E. Bailey, *Through Peasant Eyes* (Grand Rapids: Eerdmans, 1980), pp. 1–21.

30. Jack T. Sanders calls attention to the concluding verse in this pericope, Luke 5:26, in which Luke says that the audience expresses amazement and glorifies God. He understands that the Pharisees would have been included in this audience. This seems unlikely, however, in view of the continuing criticism by Pharisees that we see in several of the following pericopes. It is probable that Luke 5:26 represents for Luke the response of the Jewish public, which at this point is altogether favorable to Jesus (Sanders, "The Pharisees in Luke–Acts," in *The Living Text: Essays in Honor of Ernest W. Saunders,* ed. Dennis E. Groh and Robert Jewett [Lanham, Md.: University Press of America, 1985], pp. 141–88).

31. The persons who question Jesus in Luke 5:33 are literally unspecified in this verse, but they are clearly the same persons who had criticized Jesus in 5:30, namely the Pharisees and their scribes.

32. The conversation in Luke 10:25–28 is between Jesus and a lawyer. Pharisees are not explicitly mentioned in this pericope.

33. In the pericope of the healing of the paralytic (Luke 5:17–26) we may observe something about Luke's attitude toward Pharisees by noting that in 5:17 Pharisees and teachers of the law are present, while in 5:21 it is scribes and Pharisees who question Jesus. Luke thinks of Pharisees as the dominant group. The names of the supportive groups may vary.

34. Although the setting for both Luke 11:42–44 and 11:45–52 is the same as that of the dinner in 11:37–41, the sayings of Jesus in these pericopes are not properly responses to the Pharisaic criticism reported in 11:38. Nor is there a dialogue in these passages. It seems best to analyze them separately, while noting their placement in the Lukan narrative.

35. Luke 11:53–54 may be regarded as the conclusion to the dinner narrative that began in 11:37. In character, however, it reads more like a general summary than as part of the preceding.

36. But see Sanders ("The Pharisees in Luke–Acts"), who thinks that Pharisaic Christians are, for Luke, the real opponents of the Torah-free Christian movement that is to be identified with Jesus and Paul.

37. Luke uses the term *archiereus* in the singular to designate a specific high priest and in the plural for chief priests as a group. In this section of our study we are

mainly interested in Luke's treatment of the group. Many of the references to a particular high priest come in connection with the trials of Jesus and Paul.

38. One exception may be found in Luke 20:1, where some manuscripts read *hiereis* rather than *archiereis*. Also in Acts 4:1, in most manuscripts, ordinary priests are listed among the opponents of the apostles.

39. Some manuscripts read *hiereis*.

40. These facts would remind the reader of the connection between scribes and Pharisees in the earlier sections of Luke's gospel (5:21,30; 6:7; 11:53; 15:2), but they do not seem to hint at an association between Pharisees and chief priests in the section on Jesus in Jerusalem.

41. Josephus, *War* 2. 164–65; *Antiquities* 18. 16.

42. Josephus also speaks of a *stratēgos* in connection with the temple (*War* 6. 294). In this reference the *stratēgos* seems to be in charge of temple security. But in other places *stratēgoi* have political or military functions in Gentile cities; see *Antiquities* 14. 247, 259; 20. 131.

43. J. M. Creed (*The Gospel According to St. Luke* [London: Macmillan and Co., 1930], p. 250) implies that the scribes were connected with Pharisees, and he compares this scene with that in Acts 23:6-7. He says: "Thus Jesus has vindicated the popular belief in a future life, which was held by the Pharisees, and it is appropriate that he should receive commendation from some scribes who were present." But there is nothing in Luke 20:27–40 to suggest such a connection.

44. Note the textual variants in Acts 4:1; see Luke 20:1 and note 38 above.

Jerusalem and
the Temple

The importance of geographical settings in narrative literature generally and in the Christian gospels specifically has long been recognized. Early in the history of form criticism it was observed that geographical elements were mainly used by the final redactors of the gospels to provide links between episodes, to give a sense of movement, and to give expression to theological motifs. Karl L. Schmidt maintained that individual pericopes had been set side by side in the gospels and framed by an arbitrary geographical and chronological sequence.[1] Rudolf Bultmann recognized that the original forms of apophthegms and narratives usually did not contain indications of location. He wrote that "precise indications of place are obviously unsuited to the apophthegmatic style," although he was prepared to admit that some geographical references were "part of the very stuff of the story."[2] His general rule was: "The pointers which are necessarily presupposed by the subsequent story generally belong to the basic material. Others, especially connecting pointers, are the work of an editor."[3]

Vincent Taylor appears to have disagreed with Bultmann on this point. He reported certain experiments which showed that, in the oral transmission of miracle stories, place names tend to drop out. He believed that there was a tendency toward abbreviation at work in the miracle tradition. Nevertheless, he did not conclude from this that the presence of a place name is always an indication of a

84

primitive form or that the gospel writers never used geographical designations to support theological concepts. Taylor, in fact, set down this general proposition: "Only where details are not due to literary activity and are not subservient to doctrinal interests, can we be sure that we have to do with primitive stories."[4] This sentence suggests that Bultmann and Taylor were not far apart in their treatment of geographical elements. For Bultmann, a place designation should be attributed to secondary or editorial activity if it is not required by the story itself. For Taylor, it may be regarded as primitive if it cannot be shown that it served the doctrinal purposes of the Christian tradition or the evangelist. The difference between them is on the question of where the burden of proof lies.

The theological importance of geography was treated by Ernst Lohmeyer in his classic analysis of the relative importance and meaning of Galilee and Jerusalem in primitive Christianity and in the gospels.[5] Lohmeyer thought that, although certain geographical designations were contained in the pregospel traditions, each evangelist controlled them in his gospel and did so in line with his basic christological and eschatological assumptions.

Redaction critics have emphasized the role of the evangelists in providing such geographical notes. Indeed, in his landmark redaction-critical study of Luke–Acts, *The Theology of St. Luke*, Hans Conzelmann devoted the first major section to "Geographical Elements in the Composition of Luke's Gsopel." In this study Conzelmann traced the various geographical notes in Luke's gospel and attempted to judge their significance.

From our perspective it appears that Conzelmann's work has several major problems. In the first place, he omitted any mention of Luke's infancy narratives without fully explaining the reasons for such an omission.[6] Conzelmann felt that Luke 1–2 constituted a prologue to the gospel but not an original part of it. Second, despite the fact that he intended his book to be a study of the entire Lukan corpus, the section on geographical elements is concerned only with the gospel, not with Acts. Third, Conzelmann assumes the importance of geographical elements in the gospel but does not lay out for the reader an explanation of the importance. Finally, Conzelmann's redaction-critical work is heavily dependent upon his views on source criticism. As a matter of principle Conzelmann states in his introduction that source criticism is only of secondary importance. He states that his purpose is "to elucidate Luke's work in its present form, not to enquire into possible sources or into the historical facts which provide the material. A variety of sources does not necessarily imply a similar variety in the thought and composition of the author. How did it come about, that he brought together these particular materials? Was he able to imprint on them his own views?" Precisely at this point, however, Conzelmann is able to call upon the two-document hypothesis: "It is here that the analysis of the sources renders the necessary service of helping to distinguish what comes from the source from what belongs to the author."[7] Thus, throughout his study of the gospel Conzelmann puts special weight on a comparison of geographical notes in Luke and Mark. The most important notes are those that Luke did not find in his sources but supplied and those that he found in his sources and altered. It may be that Conzelmann did not include a section on geographical elements in Acts partly because of the difficulties of comparing this book with nonextant, hypothetical sources.

Despite these problems, Conzelmann was able to point to some significant matters relating to geographical elements in Luke's gospel. He was able to conceive of Jesus' ministry in the gospel as structured with three major sections, geographically determined as follows:

> (i) The period of the gathering of "witnesses" in Galilee, opening with the proclamation of Jesus as the Son of God.
> (ii) The Journey of the Galileans to the Temple, opening with the narrative passage containing the disclosure that Jesus must suffer and the Transfiguration.
> (iii) The period of the teaching in the Temple and the Passion in Jerusalem, opening with the revelation of his royalty at the Entry. This period closes with the dawn of the new epoch of salvation with the Resurrection and Ascension.[8]

In this outline the material on John the Baptist and the genealogy (Luke 3) are prologue. The first section of Jesus' ministry, in Galilee, includes Luke 4:1–9:50. The second, the journey section, is outlined slightly differently in Conzelmann's text from the way in which it is described in the introduction. Although he raises questions about the precise point of beginning for this second section, he finally marks it as going from Luke 9:51 to 19:27. Thus it does not include "the narrative passage containing the disclosure that Jesus must suffer [apparently Luke 9:18–27] and the Transfiguration [9:28–36]."[9] In fact, Conzelmann includes the exegesis of these two passages in the Galilean section.[10] The third section, set in Jerusalem, then goes from Luke 19:28 through 24:49.[11] Conzelmann's central insight that Luke displays the ministry of Jesus as a journey to Jerusalem appears to be sound.

William C. Robinson also maintains that Luke intended to show Jesus as engaged in a journey. He emphasizes the journey motif in Luke, calling attention to the fact that the Jesus movement was designated as a *hodos* in Acts (9:2; 19:9,23; 22:4; 24:14,22). Specifically, he looks on Luke 23:5 as the key to the geographical structure of the gospel.[12] This verse contains the charge that Jesus "stirs up the people, teaching throughout all Judea, from Galilee even to this place." The phrase translated "this place" [*heōs hōde*] clearly means Jerusalem but may also, in context, refer to the temple (see p. 108f. below). Acts 10:37,39 presents a geographical viewpoint that is consistent with that in Luke 23:5: "The word which was proclaimed throughout all Judea, beginning from Galilee after the baptism which John preached. . . . And we are witnesses to all that he did both in the country of the Jews and in Jerusalem."

In this connection one ought to note the often maintained view that the book of Acts is governed by a similar geographical scheme.[13] In Acts 1:8 Jesus gives his last words to the disciples before his departure. He assures them that they will receive power from the Holy Spirit (cf. Acts 1:4) and then says, "And you shall be my witnesses in Jerusalem and in all Judea and Samaria and to the end of the earth." The viewpoint that this verse forms a key to the geographical structure of Acts may be challenged, especially since the specificity with which the verse begins is not maintained throughout. The sequence—Jerusalem, Judea, and Samaria—generally describes the order of events in Acts 1–12. But Jesus' words in Acts 1:8 contain no mention of any of those areas subsequently visited by Paul and in which Luke must have had a lively interest. The interpretation of Acts 1:8 as a geographical key also requires us to understand the phrase "to the end of the earth" as a way of designating Rome. Although this is not a necessary interpretation, it is a plausible one. From the perspective of a movement with Palestinian roots, it is reasonable to expect that Italy would be looked upon as the end of the earth.[14]

Even if one is not fully persuaded that Luke 23:5 and Acts 1:8 (with Acts 10:37, 39) constitute geographical notes that govern the structure of Luke–Acts, these verses nevertheless represent a conception that must be reckoned with. The most noteworthy aspect of these passages is the position of Jerusalem. In Luke 23:5 it is the goal of Jesus' ministry. In Acts 1:8 it is the city in which the apostles are to receive power and in which their work of witnessing will begin. Moreover, it is the place from which the witnessing will go forth "to the end of the earth" (cf. Luke 24:47). Jerusalem appears to be the hinge of Luke–Acts.[15]

There is no doubt that, in respect to the position of Jerusalem, the passages under consideration conform to the overall structure of Luke–Acts. Among the synoptic gospels only Luke ends with postresurrection appearances of Jesus in or near Jerusalem. For him no such appearances in Galilee occurred, and none are expected. There is no departure of disciples from Jerusalem after the crucifixion; indeed, the risen Christ commands them to remain there until they have received the Spirit (Luke 24:49; Acts 1:4). At the end of the gospel the disciples are in Jerusalem (Luke 24:53); they are still there at the beginning of Acts (Acts 1:4). Leaving aside for the moment the problem of the two ascension stories, we should not overlook the fact that both narratives are located in close proximity to Jerusalem—Bethany in Luke 24:50 and the Mount of Olives (a sabbath day's journey from Jerusalem) in Acts 1:12. The centrality of Jerusalem in Luke–Acts is clear.

To discern the reasons that Luke so stressed the centrality of Jerusalem is more difficult than simply to recognize it. One may presume that Jerusalem was known to be the place of Jesus' crucifixion and thus assume that some references to the city had been retained in the oral tradition as well as in Luke's literary sources. It is notable, however, that in his letters Paul does not mention Jerusalem as the place of the crucifixion.[16] In the two places in 1 Corinthians in which he relates clearly traditional material (11:23–26; 15:3–7), there is, surprisingly, no reference to the location of the last supper, death, burial, or postresurrection appearances of Jesus. Nevertheless, Luke consistently portrays Jerusalem as the place where these events took place.

Luke also stresses the point that the church of Jerusalem was the church of the apostles. On this point he is in conformity with the indications that we have in Paul's letters. Gal 1:17–18 lets us know that Paul thought of Jerusalem as a kind of headquarters, as the place of "those who were apostles before me" and especially as the city of Cephas. Paul took up a collection for the saints at Jerusalem (Rom 15:25,26,31; 1 Cor 16:1; 2 Cor 9:1). He spoke of Jerusalem as the place from which his own missionary work began (Rom 15:19).

If Jerusalem as the place of Jesus' crucifixion and resurrection and Jerusalem as the place of the apostolic church were fixed points for Luke, it is nevertheless not obvious why he would choose to make the city the hinge of his narrative. Although Conzelmann recognizes the unique position of Jerusalem in Luke–Acts, he does not finally answer this question. More recently, however, Michael Bachmann has claimed that, for Luke, Jerusalem has significance only because it is the location of the Jewish cult and temple.[17] It is the center of Jewish life and hope, and Luke has a basically positive view of both city and temple. Bachmann writes: "Luke sees in the Temple in Jerusalem the center of Jewish service to God and thus the one earthly point responsible for the whole of Jewish life and hope (determined through the law), which directs itself in accordance with (the one) God.[18]

Although Bachmann is probably correct in showing that the connection between the city and the temple is primary for Luke, he has not shown that Luke thought of the city only in its association with the temple. It seems better to say that Luke had several conflicting associations for the city of Jerusalem: he knew it as the site of Jesus' crucifixion and resurrection, as the city of the apostles, and as the location of the Jewish temple. The conflicting and interrelated nature of these associations affects the course of Luke's narrative in complex ways.

Although suggestive and important insights are to be found in the works cited above, there is a need for a fresh analysis of the treatment of Jerusalem and the temple in Luke–Acts. The perspective of a kind of literary criticism that treats the entire Lukan corpus, emphasizes its integrity, and makes no assumptions about the author's documentary sources can provide such an analysis. Moreover, the previous chapters have shaped a perspective for raising quite specific questions about Luke's image of Jerusalem and the temple and their connection with the death of Jesus. The contention in this chapter will be that Luke presents Jerusalem, more specifically the temple, in both positive and negative ways. In particular, the temple is a place of both peace and conflict. It is likely that the Lukan treatment of the city and the temple is related to issues that he thought were involved in the execution of Jesus.

POSITIVE IMAGES OF JERUSALEM AND THE TEMPLE

The insight that Jerusalem and the temple are pivotal in Luke–Acts is quite correct. Their pivotal nature may be shown by observing that these settings create a geographical *inclusio* for the gospel. The gospel of Luke begins and ends in Jerusalem and in the temple.

The beginning in Jerusalem, specifically in the temple, immediately establishes for Luke's gospel a positive impression of these places. The Jewish temple figures prominently in Luke's infancy narratives. The narrative in which the angel Gabriel appears to the priest Zechariah is set "in the Lord's shrine" (*naos*, Luke 1:9, 21, 22), which almost certainly means the Jerusalem temple. Zechariah enters the shrine in the course of his regular priestly duties, and the angel appears "on the right side of the altar of incense" (1:11). Zechariah and his wife, Elizabeth, are described as righteous and blameless in respect to God's commandments. After his birth the infant Jesus is presented in the temple (2:22), and Simeon is led by the Spirit to enter the temple, hold the child, and pronounce a blessing. Similarly the aged widow, Anna, greets the child in the temple, speaks to those who are looking for the redemption of Jerusalem, and gives thanks. Simeon is described as "righteous and devout, looking for the consolation of Israel" (2:25), and Anna is said not to "depart from the temple, worshiping with fasting and prayer night and day" (2:37). Luke is unique among the evangelists in describing the fidelity of the holy family to the Jewish ritualistic requirements and in locating their performance in the temple—circumcision, purification, and sacrifice. Only after "they had performed everything according to the law of the Lord" (2:39) did they go to Galilee. Finally we read of Jesus at the age of twelve, who has been left behind in Jerusalem, "in the temple, sitting among the teachers, listening to them and asking them questions" (2:46).

The image of Jerusalem and the temple in the infancy narratives is an altogether positive one. Here is a place where a priest who is routinely fulfilling his duties meets an angel and receives an incredible promise. Here one associates religious devotion, piety, fidelity to God's commandments, and the righteous hope of the oppressed. The scene of Jesus at twelve (Luke 2:41–52) would seem to anticipate the material in 19:45–21:38, in which the mature Jesus teaches in the temple.

A similar phenomenon is found at the end of Luke's gospel. Indeed, the distinctiveness of Luke's reports of the postresurrection appearances of Jesus lies largely in the fact that he has located these appearances in Jerusalem and in certain neighboring villages. The first appearance occurs to the two disciples on the way to Emmaus, which is said to be sixty stadia from Jerusalem (Luke 24:13). After the risen Christ is made known to them, the two disciples return to Jerusalem, where the others are gathered and where they learn of a postresurrection appearance to Simon. The second appearance that Luke describes is to the remaining eleven disciples in Jerusalem (24:36–49), and the third is at Bethany (24:50).[19]

In addition to locating the postresurrection appearances in and around Jerusalem, Luke also emphasizes the significance of the city in the last words of Jesus in the gospel. In these parting words the risen Jesus commands the eleven to preach repentance and forgiveness of sins, "beginning in Jerusalem" (24:47), and he orders them to "stay in the city, until you are clothed with power from on high" (24:49). In the final verses the disciples "returned to Jerusalem with great joy, and were continually in the temple blessing God" (24:52–53).

The same notes of piety and great joy that pervaded the infancy narratives are also found in the last chapter of Luke's gospel. The association of Jerusalem and the temple with these very positive notes is powerful.

Before moving to the opening chapters of Acts, we must consider certain problems about the relationship between the end of Luke and the beginning of Acts. Three interrelated problems face the reader at this point. The first has to do with the text of Luke 24:51, and the second with the genuineness of Luke 24:50–53. The third problem is the question whether Luke has conflicting accounts of Jesus' ascension, one at the end of the gospel (24:50–53) and the other at the beginning of Acts (1:9–12).

Regarding the textual question about Luke 24:51, some manuscripts omit the words "and was carried up into heaven" (*kai anephereto eis ton ouranon*).[20] If this phrase had been absent from the autograph of Luke, it would be possible to regard Luke 24:51 as describing only a temporary departure of Jesus from his disciples. The final departure would be the ascension forty days later, described in Acts 1:9–12. But the third edition of the United Bible Societies' *Greek New Testament* includes the phrase, and Bruce Metzger comments that, although there was division in the committee, the majority favored its inclusion.[21] One of the points Metzger raises in defense of the longer text is that in Acts 1:2 Luke refers to a previous description of the ascension. The prologue to Acts describes the contents of the first book as including, indeed ending with, Jesus' having been taken up (*anelēmphthē*, Acts 1:2). Metzger says that Acts 1:2 "implies that he [Luke] considered that he had made some reference, however brief, to the ascension at the close of his first book."[22] Metzger also suggests that the phrase may have been omitted by a copyist who had observed the apparent inconsistency between Luke 24 and Acts 1.

The genuineness of the last verses of the gospel is a related question. Conzelmann accepts the longer text of Luke 24:51 but regards the whole of 24:50–53 as a later interpolation.[23] He maintains that if these verses had been genuine, Luke would have been guilty of writing two different ascension stories, the first set at Bethany on Easter day and the second at the Mount of Olives forty days later. Conzelmann thinks that the geographical setting at Bethany in Luke 24:50 reveals the hand of a later interpolater, since Luke consistently avoids mentioning Bethany in his gospel. There is, however, another reference to Bethany (with Bethphage), in 19:29, and Conzelmann regards this reference as having been copied by Luke from Mark 11:1.

Conzelmann's argument against the originality of Luke 24:50–53 is unconvincing. Since he accepts the argument that the longer text of Luke 24:51 was original, it is difficult to understand how he can argue that the entire section was not genuine. It must have been known to the author of Acts 1:2, and Conzelmann regards this as an authentic Lukan verse. Surely it would have been inappropriate for Luke to have written that his first book ended with Jesus' having been taken up if he did not include something like Luke 24:50–53 in the gospel.

This brings us to the third problem. If Luke 24:50–53 is to be regarded as a genuine part of the gospel, we are forced to conclude that Luke–Acts has two stories of the ascension of Jesus. But does it mean that we have conflicting ascension stories? There are apparent conflicts in terms of the settings both in place and time. The narrative in the gospel is set at Bethany, while the one in Acts is at the Mount of Olives. The time of the story in Luke 24 is apparently Easter day, while that of the narrative in Acts 1 is forty days after Easter.

As to the apparent conflict in terms of location, it is not certain that Luke thought of Bethany and the Mount of Olives as clearly distinct places. In Luke 19:29 Bethany, with Bethphage, is located *pros* the Mount of Olives. The preposition *pros* with the accusative and with verbs of motion expresses the idea of direction. We should probably translate, "he [Jesus] approached Bethphage and Bethany [moving] in the direction of the Mount called 'of Olives.' " The course of the narrative in 19:28–40 suggests that Luke pictured Bethphage and Bethany as being very close to the mountain. As Jesus approaches these villages, he sends two of his disciples to one of them (which one is unspecified) to bring a colt for him to ride. When they do so, he mounts it and rides toward the mountain, praised by his disciples. To be sure, no distances are specified, but the ride from Bethany to the Mount of Olives has the character of being a triumphal conclusion to Jesus' longer journey from Galilee to Jerusalem. One gains the impression that the ride is a short one and that no great distance separated Bethany, Bethphage, and the Mount of Olives.[24]

Furthermore, the location of the story in Luke 24:50–53 is somewhat imprecise. In 24:50 we read that Jesus led his disciples out *heōs pros Bethanian*. As in 19:29, so here, the preposition would indicate direction. I. Howard Marshall translates *heōs pros* by "right to the neighbourhood of."[25] If this phrase suggests that Jesus' ascension occurred in the vicinity of Bethany, and if Luke thinks of Bethany and the Mount of Olives as situated in close proximity to each other, there would be no essential conflict between Luke and Acts on the matter of location.

The discrepancy between Luke 24 and Acts 1 in regard to the time of the ascension is more apparent than real. Clearly the ascension in Acts happens after the many postresurrection appearances of Jesus that occurred over a forty-day period, but the setting in Luke is indefinite. Many would assume that the ascension in the gospel occurred on Easter Sunday, the same day as the other events described in Luke 24, but this assumption is not necessary. The first postresurrection appearance of Jesus that is described in Luke 24 is clearly set on Easter. In establishing the time of this appearance at Emmaus, Luke says that it was on the same day (24:13) as the discovery of the empty tomb. The day was almost over when the party arrived in Emmaus (24:29), but the two disciples started back toward Jerusalem immediately after their meal with Jesus (24:33). The second appearance of the risen Jesus then occurred in Jerusalem on the same day, apparently very late in the evening (24:36–49). All these events clearly are set on Easter Sunday, and they pack the day from early dawn to late evening. But no certain chronological connections are given in 24:50–53. It begins simply with the words: "And he led them as far as Bethany."[26] It is not necessary to conclude that Luke intended this episode to be set on the same day as the events of 24:1–49. Although Luke 24 does not clearly conform to Acts 1 in terms of the setting in time, neither does it clearly conflict with it.

While the ascension story in Luke 24 is not explicitly set forty days after Easter and is not specifically located at the Mount of Olives, it does not certainly conflict with those details in Acts 1.[27] It seems reasonable to conclude that Luke is telling the same story twice, with different but not conflicting details.

To understand why Luke might wish to tell the ascension story twice and with slightly different details is not easy. Perhaps he intended to use these narratives to create a sense of connection between the two books. It should also be observed that the overlapping is not confined to the two ascension stories but is to be found more broadly in Luke 24 and Acts 1. In both chapters Jesus gives his disciples certain orders, among them the commandment to remain in Jerusalem until they have received power or the Spirit (Luke 24:49; Acts 1:4). In both there is a priority given to Jerusalem in preaching and witnessing to Jesus (Luke 24:47; Acts 1:8). In both, the disciples return to Jerusalem after the ascension and devote themselves to pious acts (Luke 24:53; Acts 1:12–14). The overlap would give the reader a sense of continuity and an awareness that the second book begins precisely where the first leaves off. The reader would thus feel that he has missed none of the story. Literarily, Luke 24:50–53 serves as an anticipation of the fuller account in Acts 1:9–12.

In any event, the ascension story in Acts introduces a dramatic set of narratives about the apostles in Jerusalem. The early chapters of Acts (specifically 1–2), like the opening and closing chapters of the gospel, contain a very positive image of Jerusalem and the temple. Not only does Acts 1 have associations with Luke 24, but there are significant similarities between Luke 1–2 and the first two chapters of Acts.[28] In Luke's infancy narratives, for example, the prophetic spirit produces speeches by Zechariah (1:67–79) and Simeon (2:29–35). In Acts 2 the Spirit comes upon the assembled group, leads to prophetic glossolalia and to the speech of Peter, which is addressed to devout Jews in Jerusalem (2:5). Jerusalem is clearly the place where the disciples, in obedience to Jesus' word (Acts 1:4), gather to await the coming of power through the Spirit (Acts 1:12). It is perhaps of greater importance that in the first two chapters of Acts the temple is one of the gathering places for the early Christian community. In one of the general summaries that Luke uses to describe the ideal character of this community, he says that the believers attended the temple daily (Acts 2:46). In these summaries Luke emphasizes the features of harmony, peace, and unanimity in the early Christian community. Their gathering in the temple is to be seen as a demonstration of this peace and unity.

The image of Jerusalem and the temple in the infancy narratives, the postresurrection appearance accounts, and the narratives in the opening chapters of Acts is much the same. The city and its shrine are associated with pious people, who gather together in joy, peace, and blessing, and who spend their time in prayer.

Although these three sections of Luke–Acts contain the most powerfully positive images of Jerusalem and the temple, there are some notes scattered throughout the work that tend to reinforce that image. In Luke 6:17 Jesus' audience is said to be composed of people from a wide area, including Jerusalem. In Acts 3:1–10 Luke tells of an incident in the temple when Peter and John healed a lame man. He notes that these apostles had gone to the temple at the hour of prayer, and he implies that prayer was their purpose. In Acts 5:12–16, one of Luke's summary sections, he emphasizes the honor in which the apostles were held by the people, the growth of the community of believers, and the large number of healings and exorcisms that the apostles performed. He associates all this activity with the temple, as he pictures the apostles and people gathered in Solomon's portico, no doubt understood by Luke to be a part of the temple (see Acts 3:11). Again, in Acts 6:7, Luke associates the growth of the Christian movement with Jerusalem, and he even calls attention to a large number of priestly believers. And in Acts 8:27 he introduces the eunuch from Ethiopia, who was converted after a visit to Jerusalem to worship.

It is of fundamental importance that Luke pictures Jerusalem as the place of the apostles, a point that, as we have seen, is in harmony with the viewpoint of Paul. The early chapters of Acts show that, in obedience to Jesus' word, the apostles returned to Jerusalem and that, in fulfillment of his promise, they there received the Spirit at Pentecost. In all of his first main section of Acts, up to 8:3, Luke confines the Christian community to Jerusalem and stresses the apostolic leadership of the community. Moreover, even when, after the death of Stephen, persecution broke out in the city and the believers scattered, the apostles remained there (8:1). Although Peter and John later went to Samaria, they were sent there by the apostles in Jerusalem (8:14), and they returned to the city after their mission (8:25). After Paul's conversion at Damascus he came to present himself to the apostles in Jerusalem (9:26–30), and after Peter's vision and baptism of Cornelius' household at Caesarea he was required to report to the other apostles in Jerusalem (11:1–2). In 11:19–26 Barnabas was sent by "the church in Jerusalem" to investigate the conversions in Antioch. The great controversy about circumcision had to be settled by a meeting in Jerusalem. Indeed, Luke reports that Paul, Barnabas, and others were appointed by the church at Antioch to meet with the apostles in Jerusalem (15:1–2). In this incident Luke maintains that the important policies for all the churches were determined by the apostles in Jerusalem. The deliberations took place there; the agreement was regarded as binding, and it had to be communicated by letter to the church at Antioch (15:30–33) and other places (16:4).

While the setting for both the opening and the closing of Luke's gospel is the same, namely the temple in Jerusalem, in Acts the action begins in Jerusalem but ends in Rome. That fact itself signifies that we have to deal not only with positive images of Jerusalem and the temple but with negative ones as well. The conclusion of Acts in Rome signifies an alteration in the orientation of the Christian movement. It did not remain in Jerusalem, and it did not remain a Jewish movement (Acts 18:28). In Luke's presentation the negative aspects of Jerusalem and temple have a connection with this fact.

NEGATIVE IMAGES OF JERUSALEM AND THE TEMPLE

If there are passages in which the image of Jerusalem and the temple is one of peace and piety, there are others in which it appears to be associated with conflict. Probably a negative image is to be found as early as the third temptation (Luke 4:9–12), when the devil takes Jesus to Jerusalem and sets him on "the pinnacle of the temple." Although the temptation is for Jesus to jump from the temple, there is an undertone in which the city and the temple already appear as points of conflict, here between Jesus and the devil.[29]

In Acts, Jerusalem is frequently associated with the persecution of the Christian movement: Stephen is thrown out of the city and put to death (Acts 7:58); a more general persecution follows (8:1);

and the pre-Christian Paul is connected with the persecution of believers in Jerusalem (9:2,13,21; 22:5; 26:10).

The most thoroughly negative images of city and temple are
gathered around the trials of Jesus and Paul, and we shall examine
these accounts in some detail in chapter 5. But Luke has carefully
prepared for these critical sections by a number of passages that
create an aura of impending doom. Impending doom in Jerusalem
is signaled as early as the story of Jesus' transfiguration (Luke 9:28–
36). In this story Luke shows symbolically how both the law and
the prophets foretell Jesus' passion. In 9:31, a verse that is unique
to Luke, Moses and Elijah speak of Jesus' *exodos*, "which he was to
accomplish at Jerusalem."[30] It has already been observed that the
great central section of the gospel (Luke 9:51–19:44) has been organized by the evangelist as a travel narrative. It is a trip to Jerusalem, and in the narrative the reader increasingly becomes aware of
the danger that awaits the hero. From the beginning of the trip
Luke makes it clear that Jesus intentionally heads for Jerusalem. In
9:51 we have, "When the days drew near for him to be received up
[*tēs analēmpseōs autou*, cf. Acts 1:2,11,22], he set his face to go to
Jerusalem." Again, in 9:53, Luke has: "But the people [of the Samaritan village] would not receive him, because his face was set toward Jerusalem." The two references to Jesus' pending fate in Luke
9 should be taken together, although the reference in 9:31 is to his
exodos and in 9:51 to his *analēmpsis*. Both nouns may be used of
death. But the verb *analambanō*, which is used in Acts 1:2,11,22,
refers rather to Jesus' being taken up into heaven.[31] It would seem
that Luke 9:51 is an anticipation of the event that Luke describes in
Acts 1. But here there is no discernible note of joy or anticipated
victory. Why have the Samaritans refused to receive him? Although
some commentators remark that Samaritans were customarily inhospitable to pilgrims going up to Jerusalem, it is difficult to interpret the present passage along these lines.[32] The force of Luke
9:51–56 is to emphasize Jesus' determination to fulfill his destiny.
Samaritans avoid him precisely because of his sense of determination. Samaritan avoidance, determination, being taken up, fulfillment at Jerusalem—all together reinforce a sense of approaching
doom and remind the reader of the reference to Jesus' *exodos* in
Luke 9:31. Although it may be correct to say that in 9:51,53 Luke

had in mind the entire complex of events that were to transpire in Jerusalem, ending in Jesus' ascension, any implication that this should bring joy to the reader is lacking. The emphasis here and in 9:31 is on Jesus' departure, not his glorification.

At several points in the travel narrative Luke reminds the reader that Jesus is headed for Jerusalem (Luke 13:22; 17:11; 19:11, 28). At three specific points the anticipation of danger and its association with Jerusalem becomes explicit. In 13:33–34 Jesus speaks of Jerusalem as the customary place for the killing of prophets. He makes the statement that he must go to Jerusalem because "it cannot be that a prophet should perish away from Jerusalem" (13:33). In the second (18:31–34) Jesus explains that the scriptures will be fulfilled in Jerusalem—specifically the death and resurrection of the Son of man.[33] The third statement about Jerusalem is positioned by Luke just at the end of the travel narrative. Just as Jesus comes within sight of the city, thus in the first words that he directs to the citizens of Jerusalem, he utters words of apocalyptic doom.

> And when he drew near and saw the city he wept over it, saying, "Would that even today you knew the things that make for peace! But now they are hid from your eyes. For the days shall come upon you, when your enemies will cast up a bank about you and surround you, and hem you in on every side, and dash you to the ground, you and your children within you, and they will not leave one stone upon another in you; because you did not know the time of your visitation" (Luke 19:41–44).

Jesus announces that peace has been hidden from Jerusalem, and as a result its citizens will suffer siege, attack, and mass death, and the city will suffer destruction from its enemies. In 19:44 the reason for these catastrophes is said to be "because you did not know the time of your visitation." Jerusalem will experience conflict rather than peace because its citizens did not know the time of their visitation, i.e., apparently because they did not receive Jesus. The phrases in 19:42 and 44 must, in the final analysis, point to the same thing. Both speak of a lack of knowledge (*egnōs* in both cases), and in both the specific knowledge that is lacking has to do with time (*en tē hēmera tautē* in 19:42; *ton kairon* in 19:44).[34] Both these verses seem to point back to the proclamation of Jesus' disciples in Luke 19:38. There they had shouted that the King was coming, and they announced peace: "Blessed is the King who comes in the name of the Lord! Peace in heaven and glory in the highest!" (19:38). Because of the pending rejection we have the weeping of Jesus in 19:41, which contrasts with the rejoicing of the disciples in 19:37. Joy and peace should accompany the approach of the King to Jerusalem, but only weeping is appropriate for Jerusalem's rejection of Jesus.

The woes in Luke 19:41–44 anticipate the fuller apocalyptic predictions in chapter 21. In this chapter Jesus predicts the destruction of both temple (21:6) and city (21:20–24). The reason for the fall of Jerusalem is not given here, but it is clear that its fate is a fulfillment of scripture (21:22).

In several ways Paul's trip to Jerusalem mirrors that of Jesus. The first note about the trip (Acts 19:21–22) reminds one of the beginning of Jesus' journey (Luke 9:51–56). Luke emphasizes Paul's determination and the Spirit's leadership. The trip actually begins in Acts 20:13, and Luke tells us that Paul wanted to be in Jerusalem in time for Pentecost (20:16). His departure from Asian missionary work is announced by Paul in a speech to the Ephesian elders, gathered to meet him in Miletus (20:17–35). In his speech Paul speaks of his departure (*aphixis*, 20:29), and he tells the elders that they will see him no more (20:25). He speaks explicitly of Jerusalem: "And now, behold, I am going to Jerusalem, bound in the Spirit, not knowing what shall befall me there; except that the Holy Spirit testifies to me in every city that imprisonment and afflictions await me" (20:22–23). Indeed, Luke illustrates these spiritual messages as Paul makes his progress toward the city. In Tyre some disciples, speaking in the Spirit, warn him not to go on to Jerusalem (21:4). At Caesarea the prophet Agabus predicts Paul's capture at Jerusalem (21:10–14).

So in the case of both Jesus and Paul, Luke has carefully prepared the reader to expect the worst. At the same time he has emphasized the theme that divine inevitability and human determination led both the heroes to fulfill their roles.

In both the trial of Jesus and the trials of Paul the hostile character of Jerusalem is highlighted. Acts 4:27, which interprets Ps 2:1–2, serves as a summary for the trial of Jesus. The Psalm, as quoted in 4:25–26, speaks of Gentiles, the people, kings, and rulers, who have gathered together against the Lord and his Christ. In 4:27, Luke interprets the Psalm as saying that both Gentiles and Jews (*laoi*) opposed the anointed Jesus. He reads Herod for kings and Pontius Pilate for rulers. Significantly he adds a phrase that locates the gathering of these opponents of God and his anointed—"in this city." There is nothing in the quotation that would suggest this or any other location. Thus, Luke's interpretation of the Psalm reads: "For truly in this city there were gathered together against thy holy servant Jesus, whom thou didst anoint, both Herod and Pontius Pilate, with the Gentiles and the peoples of Israel" (4:27; cf. 13:27). Luke's interpretation emphasizes Jerusalem as the location of this assembly.

Similar notes are found in Luke's description of Paul's trials. A call for his arrest is recorded in the words, "Men of Israel, help! This is the man who is teaching men everywhere against the people and the law and this place" (Acts 21:28). After the conspiracy of the forty Jews was discovered, Paul was moved from Jerusalem to Caesarea for security reasons (23:23–24). After the departure of Felix and the arrival of Festus, there was a request to return Paul to Jerusalem. Luke notes, however, that this was only a pretext so that Paul could be ambushed along the way (25:1–5). And when the trial under Festus began, it was Jews from Jerusalem who brought charges against Paul (25:6–8). Although Festus gave Paul the opportunity to be returned to Jerusalem for trial, Paul appealed to Caesar (25:9–12). The image of Jerusalem in Luke's narrative of Paul's trials is one of great danger and unreasonable, vicious hostility.

In those sections of Luke–Acts in which positive images of Jerusalem and the temple are found, the city and its shrine are treated almost as a single phenomenon. In passages where there are negative images, it appears that there are some distinctions. The city receives a blanket condemnation and is associated only with doom. Luke's treatment of the temple, although negative, is more subtle. Conzelmann implies that Luke's treatment of the temple is not the same as his treatment of the city when he recognizes that in Luke 19 Jesus does not actually enter Jerusalem.[35] In view of the previous notices and predictions about Jesus' fate in Jerusalem, it is significant that Luke does not explicitly describe an entry into the city. The triumphal ride of Jesus on the colt is only from near Bethany and Bethphage (Luke 19:29) to "the descent of the Mount of Olives" (19:37). Clearly, even after this triumphal ride, Jesus is still outside the city (19:41). Moreover, in 19:45 Luke says that Jesus entered the temple, and in 21:37–38 he reports that Jesus spent his days in the temple and his nights on the Mount of Olives. Never does Luke explicitly say that Jesus entered Jerusalem, although the last supper ostensibly took place there (Luke 22:10). Conzelmann's observation seems quite correct: "He [Luke] does not connect the Entry with the city at all—according to Luke Jesus never enters it before the Last Supper, but he connects it exclusively with the Temple." In a note Conzelmann explains: "The objection might be made that in order to enter the Temple one would first have to enter the city, but Luke hardly had an accurate idea of the position of the city and of the Temple. The story in Acts iii, 1ff., for example, proves this."[36] Conzelmann may press his case a bit too hard at this point. Luke's lack of knowledge about the various parts of the temple may be seen in Acts 3, but there is no question in any of his writings about the location of the temple in Jerusalem. It was not lack of knowledge but rather literary intent that led Luke at this point. His intention was to create a distance between Jesus and the city and to associate him with the temple.

But this association of Jesus and temple, which goes from Luke 19:45 through 21:38, does not recall the positive images in Luke's infancy narratives. Rather, we now encounter a new motif, in which the temple is a scene not of peace, joy, and hope, but of conflict. The section begins with Jesus' cleansing of the temple, in which he presents the alternative possibilities for it: either to be a house of prayer or a den of robbers (Luke 19:46). Conzelmann's contention that this story is used by Luke in order to prepare the way for Jesus to teach in the temple appears to be right on target. He writes: "In Luke it is not a question of the eschatological end of the Temple, but of its cleansing; in other words, Jesus prepares it as somewhere he can stay, and from now on he occupies it as a place belonging to him."[37]

After the cleansing Jesus occupies the temple and teaches there daily. Luke calls attention to this daily practice of teaching in

19:47; 20:1; 21:37–38. In chapters 20–21 he records the teaching that Jesus gave in the temple on one day.

The teaching in Luke 20–21 starts with two pericopes that appear to deal specifically with Jesus' right to teach in the temple. In 20:1–8 the chief priests, scribes, and elders ask Jesus about his authority to do "these things." Luke is careful to say that the opponents raised their questions as Jesus "was teaching the people in the temple" (Luke 20:1). Since Jesus has begun to use the temple as the place of his teaching, his opponents ask him about his authority to do so. Jesus is able to turn them back by asking a question about John's authority, a question they are not able to answer for fear of John's large following.

The parable of the vintner (Luke 20:9–19) constitutes an even more direct answer to the question of Jesus' authority to teach in the temple. It is a parable which presents a conflict between an owner and some tenants. The absentee vintner sends three different slaves to collect rents, but the tenants refuse to pay, and they reject, beat, insult, and wound the slaves. The vintner therefore decides to send his own son, but the tenants kill him, thinking that on his death they will inherit the vineyard. The parable concludes with the expectation that the vintner will return, kill the tenants, and give the property to others. Perhaps in order to guarantee that the reader interpret the parable correctly, Luke says in 20:19 that the teaching was directed to the scribes and chief priests. This verse is a key to the understanding of the parable—or better, allegory—as it stands in Luke's gospel. If the words are spoken for their benefit, they must be understood as the tenants. The vineyard is probably the temple, that for which the chief priests are responsible. The chief priests, therefore, have had the use of the temple, but they have not rendered to God, the owner, what is due him, i.e. prayer (cf. Luke 19:46). So God has sent others, who have not been heeded, and now he has sent his beloved son. Luke must have assumed that his readers would easily be able to identify the beloved son as Jesus (see 1:32,35; 3:21–22; 9:35). We are to understand that the chief priests and their allies, as tenants, captured Jesus, the owner's son, threw him out of the temple, and killed him. Luke is here anticipating the climactic passion narrative and preparing the reader for it, as he had in the earlier predictive sayings of Jesus (9:22, 44; 17:25;

18:31–34). In the allegory of the vintner the temple is the object of conflict, and there is no doubt about the roles of Jesus, the chief priests, and their allies. As an answer to the question of authority the allegory is an assertion of Jesus' right to teach in the temple, since he is the owner's son. Not only is he there to teach but to collect what is due to God. The allegory includes an assurance that the tenants will be evicted and punished, but its main function is to defend Jesus' right to teach in the temple.

The section of temple teaching concludes with Jesus' apocalyptic discourse, in which he predicts the destruction of the temple (Luke 21:6) and the city (21:20–24).[38] In this entire section the image of the temple is one of conflict; in it the reader learns that Jesus has authority in this place and intends to make it a house of prayer. But he also learns of the challenges to Jesus' authority.

Despite the rosy picture that Luke paints of the early Christian community in Jerusalem, the image of the temple as a place of conflict and an object of conflict continues into the book of Acts. The temple appears as a battleground in Acts 5:12–42.[39] Here the author has used a literary pattern that appears frequently in the first half of Acts. [40] It is a pattern that Luke uses to deal with threats to the Christian community. The pattern has four parts—peace; threat; resolution; restoration. It begins with a statement expressing the peace and harmony of the apostolic community. Then there is a description of one or more threats to the harmony. In the third part a resolution of the threat is found, and in the fourth part Luke describes the restored peace of the community. In Acts 5:12–42 the peace of the early community is expressed in verses 12–16: signs and miracles are occurring; the apostles are all together in the temple; the community is held in high regard, and it is growing; the sick are being healed, and even Peter's shadow is thought to have healing power. But there is a threat when the high priest arrests the apostles (5:17–18). A temporary resolution occurs when the apostles escape and teach in the temple (5:19–21a). But a second threat comes when they are rearrested and brought before the Sanhedrin (5:21b–32). Then a resolution is proposed by Gamaliel, who convinces the Sanhedrin to allow the apostles to be released. The Sanhedrin agrees but adds the condition that they cease to speak in the name of Jesus (5:33–40). In 5:41–42 we have Luke's description of the restoration: "Then they left the presence of the council, rejoicing that they were counted worthy to suffer dishonor for the name. And every day in the temple and at home they did not cease teaching and preaching Jesus as the Christ."

In Acts 5:12–42 the character of the apostolic preaching is a point of controversy, since the apostles are ordered not to speak in the name of Jesus. But the location of their preaching and teaching, in the temple, is also a point of controversy. In the first and last sections of the narrative the apostles are in the temple (5:12; 5:42). In between, their right to teach in the temple is being contested. The angel who releases them from prison in 5:19–20 orders them to teach in the temple. They obey the angelic command and are later discovered, as someone reports to the *stratēgos* of the temple. "The men whom you put in prison are standing in the temple and teaching the people" (5:25). The resemblances to the story of Jesus in Luke 19:45–21:38 are striking: as Jesus taught in the temple with the authority of God his father and was challenged by the chief priests, so the apostles, obeying an angelic command, taught in the temple and were subjected to the opposition of the chief priests.

The story and the speech of Stephen (Acts 6:8–8:1) lead the reader to question the value and permanence of the temple.[41] Although Luke says it was false witnesses who accused Stephen of speaking against Moses and God, against Jewish customs, and against "this holy place" (6:13), in his speech Stephen does nevertheless speak against the temple. The speech is a lengthy recounting of early biblical history, a significant part of which is a protest against the temple. Stephen reminds his hearers that the earlier worship center was the "tent of witness in the wilderness" (7:44), and that the use of this tent was under the direction of God. Solomon built a house, "yet the Most High does not dwell in houses made with hands" (7:48). The accusation in 6:14, that Stephen said Jesus would destroy this place, should remind the reader that in Luke 21:6 Jesus had predicted the temple's destruction. The allegation that Jesus threatened to destroy the temple is absent from Luke's gospel but curiously shows up here in Acts.[42]

The strategic location of the story and speech of Stephen suggests its importance for Luke. It comes at the end of the Jerusalem section in Acts. Here is not only a representation of a struggle to control the temple, but, seemingly, a protest against its very existence. The protest involves both positive and negative evaluations of Israel's past but focuses attention upon the wilderness period. Although the wilderness period does not receive blanket approval, Stephen's speech suggests a connection between the Christian movement and the Mosaic tradition, which is regarded as the authentic Jewish tradition. The most visible aspect of that identification is the absence of a temple made with hands in both the Mosaic and Christian traditions.[43]

Despite the strategic location of the Stephen story in Acts, it must be observed that the protest about the temple involves a viewpoint that is not quite the same as in other parts of Luke–Acts. Most of the materials about Jesus, the apostles, and Paul seem to reflect a view about the proper control of the temple, while Stephen's speech is, on the one side, a protest against the temple itself and, on the other, a justification for its absence.

Logically, Stephen's speech seems to represent a later stage of the Christian argument. It is an appropriate position to take after it has become clear that control of the temple remained in the hands of the chief priests. The same may be said about Jesus' prediction of the destruction of the temple in Luke 21:6. Luke has not carefully arranged his materials so that the various stages of the argument occur in logical order. Instead, the prediction of Jesus and the speech of Stephen anticipate and justify the result, even while, in narrative time, the struggle continues.

Like Stephen, Paul was also accused of speaking against the temple and, indeed, of profaning it. During his last visit to Jerusalem Paul had gone to the temple on the advice of James and others, in order to demonstrate that he did not teach apostasy from Moses but rather lived according to the law (Acts 21:18–26). But his visit to the temple had the opposite effect, as a week later Asian Jews accused him of polluting it (21:27–28). The Lukan Paul denied the charges (Acts 24:12; 25:8). He explained that he was performing a rite of purification (24:18) and praying (22:17), but it was thought that he took Trophimus, a Gentile, into the temple (21:29). There is a nice irony here, for although Luke maintains that the specific charge is false, he nevertheless pictures Paul as evangelizing Gentiles. In any event, Paul was seized and dragged out of the temple (21:30). There is nothing here about Paul's teaching in the temple, but his right to be there is surely being contested. The image of the temple as a place of conflict becomes even more prominent here than in earlier passages, as Luke emphasizes the violent aspects of Paul's capture. His captors were in fact trying to kill him (21:31).

After this episode Luke tells of no Christian ever again entering the temple in Jerusalem. The reader follows Paul through his arrest, trials, and adventurous voyage to Rome, and there is no looking back to Jerusalem or the temple. In its larger context the words about Paul's capture in the temple are prophetic: "Then all the city was aroused, and the people ran together; they seized Paul and dragged him out of the temple, and *at once the gates were shut*" (21:30). In Acts, they never reopen for Christians.

CONCLUSION

The ambivalence of Jerusalem and the temple in Luke–Acts is striking. The presence of both positive and negative images, stories of peace, stories of conflict, and associations of both religious devotion and impending doom characterize the Lukan writing. The contrasts are deep and inescapable. Nevertheless, there appear to be significantly different nuances between the treatment of the city and of the temple. The negative aspects of the treatment of Jerusalem are totally negative, while the negative aspects of the temple treatment seem more tentative. On the negative side Jerusalem is associated with the trial and death of Jesus, the capture of Paul and his near lynching, the execution of Stephen, and the persecution of Christian believers. Its future holds more death, a siege by Gentile armies, and total destruction. On its negative side the temple is a place of conflict and an object of conflict. It is a place in which Jesus and his followers assert their right to teach and are met with harsh, sometimes violent opposition. The temple can be either a house of prayer or a den of robbers (Luke 19:46). The intention of Jesus in cleansing it and occupying it is to make it a house of prayer, and the apostles and Paul are pictured as praying in the temple on several occasions. Despite these efforts the Temple was not finally a house of prayer, since all Christians from Jesus to Paul were thrown out. It remained a den of robbers. Thus, not one stone will be left on another (Luke 21:6).

This study of Jerusalem and the temple in Luke–Acts was undertaken on the premise that the treatment of them involved certain issues that for Luke were connected with the death of Jesus. There is a powerful symbol of that connection in Luke 23:45, where it is reported that at the crucifixion "the curtain of the temple [*naos*] was torn in two." Although the words are not unique to Luke's gospel, they serve here to suggest that Jesus' death included a portent about the destruction of the temple. It also included a cosmic portent— "the sun's light failed"—and the two signs, taken together, should remind the reader of Jesus' apocalyptic discourse in Luke 21, especially verses 6 and 25 (see also Acts 2:20). Still, it remains to ask if there is a solid basis for the premise that, for Luke, the death of Jesus involved temple-related issues.

The connection betweeen Jesus' death and the city of Jerusalem is fairly plain: the trial and crucifixion occurred there. The connection with the temple must be more carefully nuanced, and the following observations should make the association clear.

First, it is significant that the temple is connected with those Jewish leaders who seem, in Luke, to be most clearly associated with Jesus' death, namely the chief priests. Although Luke did not engage in any description of the Jewish cult or the priestly activities, he would have been able to count on his readers to draw from their own religious experiences to make the association between temple, cult, and priests. The connection would have been obvious to both Gentile and Jewish readers.

Second, the conflict that Luke associates with the temple is one that involves the right to participate in the cult and the right to teach. There seems no question that Luke wants the reader to understand that, under ideal conditions, the apostles located themselves in the temple and participated in the cult. It was Paul's attempt to do so that led to his capture. More particularly, the right of Jesus and the apostles to teach in the temple is shown to be a point of major conflict. This suggests that, for Luke, Jesus' participation in the Jewish cult and his teaching in the temple were connected with his death. Indeed, it is likely that some such charge is reflected in Luke 23:5: "He stirs up the people, teaching throughout all Judea, from Galilee even to this place [*heōs hōde*]." In view of the mention of Judea and Galilee, it is plausible to interpret *heōs hōde* as a reference to the city of Jerusalem.[44] But in its context, following the long description of Jesus' teaching in the temple (Luke 19:45–21:38), it is likely that the verse includes a specific reference to the temple. Thus, here Jesus is being charged with teaching something perverted, not only in Galilee and Judea but, what is worse, in Jerusalem and specifically in the temple. Therefore, it appears that, for Luke, an underlying issue has to do with the refusal of the chief priests to accept Jesus and to recognize the role he claimed for himself as teacher.

Third, we must give full weight to the role of the temple not only as a scene of conflict but as an object of conflict. Jesus' cleansing of the temple constitutes a claim that he is the temple's lord. His teaching, especially the allegory of the vintner, emphasizes his own role as God's beloved son, who has come to collect what is due to God. As we have seen, this allegory is important as a Lukan device to assert Jesus' authority over against his challengers. In it the chief priests are seen to be wicked, irresponsible tenants, and their tenancy, hence control, of the temple has expired. We may see, then, that lurking behind Luke's treatment of the temple there is a conception about its control. For Luke, Jesus is lord of the temple, but the chief priests have not recognized him as such. Control of the temple is thus an issue that is implicit in Luke's narrative.

Fourth, Luke may use the temple as a symbol of the separation between Christianity and Judaism. He seems to have believed that such a split should never have occurred. If the chief priests had accepted Jesus and his successors, the temple would have been a house of prayer, as it was described to be in several passages in Luke–Acts. It is well known that Luke wanted to portray Jesus and his successors as persons who maintained full righteousness and fidelity to the God of Abraham. But neither Jesus nor his successors were ultimately successful, for those who opposed them denied that they were loyal Jews. The temple figures in this conception as the major symbol for the separation. Although Jesus and his successors intended to participate in the temple cult, they were not allowed to do so by the Jewish leaders. Thus Jesus predicts its destruction, and Stephen shows that its very existence did not accord with God's intentions. This appears to reflect an understanding that one cause of the separation between Christians and Jews was conflict about the temple and that the conflict started with Jesus.

We conclude that, in Luke's writing, the rejection of Jesus by the chief priests, their refusal to recognize him as lord of the temple, and their refusal to grant him his rightful control of the temple led to his death. Indeed, we may turn once again to the allegory of the vintner for a clue. In the allegory, when the wicked tenants learned that the owner's son was coming to collect the rents, they determined to kill him and take full control of the vineyard. When the son arrived, "they cast him out of the vineyard and killed him" (Luke 20:15). These words connect the death of Jesus with conflicting claims about the control of the temple.

This association between the temple and Jesus' death appears to be primary in Luke–Acts. The image of the city of Jerusalem suffers from the image of the temple, since in Luke's mind the city's significance largely resides in its being the location of the temple and the chief priests. In a secondary sense, however, as we saw in chapter 2, Luke associates Jesus' death with his rejection by the Jewish public, which occurred in Jerusalem.

As we concentrate on Jesus' trial in the following chapter, it will be important to remember that Luke approaches the death of Jesus with temple-related issues in mind. We should observe the ways in which this conception affects his report about the course of Jesus' trial.

NOTES

1. Karl Ludwig Schmidt, *Der Rahmen der Geschichte Jesu* (Berlin: Trowitzsch und Sohn, 1919).

2. Rudolf Bultmann, *The History of the Synoptic Tradition*, trans. John Marsh (New York: Harper and Row, 1963), p. 64.

3. Ibid., p. 338.

4. Vincent Taylor, *The Formation of the Gospel Tradition,* 2nd ed. (London: Macmillan and Co., 1935), p. 126.

5. Ernst Lohmeyer, *Galiläa und Jerusalem* (Göttingen: Vandenhoeck und Ruprecht, 1936).

6. In part 4 of his book, in a footnote, Conzelmann gives some of his reasons for treating the infancy narratives as prologue. He observes that outside the infancy narratives Mary plays no role, the birth of Jesus is not mentioned, and no reference is made to the genealogy (*The Theology of St. Luke*, trans. Geoffrey Buswell [New York: Harper and Bros., 1960], p. 172n.).

7. Ibid., p. 9.

8. Ibid., p. 17.

9. Ibid.

10. Ibid., pp. 55–59.

11. Conzelmann does not regard Luke 24:50–53 as an original part of Luke's gospel. On this point, see below, p. 92f.

12.William C. Robinson, Jr., *Der Weg des Herrn: Studien zur Geschichte und Eschatologie im Lukas-Evangelium* (Hamburg: Herbert Reich, 1964), pp. 30–36. The German edition of his Basel dissertation, from which the book was taken, was subtitled *Ein Gespräch mit Hans Conzelmann*.

Robinson does not find Conzelmann's three-part structure of Jesus' ministry in Luke persuasive and leans toward a fourfold division:

(1) Luke 4:14–9:50—Jesus in Galilee.

(2) Luke 9:51–19:27—Jesus' journey to Jerusalem.

(3) Luke 19:28–21:38—Jesus' final work in Jerusalem.

(4) Luke 22–24—Passion, death, resurrection.

The separation of the third from the fourth section calls attention to that unit as dealing with Jesus' teaching in the temple.

13. See, e.g., Ernst Haenchen, *The Acts of the Apostles: A Commentary*, trans. Bernard Noble et al. (Oxford: Basil Blackwell, 1971), pp. 143–47.

14. The phrase is probably drawn from Isa 49:6, which is quoted more fully by the Lukan Paul in Acts 13:47. It is probable that Rome is intended here as well as in Acts 1:8. Note, however, that Paul's own horizons extended at least to Spain (cf. Rom 15:24,28).

15. In well-chosen phrases Joseph Fitzmyer speaks of Jerusalem as Jesus' "city of destiny" and the "pivot" of Luke–Acts; see *The Gospel According to Luke (I–IX)* (Garden City, N.Y.: Doubleday, 1981), esp. pp. 164–71.

16. In 1 Thess 2:14–15 Paul writes about the persecution of Christians in Judea and about the Jews who killed Jesus. There is, however, no specific location given for Jesus' death. Although there is an implication that the crucifixion occurred in Judea, Paul is more interested in the responsible people than in the location.

17. Michael Bachmann, *Jerusalem und der Tempel: Die geographisch-theologischen Elemente in der lukanischen Sicht des jüdischen Kultzentrums* (Stuttgart: W. Kohlhammer, 1980). Bachmann pays particular attention to the two spellings of Jerusalem in Luke–Acts. He believes that *Hierosoluma* is an indication of the hand of the redactor of Luke and that *Ierousalēm* indicates traditional material. Luke was, says Bachmann, sensitive to the connotations of the Greek *Hierosoluma*, which is associated with *hieron*. When he uses this term, Luke wants to call attention to Jerusalem as a city with a temple.

18. Ibid., pp. 374–75.

19. On the location of Bethany, see below, p. 93f.

20. Note also the omission of *proskunēsantes auton* (Luke 24:52) and *eulogountes* (24:53).

21. Bruce M. Metzger, *A Textual Commentary on the Greek New Testament* (London and New York: United Bible Societies, 1971), pp. 189–90.

22. Ibid., p. 189.

23. See Conzelmann, *Theology of St. Luke*, p. 94; see also p. 94n.

24. The actual location of Bethany in relation to the Mount of Olives has no real bearing on our problem, which is literary rather than archaeological.

25. I. Howard Marshall, *The Gospel of Luke: A Commentary on the Greek Text* (Grand Rapids: Eerdmans, 1978), p. 908.

26. The RSV translation, "Then he led them out as far as Bethany," suggests a chronological link that is not present in the Greek. The NEB translation is the same as the RSV.

27. Haenchen rightly remarks that "Luke does not set as much store as we upon consistency in the story" (*Acts of the Apostles*, p. 146). He cites as evidence the differing details in Luke's thrice-told narrative of the conversion of Paul (Acts 9:1–22; 22:4–16; 26:9–18).

28. See Raymond E. Brown, *The Birth of the Messiah* (Garden City, N.Y.: Doubleday, 1977), pp. 239–43.

29. Fitzmyer believes that Luke's "preoccupation with Jerusalem . . . accounts for the order of the temptation scenes" (*The Gospel According to Luke*, p. 165). Luke's account puts Jerusalem in the climactic position.

30. See David P. Moessner, "Luke 9:1–50: Luke's Preview of the Journey of the Prophet Like Moses of Deuteronomy," *Journal of Biblical Literature* 102 (1983): 575–605. As his title suggests, Moessner believes that Luke 9:1–50 is a preview of the journey of Jesus, which begins at Luke 9:51.

31. The noun *analēmpsis* is found only in Luke 9:51 in the Greek Bible. See W. F. Arndt and F. W. Gingrich, *A Greek-English Lexicon of the New Testament*, 2nd ed. (Chicago: University of Chicago Press, 1979), in loc.

32. See Marshall, *The Gospel of Luke*, p. 406.

33. Luke 18:31–34 is the fourth and last in the series of Lukan passion predictions (9:22,44; 17:25) and the most specific of the four. It is the only one that explicitly mentions Jerusalem as the place of the passion.

34. In Luke 19:44 Jesus says that the citizens of Jerusalem did not know *ton kairon tēs episkopēs*. *Episkopē* means visitation, but it may also be used to refer to the office of an overseer or bishop (Acts 1:20; 1 Tim 3:1). In Luke 19:44, as in 1 Pet 2:12, the emphasis is on an event; otherwise the reference to time would lose significance. But there may be a connotation in Luke 19:44 that suggests Jesus' position as overseer of Jerusalem.

35. Conzelmann, *Theology of St. Luke*, pp. 75–78.

36. Ibid., p. 75.

37. Ibid., p. 77.

38. See Luke 13:35, which is frequently understood to be a statement about the destruction of the temple. See also Luke 19:43–44, a prediction of the destruction of Jerusalem.

39. Acts 4:3, if the arrest of Peter and John occurs in the temple, also pictures the temple as a battlefield.

40. See my article "Acts 6:1–7 and Dietary Regulations in Early Christianity," *Perspectives in Religious Studies* 10 (1983): 145–61, where this literary pattern is discussed in greater detail.

41. The speeches in Acts have generated a great deal of scholarly concern. Questions about the authenticity of the speeches continue to be raised, and views range widely on this matter. Such questions are not, however, relevant to the present study. As in the case of the traditions about Jesus that were used in the gospel of Luke, so here, we need not attempt to go behind Luke's writing to determine historicity or authenticity. Rather, we work within the world of the text itself and ask questions about the place of the speeches in the overall context of Luke–Acts. For this purpose it is better to approach the speeches as communications from Luke to the reader than from an apostle to his contemporaries. If, however, we find some point of view in the speeches that appears to be at variance with Luke's views as otherwise determined, there may be some cause to raise a question about source material. On the speeches see Martin Dibelius. "The Speeches in Acts and Ancient Historiography," in *Studies in the Acts of the Apostles*, ed. Heinrich Greeven (New York: Charles Scribner's Sons, 1956), pp. 138–85; Ulrich Wilckens, *Die Missionsreden der Apostelgeschichte* (Neukirchen kreis Moers: Neukirchener Verlag, 1961).

42. Luke must have been thoroughly convinced that Jesus had made no threats about the destruction of the temple. Not only is that charge missing in the gospel, but it is clearly labeled as false in Acts 6:14. It is necessary to have a grasp on the principles that guided Luke in his reporting of the trials of Jesus in order to make a judgment about the omission of this threat in the gospel. See chapter 5 below.

43. See Earl Richard, *Acts 6:1–8:4: The Author's Method of Composition* (Missoula, Mont.: Scholars Press, 1978).

44. But see Robinson, *Der Weg des Herrn*, pp. 30–36.

FIVE

The Trial
of Jesus

The narratives about the trial of Jesus naturally form the heart of our investigation. They are climactic for Luke-Acts as well. The preceding chapters here have shown that, for the author of these books, dramatic shifts occurred in connection with the complex of events surrounding the trial. The opposition of Pharisees to Jesus gives way precisely as he comes within sight of the city of Jerusalem. At the same time the reader's attention is focused upon the chief priests as Jesus' opponents in the narratives that deal with his teaching in the temple and those that report his trial. Precisely at the point of Jesus' arrest the attitude of the Jewish public suddenly changes from support to opposition. The association of the city of Jerusalem with Jesus' trial and death has been anticipated and developed, and Luke has shown that temple-related issues are connected with the death of Jesus. We have seen that these points served as literary devices for Luke in his presentation not only of the life of Jesus but also the stories of the early Christian community and the life of Paul. Indeed, the parallels between Jesus, the apostles, and Paul have frequently been noted.

We may therefore approach the trial narratives with the prior understanding that a first- or second-century reader of Luke probably would have had. It seems likely that such a reader, if he had no familiarity with another gospel, would have prepared to read, or hear, these narratives with certain expectations in mind. This reader would expect the chief priests and their allies to be the major culprits, and he would expect Jesus to be charged with some crime relating to his attempt to take control of the temple. Would this hypothetical reader be perplexed to find that, although the chief priests lead the prosecution against Jesus, issues about control of the temple do not come to the surface and that, in addition to a hearing before the priests, Luke portrays a trial before a Roman governor over political issues? Such questions remind us of the complexity of the Lukan narratives about the trial of Jesus and of the need for a careful investigation of them.

Although we customarily speak of the trial of Jesus in the singular, it is necessary to note that Luke has four stages or components that make up the proceedings. In this light it is important to observe that some scholars have called attention to certain parallels between the trials of Jesus and Paul.[1] One of the significant parallels is found in the fact that each is made up of four components, as can be seen in the following table:

Jesus	Paul	
Luke 22:66–71	Acts 23:1–10	Before the Sanhedrin
Luke 23:1–5	Acts 24:1–23	Before Roman governor
Luke 23:6–12		Before Herod
Luke 23:13–25	Acts 25:6–12	Before Roman governor
	Acts 25:23–26:32	Before Herod

The parallelism is impressive but not exact. In the trial of Jesus the appearances before the Roman governor are both before the same Roman governor, Pontius Pilate. In the case of Paul two Romans are involved, Felix and Festus. The order of the four components is not the same, since Jesus' hearing before Herod forms something of an interlude in the trial before Pilate, while Paul's appearance before Herod and Bernice is the final one in the series, and the Roman governor Festus is in attendance on this occasion. Finally, the proceedings against Paul consume over two years, while those involving Jesus occur in the space of a few hours. Still, when one understands that for both Jesus and Paul there were hearings before the Sanhedrin, Roman officials, and Herods, and that for each there were four hearings, there is an impressive similarity.

Anton Büchele has recently shown that Luke carefully crafted much of the material about the trial of Jesus. He concentrates on Luke 23 and shows that the structure of this chapter (what Büchele calls the outer or formal structure) follows a three-part architechtonic plan. According to him, Luke 23 is composed of three major sections, the first (Luke 23:1–25) dealing with Jesus' trial before the political authorities, the second (23:26–49) treating the crucifixion and death of Jesus, and the third (23:50–56), Jesus' burial. In turn, the three major sections are each made up of three subsections, and each of the three subsections in the middle section includes three parts. Büchele's outline of the entire chapter is as follows:

I.   Jesus' political trial (Luke 23:1–25)
   a.   Jesus before Pilate (23:1–5)
   b.   Jesus before Herod (23:6–12)
   c.   Pilate and the will of the people (23:13–25)
II. Jesus' crucifixion (23:26–49)
   a.   Jesus on the way to crucifixion (23:26–32)
      1.   Simon of Cyrene (23:26)
      2.   The crowd and the wailing women (23:27–31)
      3.   The two thieves (23:32)
   b.   The crucifixion (23:33–43)
      1.   Mocking by the leaders (23:35)
      2.   Mocking by the soldiers (23:36–38)
      3.   Mocking by the thieves (23:39–41)
   c.   The death of Jesus (23:44–49)
      1.   Testimony of the Roman centurion (23:47)
      2.   Testimony of the people (23:48)
      3.   Testimony of the Galileans (23:49)
III. The Burial of Jesus (23:50–56)
   a.   Joseph of Arimathea (23:50–53)
   b.   Note about the sabbath (23:54)
   c.   The women from Galilee (23:55–56)[2]

Büchele believes that the structure Luke uses in this chapter has been influenced by Deut 19:15 (cf. 17:6–7), which requires the testimony of two or three witnesses for a charge to be sustained. That is to say, Luke intends to provide three witnesses for each phase of the trial, death, and burial of Jesus.

Büchele's explanation of Luke's use of the three-part architechtonic structure is not totally convincing. If Deut 19:15 did in fact influence Luke at this point, the absence of a quotation of this verse or an allusion to it is surprising. Moreover, even if Deuteronomy influenced Luke here, that influence would not have required the very rigid structure that Büchele has. Occasionally Luke could have had two witnesses. It also stretches the point to refer to some parts of the Lukan narrative as witnesses, such as the various acts of mocking (Luke 23:35,36–38,39–41) and the note about the sabbath (23:54). Finally, although he finds some connections between Luke 23 and the Sanhedrin session reported in Luke 22:66–71, this session does not really concern Büchele. Yet it forms an integral part of the Lukan narrative of Jesus' trial, and its significance in Luke-Acts should not be minimized. Nevertheless, Büchele has put us all in his debt by his very close analysis of Luke 23. His structural analysis is, for the most part, convincing and brings to light a major aspect of Luke's literary artistry.

Although Büchele's comments are helpful for understanding Luke's literary procedures in composing chapter 23, it is necessary to examine a somewhat broader range of material and to become attuned to the dominating themes that Luke used in presenting the trial of Jesus. Clues to the ways in which Luke conceives of the trial are to be found in the so-called passion predictions in the gospel. Similarly, Acts contains a few summaries of the trial, and in these summaries there are certain indications of themes that are more fully developed in the trial narratives. An analysis of these passages should provide a useful approach to these narratives.

Taken together the four passion predictions in the gospel of Luke (9:22; 9:44; 17:25; 18:31–34) seem to be shaped around a limited number of motifs, although all the motifs do not appear in all the predictions. The suffering of the Son of man is stated generally in Luke 9:22 and 17:25 and specified as mocking, shameful treatment, spitting, and scourging in 18:32–33. Scriptural prediction of the suffering and death is stressed in 18:31. The rejection of the Son of man by elders, chief priests, and scribes in 9:22 becomes rejection by "this generation" in 17:25. The delivery of the Son of man is to be into the hands of men (9:44) or to Gentiles (18:32). The death and resurrection on the third day (*tē tritē* [*tē*] *hēmera*) are forecast in 9:22 and 18:33. Only in the fourth of the predictions is there a reference to Jerusalem (18:31).

In Acts several of the statements about the death of Jesus occur in speeches, by Peter (2:14–36; 3:11–26; 4:8–12; 10:34–43; cf. 5:27–32), Stephen (7:2–53), and Paul (13:16–41; cf. 17:1–9).[3] One appears in a liturgical section in which the community of Jerusalem Christians gives thanks for the release of the apostles Peter and John (4:25–27). Some of the same themes that are found in the passion predictions in the gospel are also found in Acts. The crucifixion, death, and resurrection of Jesus are announced in Acts 2:23; 10:39–40; 13:29–30, but with a reference to the third day only in 10:40. Postresurrection appearances are included in the statements in 10:39–40 and 13:31. Divine necessity and the fulfillment of prophecy are stressed in 2:23; 4:27–28; 13:29; and 17:3, and the delivery of Jesus into the hands of the lawless (*anomōn*) comes up in 2:23 (cf. 3:13). Acts 4:27 and 13:27 specifically mention Jerusalem as the setting for the death of Jesus. Pilate is mentioned in 3:13; 4:27; and 13:28, but Herod only in 4:27. In several statements Jews in general are blamed for Jesus' death (4:10; 5:30; 7:52). In 13:27–28, however, Paul's statement is more specific. He appears to summarize Jesus' hearing before the Sanhedrin and his delivery to Pilate when he contends that the residents of Jerusalem and their leaders condemned Jesus, despite the fact that they could find no basis for a death penalty, and asked Pilate to have him killed. The ignorance of the Jews and their rulers is mentioned in 3:17 and 13:27.

As an approach to Luke's treatment of the death of Jesus, these anticipatory and retrospective passages are exceedingly important. The ones in the gospel provide signals about what to expect in the climactic narratives, and the ones in Acts remind us of themes developed in those narratives. In order to approach the trial narratives most fruitfully, we should highlight certain themes that appear in these passages. One such theme is that of rejection; it is expected that Jesus will be rejected by certain Jewish leaders, namely elders, chief priests, and scribes (Luke 9:22). Those rejecting Jesus are referred to as "this generation" in Luke 17:25, and as we saw in our examination of Luke 7:31, the designation "people of this generation" is a technical term used by Luke to refer collectively to Jesus' opponents. Thus, the passion predictions in Luke anticipate the rejection of Jesus by those leaders who opposed him, specifically the priestly block of opponents.

The delivery of Jesus into the hands of others is another theme that emerges in these passages. Those to whom he is delivered are variously designated: people (Luke 9:44); Gentiles (Luke 18:32); the lawless (Acts 2:23). "The lawless" may be a way of designating Gentiles, i.e., people who do not have Torah. Although the passages under examination contain references to both Jewish and Roman responsibility for the death of Jesus, the weight falls on the Jewish side. Sometimes that responsibility is defined as turning Jesus over to the authorities and asking for a death penalty; at other times Jews are made directly responsible.

Probably the most important of the passages is Acts 4:25–27. Some scholars believe that this passage influenced Luke's description of Jesus' trial.[4] As we saw in chapter 4, the passage is an interpretation of Psalm 2:1–2, which is quoted in 4:25–26. The interpretation says that the opponents of Jesus, gathered in Jerusalem, are Herod, Pilate, Gentiles, and Jews. The presence of all four in Luke's account of Jesus' trial clearly conforms to the requirements of the passage in Acts, but just as certainly three of the four declare Jesus to be innocent. Only the Jews do not. Thus, only in a limited sense is it correct to say that Acts 4:25–27 affects Luke's treatment of the trial of Jesus.

As we approach a more detailed analysis of the trial narratives themselves, we may expect some reference to the rejection of Jesus by Jewish leaders and his delivery into the hands of Gentile authorities. We may also expect major roles to be played by Pilate and Herod. The balance of this chapter will be organized around certain aspects of the trial narratives that should illustrate the dominant themes and the ways in which Luke utilizes them. Attention will thus be focused on the arrest of Jesus, the nature of the Jewish Sanhedrin, Jesus' hearing before that body, the charges against him, and the characterizations of Herod and Pilate. In the process of this study additional Lukan themes should emerge.

THE ARREST OF JESUS

In the analysis of the shift on the part of the Jewish public, the importance of the scene of Jesus' arrest has been noted (Luke 22:47–53; See above, page 37f.). We observed that Judas' intention to betray Jesus had been reported earlier (22:3–6) and that Judas "sought an opportunity to betray him to them [chief priests and *stratēgoi*] in the absence of the multitude" (22:6). In describing the scene at the arrest, Luke pictured Jesus in almost total isolation. His disciples were present, but as he prayed alone, they slept. Just as he addressed his sleeping disciples, "there came a crowd" (Luke 22:47). It is at this point that the crowd is presented as opposed to Jesus and in support of Judas and the arresting party.

The most interesting single figure at the arrest of Jesus is Judas, but Luke does not develop his character in the gospel. Twice in Chapter 22 he reminds us that Judas was one of the twelve (22:3,47). When he first introduces him, he tells the readers that Judas will be a traitor (6:16). The manner of his death is reported in Acts 1:18, but at that point the author is more interested in the process by which the number of the twelve was refilled. In the words of Peter, Judas "was numbered among us, and was allotted his share in this ministry" (Acts 1:17). Because of his treachery and death, a new apostle had to be chosen, and Matthias took his place (Acts 1:26). Luke does not hesitate to picture Judas in the worst possible light. Satan entered him (Luke 22:3) when he engaged in conspiracy with the chief priests.[5] His death is described as fittingly grotesque (Acts 1:18). His status as traitor is highlighted, and the irony of betrayal with a kiss (whether or not the kiss was actually performed) is powerful. But Luke is not interested in telling us precisely what it was that Judas betrayed. Surely it was not the identity of Jesus, for, as Jesus himself said (Luke 22:53), he had taught daily in the temple. Perhaps it was the whereabouts of Jesus on the Mount of Olives. Luke had said that Jesus customarily spent his nights there (Luke 21:37; 22:39), but there had been no hint that the mountain served Jesus as a hiding place. The story of the arrest does not suggest that Judas betrayed to the authorities something about Jesus' messianic conceptions.

Luke's handling of the arrest scene is more subtle than has been generally recognized. Although Judas' service as a guide (*hodēgos*) is mentioned in Acts 1:16, his role in Luke 22 is that of isolating Jesus from the crowd. That is what he intended to do, according to Luke 22:6, and, when he approached Jesus at the Mount of Olives (22:47), he did so accompanied by a crowd.[6] Jesus himself commented on the situation when he asked why he was not arrested in the temple. The reader knows quite well that he was not arrested in the temple because there he had been surrounded by a supportive crowd (Luke 19:47–48; 20:19). Although Luke gives us no details about Judas' betrayal, there are significant hints that he accomplished a difficult feat offstage, that of driving a wedge between the crowd and Jesus.

Although Judas is the featured actor at the arrest of Jesus, it is important to take note of the other members of the arresting party. The presence of an unnamed servant of the high priest is especially noted (Luke 22:50), but the others are also designated by class terms, as chief priests, *stratēgoi*, and elders (22:52). This means that Jesus has fallen into the hands of the priestly block of opponents, the ones who had determined to capture him but up to now had been prevented from doing so by the crowds who listened to him and supported him.

To confirm that the hero has now fallen into the hands of this powerful and malevolent block of opponents, Luke tells us that as soon as Jesus was captured he was taken to the house of the high priest (22:54), where he was mocked and beaten (22:63–65). The sad story of Peter's denial (22:54–62) prepares the way for the climactic confrontation between Jesus and his accusers.

THE JEWISH SANHEDRIN

Jesus' appearance before the Jewish Sanhedrin is set on the morning following his arrest at the Mount of Olives. Apparently he was to be detained at the home of the high priest only for the one evening and in order to assure his presence at the session the following morning.[7]

In 22:66 Luke writes: "When day came, the assembly [*presbuterion*] of the elders of the people gathered together, both chief priests and scribes; and they led him away to their council [*sunedrion*]." The Greek word *presbuterion* is an unusual one and somewhat unexpected. Other than in Luke 22:66 it is found in the NT only in Acts 22:5 and 1 Tim 4:14, where it refers to a Christian council. In Acts 22:5 the *presbuterion* is associated with the high priest, but it is not clear whether Luke thought of it as somehow separate from the Sanhedrin or synonymous with it. In Luke 22:66 it appears to be separate from it and composed of chief priests and scribes. Etymologically, however, it would be difficult to conceive of a *presbuterion* without *presbuteroi*.

Although Luke uses the term "Sanhedrin" only here in the gospel, it is found frequently in Acts. In Acts 4:15 the Sanhedrin deliberates the fate of Peter and John, who healed in the name of Jesus. The two apostles were arrested by the *stratēgos* of the temple and by Sadducees (Acts 4:1). The deliberating body is made up of rulers, elders, scribes, Annas the high priest, Caiaphas, John, Alexander, and all those who were of high priestly descent (Acts 4:5–6). In Acts 5:21–42 Luke tells of a summoning of "the council [*sunedrion*] and all the senate [*gerousia*] of Israel." As with *presbuterion* in Luke 22:66, so with *gerousia* in Acts 5:21; it is not clear whether these bodies are thought of as identical to the Sanhedrin, separate from it, or constituent parts of it, although the last seems most in accord with the phrasing in both places. In any event the meeting in Acts 5:21 is called by the high priest, who seems to preside (5:27), and by those with him, i.e., Sadducees (5:17). We find later that not only are the chief priests present but also the *stratēgos* of the temple; and in 5:34 a Pharisaic member, Gamaliel, addresses the Sanhedrin. He is described as a teacher of the law (*nomodidaskalos*), esteemed by all the people.

In Acts 6:12 we read of the arrest of Stephen, who is brought before the Sanhedrin. The composition of the body is not described, but elders and scribes are connected with Stephen's arrest, and the high priest does the questioning (7:1).

In Acts 22:30 a Roman military tribune, later identified as Claudius Lysias (23:26), ordered the chief priests and the Sanhedrin to meet. The purpose of the meeting was to give the tribune accurate information about Jewish opposition to Paul, and the session that is described in 23:1–10 forms the first phase of Paul's trial. In 23:6 we find that the Sanhedrin was made up of Pharisees and Sadducees. Luke points out that some of the scribes of the Pharisees who were in the Sanhedrin turned out to be sympathetic with Paul's views. Although in 22:30 the Roman tribune called the Sanhedrin into session, it is implied in 23:14–15 that the chief priests and elders could do so, and in a letter to the procurator Felix the tribune refers to the body as "their" Sanhedrin (23:28). When Paul is subsequently taken to Caesarea, the high priest and some elders appear before Felix to bring charges, but Luke does not use the term "Sanhedrin" to designate this group.

The pericope in Acts 23:1–10 that reports Paul's appearance before the Sanhedrin is notoriously difficult, especially for those scholars who search for the historical background of the incident. As soon as the session begins, Paul addresses the group with a defense, and the high priest Ananias orders him to be struck. Paul responds with a curse, "God shall strike you, you whitewashed wall" (Acts 23:3), and he claims that he was struck contrary to God's law. But when he is told that it is the high priest he has cursed, Paul abjectly apologizes, explaining that he did not recognize the high priest. The situation abruptly changes when Paul realizes that the Sanhedrin is made up of both Pharisees and Sadducees. He is able to create a division between the two groups by asserting that he is on trial for maintaining a Pharisaic belief, namely belief in the resurrection of the dead. This assertion causes such an uproar that the Roman tribune, with military support, rescues Paul and brings him back to the barracks.

Not only are there great difficulties in interpreting Acts 23:1–10 with historical questions in mind; there are problems in a literary approach to the passage. Its structure seems loose, and the characterization of Paul in the passage is puzzling. There seems to be a good deal of activity, but there is no real conclusion, and the function of the narrative is by no means clear. Ernst Haenchen stresses the literary context of this section of Acts. He claims that the Sanhedrin session must be preliminary, because the climactic narrative must be Paul's appearance before the officials: "As an author and narrator Luke knows about the laws of climax. Discussion on the highest level—i.e. before governors and kings—may not stand at the beginning; it can only form the crowning conclusion."[8] Thus, Haenchen speaks of this session as a "curtain raiser, which however already allows the reader to experience a dramatic conflict."[9] Similarly, Jürgen Roloff calls attention to Acts 23:11, which he understands to be Luke's clue to the reader about how to read this incident.[10] The word of the Lord in this verse helps the reader to understand that the great commission which has been given to Paul is to testify to the Lord in Rome. The Jerusalem incident is only preliminary to that.

We cannot conclude, however, that the pericope is without literary significance. Although there are certain difficulties in following the course of the narrative, there appear to be several impressions that a reader would gain. The first is that Paul's single major foe is the Jewish high priest. Whatever hostility and violence there is occurs between these two characters. Luke wants to show that, although Paul is able to pronounce a curse against the high priest, he is still a law-abiding Jew, whose life is governed by the scriptures (see Exod 22:28). Paul's failure to recognize the high priest is difficult to understand, either as a historical statement or a literary device. As a historical statement it has been interpreted to mean that Paul's eyesight was not good, that Ananias had not been high priest very long, that Paul's view of him was blocked, or that Ananias was not on that occasion dressed in the garb of the high priest.[11] As a literary device Paul's words in Acts 23:5 serve to explain how he could, on the one hand, pronounce a curse and, on the other, present himself as a law-abiding Jew. At best, the device must be regarded as weak.

Another impression that a reader would probably gain from this passage is that of Paul's cleverness in dividing the Sanhedrin and hence rendering it unable to act in its proper judicial role. The competing roles of Pharisees and Sadducees would also be impressive. We have already taken note of this passage in dealing with the Jewish leaders and have observed the almost totally positive view of the Pharisees that is presented in Acts (see above, page 70f.). Here, of course, is one of the main passages on which that case was built.

Above all, however, a reader would probably be deeply impressed with the contrast between the disorganized, noisy, disorderly, and even violent session of the Sanhedrin and the orderly, prudent, and careful deliberations under the Roman procurators (despite the delays and the expectation of bribery; see Acts 24:26–27). We may, therefore, say that the literary purpose of the session of Paul before the Sanhedrin is to discredit that body as a judicial entity.

Although Luke, in Acts 23, thinks of the Sanhedrin as including Pharisees, for the most part he has associated it with the chief priests and the priestly block of opponents. He seems to think that it can be called into session by a Roman official, the high priest, or the chief priests, scribes, and elders collectively. The high priest is the presiding officer, and the body meets in Jerusalem. Except for the inclusion of friendly Pharisees in Acts 23, the Sanhedrin is associated with the opposition to Jesus and his followers and with the city of Jerusalem.[12]

JESUS' HEARING BEFORE THE SANHEDRIN

Although both Jesus and Paul appeared before the Jewish Sanhedrin, the resemblance between the two reports just about ends there. Jesus simply responds to questions, while Paul aggressively defends himself and accuses his accusers. Jesus is met with unanimous opposition, while Pharisees, whose presence on the Sanhedrin is not noted in Jesus' case, support Paul.[13] In the case of Jesus the Sanhedrin agrees to take him to Pilate; in the case of Paul the Roman tribune is forced to intervene and rescue his prisoner. In Jesus' case the Sanhedrin meets on the initiative of the Jewish leaders, while in Paul's it is summoned by the Roman tribune. Virtually the only resemblance between the two hearings is that both Jesus and Paul appeared before the Jewish body.

Jesus' hearing before the Sanhedrin is reported in Luke 22:66–71. In this passage the groups that make up the body are described as elders, chief priests, and scribes.[14] The entire proceeding involves two sets of questions and answers followed by a conclusion. In the first question (Luke 22:67), apparently asked by the council as a whole, Jesus is asked if he is the Messiah. To this question he gives a seemingly ambiguous answer (22:67–68). He suggests that if he should make a messianic claim, it would not cause belief on the part of the members of the Sanhedrin, and that if he should ask for their verdict, they would not give it.

The question addressed to Jesus implies that he is being accused of claiming to be Messiah. In this connection it is useful to recall what Luke has previously said about this subject. Without question, he presents Jesus as the Christ. He is proclaimed as such in the birth narratives by an angel (Luke 2:11) and by the Holy Spirit

(2:26). Demons have knowledge about Jesus (Luke 4:41), although Jesus will not allow them to speak. In Luke 9:20 Peter confesses his own belief that Jesus is God's Messiah, but Jesus requires him to be silent. In Luke 20:41–44 Jesus himself questions the identification of Messiah with son of David. One is struck by the fact that, although the reader of Luke is given information about Jesus' status, there is never an occasion on which Jesus himself affirms that he is the Messiah, allows his followers to announce it, or confirms the opinion of anyone who confesses it. Luke's intention appears to be to enlighten the reader about Jesus but not to picture him as making any claims about himself. Thus, Jesus' seemingly ambiguous and irrelevant answer to the Sanhedrin in 22:67–68 is consistent with the ways in which Luke has addressed the matter of Jesus' messiahship up to this point. The reader knows that Jesus is in fact God's Messiah, but he also knows that Jesus has made no such claim.

After the initial answer Jesus continues with a proclamation, "But from now on the Son of man shall be seated at the right hand of the power of God" (Luke 22:69). This statement, probably an allusion to Ps 110:1, does not appear to be a response to the first question, nor does it lead naturally to the second. It does, however, constitute an announcement to the reader. The reader of Luke's gospel has become accustomed to the phrase, "Son of man," as a designation of Jesus.[15] Thus, Luke 22:69 is a statement about Jesus' imminent glorification, although it is not to be assumed that the Sanhedrin could rightly regard it as a messianic claim.

The second question is also asked by an anonymous "they": "Are you the Son of God, then" (Luke 22:70)? Luke's use of the connective "then" [oun], must mean that he felt there was a connection between verses 69 and 70 and that Jesus' statement about the glorification of the Son of man was understood by the Sanhedrin to be a claim to be the Son of God.[16] Thus, the second question, like the first, implies an accusation that Jesus has made some claim about himself. But Luke is not taking this occasion to explore these accusations with any depth. Nor are we to see any explicit attempts at precise definition. Rather, Luke has brought together three titles that, for him, are appropriate for Jesus: Christ, Son of man, and Son of God. Conzelmann's comment on this passage is probably correct: "These verses are meant to set out explicitly the fundamental identity of the current Christological titles. . . . The thing to note is that they are assimilated to one another."[17] In a note Conzelmann adds that "Luke makes out of the trial a compendium of Christology for his readers."[18]

Jesus' answer to the second question is, "You say that I am" (*humeis legete hoti egō eimi,* Luke 22:70). It seems likely that Luke wants to emphasize the ambiguity of the answer and, hence, imply that even under the direct questioning of the Jewish body, Jesus made no claims about his status. The answer is interesting because it is almost identical to Jesus' later response to Pilate in Luke 23:3. There Pilate asks, "Are you the king of the Jews?" and Jesus answers, "You are saying it" (*su legeis*).[19] But whereas Pilate concludes from this that Jesus is innocent, the members of the Sanhedrin agree that the answer is an admission of guilt. The ambiguity of Jesus' response in both cases offers Luke an opportunity to contrast Jewish and Roman justice. Throughout the trial narratives Luke stresses the goodwill of Pilate and the malevolence of the Jewish leaders. But there is irony as well. The Sanhedrin apparently agrees that Jesus is guilty of claiming to be God's son, although he has not made any such claim. In fact, however, the reader knows that, within the world of the text, Jesus is God's son. Pilate regards Jesus as not guilty of claiming to be king of the Jews, and it is true that the Lukan Jesus has made no such public claims. Again, however, the reader knows that, in Luke's narrative, Jesus deserves this title. The Sanhedrin is wrong and Pilate is right if one merely focuses on Jesus' claims about himself: he has not claimed to be either God's son or king of the Jews. But both the Jewish and Roman authorities are wrong at another level. Both refused to recognize him for what he was: God's son and king of the Jews. If the Sanhedrin had known that he was God's son, it could not have regarded him as guilty; if Pilate had known that he was king, he could not have regarded him as innocent.

From one point of view we might expect Jesus' appearance before the Sanhedrin to be the climactic one. He has finally arrived in Jerusalem and has been challenged for teaching in the temple. After his arrest, with the defection of Judas, the weakness of Peter, and the loss of popular support, Jesus finally meets his most malevolent opponents, the chief priests and their allies. The setting appears to be a formal meeting of a judicial body that is composed of Jewish leaders who are concerned for and informed about religious matters. Thus we might expect a full-scale debate between the chief priests and Jesus about the temple and its proper control. Instead, however, we get a "compendium of Christology."

Whatever else the hearing before the Sanhedrin is, it is not a trial. There is neither formal charge nor testimony. There is no reference to a presiding officer. There is only the vaguest of verdicts—"We have heard it ourselves from his own lips" (Luke 22:71). No punishment is inflicted or even mentioned. The only substantive decision that the members of the Sanhedrin made was to take Jesus before Pilate (23:1). This hearing, therefore, is only preliminary, a kind of curtain raiser, and we know that the climactic judgment is yet to come in the appearance of Jesus before Pilate.

But to understand the hearing before the Sanhedrin simply as a curtain raiser and a "compendium of theology" does not exhaust its literary functions. It may be possible to judge these functions if we ask why Luke has this pericope at all. After all, the climactic narrative involves questions about Roman justice, not Jewish, and there is only the slimmest connection between the Sanhedrin session and the session before Pilate. The session before the Sanhedrin is not dictated by Luke's interpretation of Psalm 2, which requires only the presence of "Herod and Pontius Pilate, with the Gentiles and the peoples of Israel" (Acts 4:27).

The function of Luke 22:66–71 must be understood by reference to its position in the narrative as a whole. This pericope is the fulfillment of what had been anticipated in the passion predictions, which taught the reader to expect the rejection of Jesus by the priestly block of opponents and his delivery to Gentiles (Luke 9:22,44; 17:25; 18:31–34). It brings Jesus up against the chief priests, and, as in the teaching in the temple, the controversy is over Jesus' authority. The reader thus would see the Jewish Sanhedrin as composed of Jesus' opponents, who refused to grant him the authority that belongs to the Christ, the Son of man, and the Son of God. So far as the gospel of Luke is concerned, the Sanhedrin session is the official rejection of Jesus by the chief priests.

It is also the key to the death of Jesus. Although the Sanhedrin in Luke did not conduct a formal trial, issue a conviction, or determine a penalty, the act of turning Jesus over to Pilate sealed his fate. As it turned out, the judge in the Roman court declared Jesus innocent, but he was pressured into giving permission for him to be crucified. Luke does not explicitly identify the source of that pressure as the Sanhedrin, but he clearly associates it with the Jewish leaders who made up that body, especially the chief priests. If, therefore, it had not been for the chief priests and the Sanhedrin, Jesus would not have been executed. Thus, the session before the Sanhedrin, although preliminary, looms large in Luke's narrative. This hearing accords perfectly with the anticipations of the trial that we examined earlier, even if it is not required by Acts 4:27.

THE CHARGES AGAINST JESUS

Several motifs inform the section of Luke that deals with the so-called Roman trial of Jesus. Although these motifs were implicit in the Sanhedrin hearing, they become explicit in Luke 23, where Luke is clearly interested in showing that Jesus' trial was irregular, the charges were false or unjust, and Jesus was innocent. The irregularity of the trial is seen in the fact that the kind of examination the Sanhedrin conducted had little relationship to the charges that were brought before Pilate. It is also seen in the fact that a declaration of innocence by the emperor's representative in Jerusalem carried less weight than the insistent outcries of chief priests and crowd. The injustice of the charges is a particularly significant motif.

One of the distinctive features in the Lukan trial narrative is that there is a clear statement of the charges that were brought against Jesus before Pilate.[20] Three charges were formally presented by the Sanhedrin in Luke 23:2; the fourth is offered by the chief priests and the crowds in 23:5.

In the first charge Jesus is accused of "perverting our nation" (*diastrephonta to ethnos hēmōn*, Luke 23:2). The verb literally means to turn away, but it is also used to designate the act of misleading someone or misshaping something. Pilate reviews the charge in 23:14: "You brought me this man as one who was perverting the people" (*apostrephonta ton laon*). The verbs are cognates and approximately the same in meaning, although *diastrephō* may express greater intensity than *apostrephō*. In either case the context suggests that the charge is political in nature. It probably means that Jesus has been trying to turn the nation away from the political alignment that Pilate would have regarded as proper, i.e., alignment toward Rome.

In the second charge there is an accusation about Jesus and Roman taxation. The charge is usually translated to say that Jesus forbade the people to pay taxes to Caesar (RSV: "forbidding us to give tribute to Caesar," *kōluonta phorous Kaisari didonai*, Luke 23:2). The verb *kōluō* means to hinder, prevent, forbid, or refuse. The pronoun "us" does not appear in Luke 23:2, and the charge may be read as indicating that Jesus refused to pay his own taxes. It is more likely, however, that the charge is intended in a broader sense as an objection to some aspect of Jesus' teachings. The first two charges are related; Jesus' policy on taxation would be part of his general effort to turn the nation against Rome.

In the third charge Jesus is accused of claiming to be Christ a king (*legonta heauton Christon basilea einai*, Luke 23:2). The charge about the Christ connects the trial before Pilate with the earlier investigation of the Sanhedrin. The association of messiahship and kingship is found only here in Luke-Acts, although Acts 17:7 has something that reminds us of this charge. The use of king as an appositive to Christ shows that the members of the Sanhedrin are making an effort to convert their own charges against Jesus (22:67) into charges of a political nature. Apparently Pilate is interested only in this charge, since he questions Jesus about kingship in Luke 23:3–4 and finds him innocent.[21]

The fourth charge comes up in the course of the trial before Pilate. In Luke 23:5, in an accusation that presumably comes from the chief priests and the crowds, we read that "he stirs up [*anaseiei*] the people, teaching throughout all Judea, from Galilee even to this place."[22] In chapter 4, we saw that William C. Robinson and others regard this verse as a clue to the geographical structure of Luke. We also noted a certain ambiguity in the wording *heōs hōde*. The accusation surely means that Jesus has taught in Jerusalem, but, in view of the attention paid to his teaching in the temple in Luke 19:45–

21:38, it probably also reflects an objection about his teaching there. The words seem to indicate that there is something more serious at stake than the earlier teaching in Galilee and Judea. The charge does not suggest any change in the content of the teaching but in the location. If this is a charge about Jesus' teaching in the temple, it reflects a consistent Lukan motif about the conflicting claims of the chief priests and Jesus over the control of the temple. We might paraphrase this fourth charge to say: "This man, who previously taught in Galilee and Judea, has now shown up here and has taken upon himself the authority to teach in the temple." Of course, the mention of Galilee connects this verse with the hearing before Herod, which follows immediately (23:6–12).

Once we isolate the charges in the Lukan account, it becomes clear that our author has been concerned to prepare for the trial by presenting certain aspects of Jesus' life as defenses against the charges. This is most obvious in the case of the second charge, the one about tax policy. In Luke 20:20–26 Jesus' opponents had tried to trap him by asking a direct question about taxation, and he had been able to answer them without falling into the trap. Thus, the reader knows that Jesus neither refused to pay taxes nor advised anyone else to do so, and the charge would be viewed by the reader as totally false.

In more subtle ways Luke has prepared the way for the reader to understand the injustice of the third charge, that of claiming to be Christ a king. Jesus' response to the question of the Sanhedrin formed part of this preparation (22:67–68). In respect to kingship, however, the story of Jesus' ride on the colt in 19:28–40 may be damaging, for it reads very much like a description of a royal parade. Jesus' approach to Jerusalem is announced by the rejoicing disciples, "Blessed is the King who comes in the name of the Lord!" (19:38). The image of Jesus riding toward Jerusalem, his way being prepared by disciples, to the accompaniment of their shouting, suggests the approach of a conquering king. Only in Luke 19:38 and Acts 17:7 is the title *basileus* used of Jesus, and it is notable that in Luke 19:40 Jesus refused to prevent his disciples from using it.[23]

The idea of kingship also played a prominent part in the conversation between Jesus and his disciples at the last supper. There he claimed to have a kingdom which came from God. He made the disciples a part of his kingdom and granted a royal throne to each of them (Luke 22:29–30).[24] These verses should leave no doubt in the reader's mind that Jesus is a king in some fashion and that the kingdom is in some way connected with Israel, since the disciples are to be given the responsibility to judge the twelve tribes of Israel. We are probably to understand Jesus' promise to the disciples as a reminder of the social revolution that was anticipated as early as Luke 1:52: "He has put down the mighty from their thrones, and exalted those of low degree." Although one may be inclined to think of the completion of the revolution as eschatological, Jesus' claim to have a kingdom is fundamental in his words at the last supper. But Luke reports these words as part of a private conversation, and he does not have Jesus make any kind of royal claim in his public speeches. Thus, strictly speaking, Jesus is innocent of the charge of publicly claiming to be a king.

The same is true of the accusation that Jesus claimed to be Christ, as we have seen in examining the appearance before the Sanhedrin. Prior to the resurrection all uses of the word in reference to Jesus are on the lips of others—an angel in Luke 2:11; Peter in 9:20; elders, chief priests, and scribes in the question asked in 22:67; leaders in 23:35; and a crucified criminal in 23:39. It also appears in two explanatory sentences (Luke 2:26; 4:41) and once in connection with John the Baptist (3:15). In one pericope where we might reasonably have expected such a proclamation, Luke 20:41–44, it is lacking. It is only after the resurrection that Jesus uses the term in apparent reference to himself, as he explains to the disciples that the Christ was required to suffer (Luke 24:26,46). The lack of a preresurrection claim on Jesus' part is surely significant and has a bearing on how one should understand this particular charge in the hearing before Pilate. Although, according to Luke, Jesus is the Christ, it is not true that he claimed to be.

The fourth charge, as we interpret it, was that Jesus has taken upon himself the authority to teach in the temple. As we have seen in the long section that runs from 19:45 through 21:38, Luke makes no effort to deny the accuracy of this charge. His narrative was not intended to deny that Jesus taught in the temple but to show that he did so daily and openly and that he had every right to do so. Luke thus offers a christological defense against the fourth charge: as God's son, Jesus has authority over the temple (see Luke 20:9–19).

Thus, Luke has prepared the way for the reader to see the injustice at Jesus' trial. The reader knows that Jesus has not advised people against paying the Roman tax. He knows that Jesus has not publicly claimed to be Christ or king of the Jews, although he has been shown that he is both. He knows that he has every right to teach in the temple. Although there is no distinct treatment of the charge of perverting the nation, the reader would have little difficulty in understanding both the irony and the injustice of the charge. Jesus is indeed both king and Christ, but he has said nothing against the imperial government.

THE CHARACTERIZATION OF HEROD

The session of Jesus before Herod is unique to Luke, and it is consistent with the interpretation of Ps 2:1–2 in Acts 4:25–27. This Herod is evidently the same as the one whom Luke usually calls Herod the tetrarch. He was first mentioned in Luke 3:1, in the elaborate chronological setting that introduced the appearance of John the Baptist, where it was said that Herod was tetrarch of Galilee. Thus, when Pilate learns that Jesus is from Galilee, he knows that he has lived under the jurisdiction of Herod, whom we know as Herod Antipas. This Herod will be remembered as the one who, by his action in imprisoning the Baptist, had been explicitly identified as an opponent of the gospel (Luke 3:18–20). He is known as the one who killed the Baptist (Luke 9:7–9) and intended to do the same with Jesus (13:31).

The malevolent position of Herod the tetrarch is gradually revealed in Luke's gospel. From observing his oppression of John the Baptist the reader learns early in the gospel that Herod is also to be grouped with the opposition to Jesus. His reflection on the ministry of Jesus as reported in Luke 9:7–9, however, presents a certain ambiguity. The reader learns here for the first time that John is dead and that it was Herod who beheaded him. But what is the meaning of Herod's observation about Jesus? Luke characterizes him as being greatly perplexed because of what he had heard about Jesus' reputation, "because it was said by some that John had been raised from the dead, by some that Elijah had appeared, and by others that one of the old prophets had risen" (Luke 9:7–8).[25] All three possibilities involve the coming back to life, or reappearance, of one who had ceased to live, but Herod only comments on the expectation of the return of John the Baptist, "John I beheaded; but who is this about whom I hear such things?" (Luke 9:9). Luke comments that Herod wanted to see Jesus. Perhaps Luke means to imply that Herod wanted to expose the rumors that Jesus was a resurrected John the Baptist. Perhaps we are to think of Herod as simply curious to see the kind of person about whom such rumors could circulate.[26] Although these are possible interpretations of the Lukan passage, it is more likely that the words involve a greater malevolence than these interpretations would suggest. While all three of the rumors imply resurrection, they also imply a continuity— between Jesus and Elijah, the prophets, and John. Since Herod mentions only John, it is reasonable to infer that his perplexity is about the connection between Jesus and John. Perhaps we are to understand that Herod is interested to see the kind of person Jesus is, but he appears here to be more interested in the relationship between the two persons. Since he now is the self-confessed executioner of John and since he expresses interest in the supposition that Jesus is the resurrected Baptist, Herod the tetrarch wishes to see Jesus. Why? In order to do to him as he had done to John.

If any reader is in doubt about this interpretation, he has only to read on to Luke 13:31, where Pharisees, also part of the opposition to Jesus, warn him to flee, "for Herod wants to kill you." Jesus' reply to the warning, not without ambiguity, is essentially that this is neither the time nor the place for his death. He will continue his work for two or three days, and his execution, like that of all the prophets, will take place in Jerusalem (13:32–33).

Thus, when Jesus and Herod Antipas finally meet in Luke 23:6–12, the reader expects a climactic confrontation. Luke 23:8 reminds us of 9:9, although the former verse seems to express only curiosity. The hearing before Herod is similar in form to the hearing before Pilate. Herod questions Jesus, the chief priests and scribes bring their accusations, and Jesus is found to be innocent (23:15). But there are differences. There is no dialogue; Luke reports that Herod questioned Jesus, but he does not report the questions that were asked. Jesus himself does not respond to the questions.[27] Although the same groups are present in the role of prosecutors, Luke does not tell us what charges they brought to Herod's attention. The brief scene concludes with a mocking by Herod and his soldiers and the return of Jesus to Pilate. The comment in 23:12, that Herod and Pilate became friends that day, seems gratuitous.

From a literary perspective the most interesting thing about the pericope Luke 23:6–12 is the shift in the characterization of Herod the tetrarch. He does not play the role that we might have expected him to play. Instead of a climactic confrontation between the hero and one of the chief villains, there is a pale description of what we today might call a nonevent. Herod does not even fill the role that Luke assigned to him in his interpretation of Psalm 2. Although he is one of the rulers who gathered in Jerusalem against God's anointed (see Acts 4:25–27), he does not cast his vote against him. This is not to say that Herod has shifted sides from being an opponent of Jesus to being a supporter. He has, however, become dissociated from those who now have become Jesus' major opponents, the chief priests.

Thus far we have dealt with three components of Jesus' trial. After the first (Luke 22:66–71), there was an agreement to take Jesus to Pilate. In the second (23:1–5) and the third (23:6–12) he has been declared innocent.

THE CHARACTERIZATION OF PILATE

The fourth and final component of the trial (Luke 23:13–25) begins with Pilate's review of the situation. In words addressed to the chief priests, rulers, and people, Pilate states that, although Jesus had been charged with perverting the people (*apostrephonta ton laon*, Luke 23:14), neither he nor Herod found him guilty. Pilate then reaffirms his earlier verdict, declares Jesus innocent (23:15), and states his intention to release him (23:16). This pronouncement is met with an insistent demand for the release of Barabbas and the crucifixion of Jesus. Pilate repeats his verdict and his intention to release Jesus, but the cries for his crucifixion are all the more urgent. Luke concludes the narrative by saying that the voices of the crowd prevailed and that Pilate finally "gave sentence that their demand should be granted" (23:24). He released Barabbas, "but Jesus he delivered up to their will" (23:25).

The lines of opposition come into focus in the climactic narrative in Luke 23:13–25. Those who call for the crucifixion of Jesus are designated by an anonymous third person plural (23:20,23), but in context this must mean the chief priests, rulers, and people (23:13; cf. Acts 4:27). The only defender that Jesus has is the Roman official, Pontius Pilate, but his verdict does not prevail, and finally he turns him over to his enemies.

Pilate has not been even a peripheral character in Luke's narrative to this point. Outside the formal identification in Luke 3:1 he has been referred to only once. That reference was in 13:1, where Jesus was questioned about Pilate's action in the assassination of some Galileans during the performance of their sacrifices. The brief reference conveys an impression of Pilate as ruthless, insensitive, unjust, and even antireligious. But in the trial of Jesus we meet a character of some complexity. He is convinced of Jesus' innocence and even insists on it. He gives his judgment in 23:4,15, 22, and the last is expressly referred to as the third declaration of Jesus' innocence. In 23:14 he recalls the judgment he made in 23:4, and in 23:16,20,22 he proposes to release him. But Pilate lacks the will to carry out his own conviction. He is pressured by the crowd and its leaders, and at the critical moment he effectively resigns his authority and turns Jesus over "to their will" (23:25).

Herod and Pilate are not treated in positive ways in the trial narratives, but they come off looking better than the chief priests and their allies. They gain by comparison with the more unprincipled opponents, but they are still Jesus' opponents. Pilate had in fact expressed his intention to punish Jesus (Luke 23:16,22), and Herod had "treated him with contempt" (23:11). But what is operative in the trial scenes is the insistence on the part of the priestly block of opponents and the crowd that Jesus is guilty and must be put to death. It is they who make the charges and press their case before both Pilate and Herod. Luke is careful to conclude the trial scenes by emphasizing Pilate's accession to the will of the chief priests and the people. Pilate neither changes his mind about Jesus' guilt nor does he sentence him. Rather, he turns him over to their will—i.e., the will of the priestly block of opponents, now including the crowd.

CONCLUSION

Taken as a whole, Luke's trial narratives portray Jesus' opposition as unprincipled and his execution as unjust. The irregularity of the various components of the trial, the false charges, the official but ineffective declarations of innocence, and the shifts in characterization all fit together to create a powerful impression about the processes that led to the death of Jesus.

The theme of the innocence of Jesus dominates the entire narrative and affects the way in which Luke composes his story. The reader is compelled to observe that Jesus' innocence was recognized and affirmed by the Roman governor and by Herod but not by the Jewish leaders and people.

A similar motif is consistently pursued by Luke in telling of Jesus' successors in Acts. Luke wants to show that, not only did Jesus and his followers do nothing against Roman law, but that, whenever possible, the officials recognized their innocence. The innocence of Paul and his companions is explicitly maintained at a number of points in Acts. Magistrates at Philippi release Paul and Silas from prison and apologize for their arrest (Acts 16:35–40). At Corinth, Gallio refuses to hear a case brought against Paul by the local Jews (18:12–17). At Ephesus the city clerk pronounces that Paul and his companions did nothing sacrilegious or blasphemous against Artemis, and he dismisses the assembly that formed in opposition to them (19:28–41). Finally, both Festus and Herod Agrippa agree that Paul had done "nothing to deserve death or imprisonment" (26:31). Agrippa's statement to Festus, occurring as it does just at the end of the long series of Paul's trials, is surely intended to be climactic: "This man could have been set free if he had not appealed to Caesar" (26:32). Throughout the long story of Paul the theme is crystal clear; namely, that Paul was totally innocent of any infringement of Roman law or of any local laws in any of the places he visited. His troubles all came from Jews and involved disagreements about the interpretation of scripture, especially disagreements about the resurrection of the dead.

This same theme, so abundantly explicated in the story of Paul, also dominates the Lukan report of the trial of Jesus. Jesus was innocent of all alleged crimes against the Roman state, and he was pronounced not guilty by both Pilate and Herod.

The dominance of the theme of innocence would seem to explain the ways in which Luke presented the charges against Jesus. He used them in order to demonstrate not only the character of Jesus but also the character of his opponents and the issues between him and them. The charges that Jesus perverted the nation, forbade the payment of taxes, and claimed to be Christ a king are all, for Luke, smoke screens. They have no validity and no basis, so far as a reader of Luke is able to determine. When we recognize that these are all charges that might reasonably be brought in a Roman court of law, then we recognize the relationship that Jesus' trial has to the theme of innocence, as we observed it at work in Acts. In relationship to the charges brought against him, charges of treason, Jesus was innocent. He did not try to turn Israel against Rome; he did not oppose the payment of Roman taxes; nor was he a royal pretender.

If the charges involving treason are hollow, the substantive accusation against Jesus remains somewhere beneath the surface. Much of the material leading up to the trial had suggested that there was a connection between the opposition to Jesus and his teaching in the temple. If one is willing to grant that this connection is reflected in the fourth charge—that Jesus' teaching has come to this place (Luke 23:5)—it then becomes plausible to see yet another connection between the trial of Jesus and that of Paul. In the final stages of Paul's trials it became clear that the accusations against him did not involve violations of Roman law but rather reflected Jewish religious disagreements. Similarly, in the case of Jesus the issues did not involve Roman law but religious disagreement, specifically involving the control of the Jewish temple.

There should be no doubt about the group that Luke blames for putting Jesus to death. It was not the Romans, who officially declared him innocent. Not even Herod the tetrarch is implicated. The Pharisaic block of Jesus' opponents is not present at the crucial moment. The foes of Jesus who are to blame are those who formed the priestly block, who officially rejected him in his hearing before the Sanhedrin, who delivered him to Roman authority, prosecuted his case before Pilate, and, with the support of the Jewish public, pressured the Roman governor to violate all semblances of justice and assent to his crucifixion.

There is a sense in which Acts 4:25–27 controls Luke's trial narratives. His interpretation of Ps 2:1–2 requires him to bring together in Jerusalem Pilate, Herod, Gentiles, and Jews, all arrayed against Jesus. But their assembling against the Lord's anointed does not mean that in every case they remained opposed to him. Pilate repeatedly declared Jesus to be innocent (Luke 23:4,15,22), as did Herod (23:15). The verdict of the Gentiles appears to be placed on the tongue of the Roman centurion in Luke 23:47: "Certainly this man was innocent!" Only the Jews, led by the chief priests, withheld this verdict.

NOTES

1. See e.g., Charles H. Talbert, *Literary Patterns, Theological Themes and The Genre of Luke-Acts* (Missoula, Mont.: Scholars Press, 1974), pp. 15–23.

2. Anton Büchele, *Der Tod Jesu im Lukasevangelium: Eine redaktiongeschichtliche Untersuchung zu Lk 23* (Frankfurt am Main: Josef Knecht, 1978), pp. 70–75.

3. On the speeches in Acts, see above, chapter 4, n. 41.

4. See, e.g., Rudolf Bultmann, *The History of the Synoptic Tradition,* trans. John Marsh (New York: Harper and Row, 1963), p. 273.

5. Hans Conzelmann described Jesus' ministry as a time when Satan was absent, an absence that extended from the end of the story of Jesus' temptation (Luke 4:13) to Judas' conspiracy with the priests (22:3). See Conzelmann, *The Theology of St. Luke,* trans. Geoffrey Buswell (New York: Harper and Bros., 1960), p. 16 et passim.

6. It is probably incorrect to translate Luke 22:47, as does the RSV, to say that Judas was leading the crowd. A better translation would be: "While he [Jesus] was still speaking, a crowd, together with the one called Judas, approached them."

7. The differences between Luke and the other synoptic gospels are significant at this point and will be noted in chapter 6.

8. Ernst Haenchen, *The Acts of the Apostles: A Commentary,* trans. Bernard Noble et al. (Oxford: Basil Blackwell, 1971), pp. 641–42.

9. Ibid., p. 642.

10. Jürgen Roloff, *Die Apostelgeschichte* (Göttingen: Vandenhoeck und Ruprecht, 1981), p. 327.

11. In reference to these attempted explanations Haenchen says, "Paul's answer, that he did not know that it was the High Priest, is so unbelievable that it has driven the theologians to desperate efforts" (*The Acts of the Apostles,* p. 640).

12. For a discussion of the historical nature of the Sanhedrin at the time of Jesus see Solomon Zeitlin, "The Political Synedrion and the Religious Synedrion," *Jewish Quarterly Review* 36 (1945):109–40; Ellis Rivkin, "Beth Din, Boulé, Sanhedrin: A Tragedy of Errors," *Hebrew Union College Annual* 46 (1975):181–99.

13. In Luke 23:50–51 we meet Joseph of Arimathea, who is said to be a member of the council (*bouleutēs*) but "who had not consented to their purpose and deed." But there is no mention of this character or any other sympathizer with Jesus in Luke 22:66–71. Although Luke does not use the term *sunedrion* in Luke 23:50, the reference is clearly to the session of that body described in 22:66–71.

14. On scribes, see above, p. 63f.

15. A number of uses of the phrase "Son of man" do not unquestionably refer to Jesus (e.g., Luke 6:22; 12:10). But a sufficient number do (e.g., Luke 5:24; 6:5; 7:34; 9:22,44,58; 11:30; 18:31; 19:10; 22:22,48). In Luke 22:69 the reference is probably to the apocalyptic Son of man, which had not earlier been clearly identified with Jesus (see 9:26; 12:8,40; 17:24,26,30; 18:8; 21:36).

16. For Luke's use of the phrase, Son of God see Luke 1:32,35; 3:22; 4:3,9,41; 8:28; 9:35; 10:22.

17. Conzelmann, *Theology of St. Luke*, pp. 84–85. Helmut Flender agrees that the emphasis in the passage is christological but disagrees with Conzelmann's contention that the various titles are to be assimilated (*St. Luke: Theologian of Redemptive History,* trans. R. H. and Ilse Fuller [Philadelphia: Fortress Press, 1967], pp. 44–46). For a detailed analysis of Luke 22:66–71 see David R. Catchpole, *The Trial of Jesus* (Leiden: E. J. Brill, 1971), pp. 153–220.

18. Conzelmann, *Theology of St. Luke*, p. 85n.

19. The RSV translates Luke 23:3 "You have said so." For a discussion of the meaning of these phrases see David R. Catchpole, "The Answer of Jesus to Caiaphas (Matt. XXVI. 64)," *New Testament Studies* 17 (1970–71): 213–26. Catchpole designates the meaning as "affirmative in content, and reluctant or circumlocutory in formulation" (p. 226).

20. In Matt 26:65 and Mark 14:64, at the end of the Sanhedrin session, the high priest concludes that Jesus has committed blasphemy. But when Jesus is taken before Pilate, no definite charges are mentioned. Matt 27:12 says that he was "accused by the chief priests and elders," and Mark 15:3 says that "the chief priests accused him of many things." These gospels lack the specificity that is found in Luke's formulation of the charges.

21. Cf. Acts 17:7, where the charge of proclaiming Jesus as king is presented as a crime against the decrees of Caesar.

22. Cf. Acts 17:6, where a mob in Thessalonica captures Jason and accuses him of acting as host to Paul and Silas, who "have turned the world upside down [and] have come here also."

23. In the infancy narratives Luke referred to Jesus' throne and kingdom but did not use the title *basileus* of him. See Luke 1:32–33.

24. The number of thrones is given as twelve in Luke 22:30, and this number would include Judas (see 22:21). Although Judas is "of the number of the twelve" (22:3), it cannot be that Luke intends for him to occupy one of the thrones. This

problem is not resolved until Acts 1:15–26, when Matthias is selected to take the place of Judas among the twelve.

25. Cf. Luke 9:19, where Jesus' disciples report to him about the same speculations.

26. I. Howard Marshall, *The Gospel of Luke: A Commentary on the Greek Text* (Grand Rapids: Eerdmans, 1978), p. 357, describes Herod's desire to see Jesus as "a feeling prompted by curiosity or malice, not by faith."

27. Paul's hearing before Herod Agrippa (Acts 25:23–26:32) forms a dramatic contrast to Jesus' appearance before Herod Antipas. Whereas Jesus is silent, Paul gives a vigorous defense that consumes almost all of Acts 26.

The Distinctiveness
of Luke

T he preceding chapters have been devoted to a reading
of Luke–Acts with particular emphasis on the literary
composition and meaning of these books. The reading
has suggested that Luke carefully crafted his material dealing with
the circumstances surrounding the death of Jesus. In this reading a
conscious effort was made to ignore source-critical theories in
regard to Luke's gospel and to deemphasize comparisons among
the three synoptic gospels. Now that the reading has been com-
pleted, it seems appropriate to raise questions about the distinctiveness of Luke as an author. Is his treatment of the death of Jesus fundamentally the same as that in the comparable gospels? Are his
literary themes to be found also in the other synoptic gospels, or
are they unique? These questions require a comparative analysis
of those gospels that, by all accounts, have fundamental similarities and are related to one another in some fashion. Without
resorting to assumptions about the precise literary relationships
among the synoptic gospels, it is nevertheless possible to draw
some comparisons.

The result of this comparative analysis will not be a validation of
what we have found in reading Luke–Acts. Such validation is not
strictly necessary, since the existence of certain themes in one book
does not depend on their appearance or nonappearance in another.
But since there are obvious similarities among the synoptic gospels,
some comparison is unavoidable. Thus, the purpose here is to raise

questions about the distinctiveness of Luke's literary approach vis-à-vis Matthew and Mark.

Certain limits to comparing these documents immediately present themselves. A full-blown comparison of Luke with the other synoptic gospels on the subject of the death of Jesus must await a literary-critical analysis of these gospels, which should be examined in the way that Luke has been examined here. The questions that were addressed to Luke should be addressed in the same way to Matthew and Mark, without presuppositions about sources.

In addition, Luke–Acts is comparable with Matthew and Mark only in respect to the gospel component. The student of Luke–Acts is able to trace themes, characterizations, and plot devices in a document whose scope is very different from that of Matthew or Mark. In this sense a comparison of Luke–Acts with the other synoptic gospels is faulty, since the terms of comparison are not commensurate. The definition of our task, then, will be to take what we have learned from reading Luke–Acts and to concentrate on those matters that appear to be comparable with aspects of Matthew and Mark.

The present chapter does not pretend to be a literary-critical analysis of Matthew and Mark. Nor is it an attempt to examine all aspects of the viewpoint about the death of Jesus that informs these gospels. Rather, the procedure will be to raise questions about the distinctiveness of Luke's treatment by making selective comparisons with the other two gospels. But first it will be necessary to review the main points that have been made about Luke's view of the death of Jesus.

Four major areas have been investigated and have yielded pertinent material for understanding Luke's viewpoints. The first related to Luke's use of the Jewish public in the various scenes that make up his gospel and its sequel. It appears that he employed a particular kind of literary device in the stories that dealt with the public reception of Jesus and that of his successors. In these stories, and in Luke–Acts as a whole, the public reception was initially favorable but finally hostile; i.e., initial acceptance was followed by final rejection. The Jewish public that responded favorably to Jesus almost up to the end finally joined the Jewish leaders in calling for his death. The crowd that responded so favorably to the apostles at the beginning of Acts finally called for the death of Paul.

The second area related to Luke's treatment of the Jewish leaders. Here we found that there was a basic division of the leaders into two blocks, one headed by Pharisees and the other by chief priests. Although both blocks were grouped among Jesus' opponents, significant differences appeared between them. The opposition of the Pharisees revolved around certain issues relating to the application or interpretation of Torah. Controversies between them and Jesus occurred outside Jerusalem, and Luke did not suggest any connection between Pharisees and Jesus' death. The opposition of the chief priests, by contrast, seems to have revolved around temple-related issues, and all of Jesus' controversies with them occurred in Jerusalem, specifically in the temple. Chief priests are explicitly connected with the death of Jesus. Luke shows that they were present at the various stages of his trial and called for his crucifixion.

Third, it was found that Luke demonstrates an ambivalent attitude toward Jerusalem and the temple. In some passages he associates the city and the temple with piety, joy, and religious devotion. In others there are only dark colors. Jerusalem is known to be the place of Jesus' death, but it is also the city of the apostles. The city's significance lies mainly in its being the location of the Jewish temple, which is pictured in some passages as a battleground and, indeed, as the object of conflict. Although, in Luke's perspective, Jesus was Lord of the temple, the chief priests refused to recognize him, nor did they recognize his right to teach in the temple. His attempt to exercise authority in the temple lies behind their opposition to him.

Fourth, Luke's treatment of the trial of Jesus is a complex of four components, all governed by certain themes. The dominant themes are that Jesus was innocent of the charges brought against him, his trial was highly irregular, and he was pronounced innocent by those in authority. The hearing before the Sanhedrin was the official rejection of Jesus by the chief priests and their associates, and it was they who, with the support of the Jewish public, insisted on his execution.

THE JEWISH PUBLIC

All three gospels emphasize the enthusiastic acceptance that initially greeted Jesus from crowds of Jewish people. At the end of his sermon on the mount Matthew summarizes the response to Jesus by calling attention to the astonishment of the crowd and its impression of Jesus' great authority, which is favorably compared with the authority of the scribes (Matt 7:28–29; cf. Mark 1:21–22; Luke 4:31–32). When they see the healing of the paralytic, the people likewise express admiration for Jesus' authority, as well as fear, and they glorify God (Matt 9:8; Mark 2:12; Luke 5:26). Both Matthew and Mark call attention to the large crowd that followed Jesus when he went to Judea (Matt 19:2; Mark 10:1) and when he left Jericho (Matt 20:29; Mark 10:46; cf. Luke 18:35). Both gospels frequently call attention to the pressure exercised on Jesus by the great throngs that came to hear him teach and to be healed (e.g., Matt 12:46; 13:1–2; 14:13; 17:14; Mark 1:35–38,45; 2:4; 3:9; 4:1–2; 5:21,27,31; 6:33; 9:14). Matthew emphasizes the enthusiastic public support Jesus received on his entry into Jerusalem (Matt 21:8–9; cf. Mark 11:8–10). Luke calls attention to the protection that was afforded Jesus by this mass support as he taught in the temple (Luke 19:48; 20:19,26; 22:2). The chief priests and their associates would have arrested Jesus in the temple if it had not been for this support. This Lukan emphasis is also found in Matthew (21:46; 26:5) and Mark (11:18; 12:12; 14:2).

In Matthew and Mark, as in Luke, the crowd, incited by the chief priests, turns against Jesus at his trial. Although the crowd does not join the chief priests in bringing charges against Jesus, as in Luke, it nevertheless joins them in opposing him. In Matt 27:15–20 the evangelist describes the practice of the Passover amnesty, which is not mentioned in Luke, and then says that the chief priests and elders persuaded the people to ask for Barabbas rather than Jesus. In Mark 15:6–11 the crowd reminds Pilate of the usual amnesty, and then the chief priests stir up the populace on behalf of Barabbas. In both gospels the crowd insists that Jesus be executed. In Mark 15:15 the author explains that Pilate submitted to their will in order to satisfy the crowd, and in Matt 27:25 all the people take responsibility for Jesus' death.

Unquestionably, both Matthew and Mark present a Jewish public that initially accepts Jesus but finally rejects him. Indeed, many of the passages that illustrate this approach are parallel in two and in some cases all three gospels. But there are two Lukan passages that tend to make this theme somewhat more dramatic in that gospel than in the other two.

One of the passages relates to Judas' betrayal of Jesus. In Luke's description of the arrangements that Judas made with the chief priests (Luke 22:3–6), he notes that Judas "sought an opportunity to betray him to them in the absence of the multitude" (22:6). The parallels in Matt 26:16 and Mark 14:11 say only that Judas sought an opportunity to betray Jesus. The difference may not appear to be important, but in the context of Luke's narrative it is significant, as we have seen. Jesus' popular support created a difficulty for the chief priests that had to be neutralized or, better, overcome. Luke wants the reader to be keenly aware that Judas could not have accomplished his purpose if he had not been able to solve this problem. Thus, Judas must look for an opportunity to betray Jesus at a time when the supporting crowd is not present. In all three gospels the arrest of Jesus is accomplished with the help of Judas, accompanied by a crowd (Matt 26:47–56; Mark 14:43–52; Luke 22:47–53), but only in Luke is there a statement about the need to isolate Jesus from the crowd.

Of greater importance is the programmatic pericope in Luke 4:16–30, Jesus' initial sermon in Nazareth. As we have seen, this passage appears to set out the theme of acceptance and rejection in miniature. It anticipates the fate of both Jesus and Paul and connects their fates with the evangelizing of Gentiles. Although there are fragmentary parallels in Matt 13:53–58 and Mark 6:1–6, Luke's fundamental emphases are unique. Matthew and Mark are quite similar in this passage, but there is very little verbal agreement between Luke and the other two. In all three gospels the location of the episode is in a synagogue (Matt 13:54; Mark 6:2; Luke 4:16), and both Mark and Luke set it on a sabbath. Matthew and Mark give no name to the location, speaking of it only as Jesus' *patris*. Luke calls it Nazareth, but in view of the saying in 4:23–24 Luke must think of Nazareth as Jesus' *patris*. Some part of the audience's response is found in all three gospels, although even here there is a difference. In Matt 13:55–56 and Mark 6:3 the crowd raises a question about Jesus' relatives, and they name Mary, four brothers, and an indefinite number of sisters. In Matthew the father is designated simply as the carpenter, while in Mark nothing is said about the father, and Jesus is called the carpenter.[1] In Luke, however, the question is: "Is not this Joseph's son?" (Luke 4:22). The only other contact between Luke and the other two synoptic gospels is in Jesus' saying in Luke 4:24—"No prophet is acceptable in his own country"—a saying which appears in a slightly different form in Matt 13:57 and Mark 6:4. Other than these few fragmentary similarities, there are no significant parallels between Luke and the other two synoptic gospels, and Luke's narrative is far more detailed and dramatic.

The theme of initial acceptance followed by rejection may be suggested in a rudimentary way in the Matthew/Mark story. In these gospels the congregation initially expresses amazement at Jesus' wisdom and power and finally is scandalized (*eskandalizonto*, Matt 13:57; Mark 6:3) by him. But it is not clear that this story presents two contrasting attitudes, as does Luke. Those who heard Jesus were amazed, because they did not understand how he, whose relatives were known, could have obtained the power and wisdom that he had demonstrated to them. This amazement led to their being scandalized. It seems that we ought to read Matt 13:54–57 and Mark 6:2–3 as expressing a single crowd response, essentially a negative one. But Luke's story makes the contrast between initial acceptance and final rejection exceptionally vivid. At first the people speak well of Jesus and wonder about his words of grace; at the end they take him out of the synagogue and attempt to put him to death. In addition, the position of the Nazareth pericope in Luke, as Jesus' opening sermon, gives the story a significance that is lacking in Matthew and Mark.

The inclusion of the Nazareth pericope, the note about the crowd in Luke 22:6, and the other notes in both Luke and Acts that we have observed suggest that the theme of initial acceptance and final rejection has a more definite character in Luke than in the other two synoptic gospels. This brief glance at Matthew and Mark has shown that the theme is not unknown in those gospels. The number of parallels between Luke and the other two confirms the view that Luke's treatment of the Jewish public is not unique. Matthew and Mark both seem to agree that initial acceptance turned finally into rejection. Luke's distinctiveness in regard to his treatment of the Jewish public lies in the consistency with which he used this theme throughout the gospel and Acts and in the clarity with which he announced the theme in the Nazareth pericope. More than the other gospels Luke has implied that there was some offstage maneuvering that finally isolated Jesus from the crowd and turned the Jewish people against him. Moreover, only Luke gives a hint that the dramatic alteration on the part of the Jewish people had something to do with the Christian mission to the Gentiles (see Luke 4:25–27).

THE JEWISH LEADERS

We observed in Luke that the opposition to Jesus was divided into two groups, one whose most prominent members were Pharisees and the other headed by the chief priests. The same kind of arrangement seems to be the case with Matthew and Mark as well. As in Luke, scribes seem to be attached to both Pharisees (Matt 5:20; 12:38; 15:1; 23:2,13,15,23,25,27,29; Mark 2:16; 7:1,5) and chief priests (Matt 2:4; 20:18; 21:15; Mark 10:33; 11:18; 14:1; 15:31). Elders are predominantly grouped with chief priests (Matt 21:23; 26:3,47; 27:1,3,12,20), and frequently scribes, elders, and chief priests appear together (Matt 16:21; 26:57; 27:41; Mark 8:31; 11:27; 14:43,53; 15:1). For the most part these are the same kinds of arrangements that we saw in Luke; indeed, many of the pericopes in which these groups express their opposition are paralleled in all three gospels. Moreover, it should be noted that in all three gospels Pharisees and chief priests frequently appear without allies.

There are some significant differences, however. Both Matthew and Mark bring certain groups into the action in ways that differ from Luke's treatment of the opposition to Jesus. Whatever is meant by the references to Herodians, it is notable that Mark groups them with Pharisees on two occasions (Mark 3:6; 12:13) and that Matthew does so in 22:15–16, a parallel to Mark 12:13. Sadducees appear once in Luke's gospel (Luke 20:27; cf. Mark 12:18; Matt 22:23) and occasionally in Acts, but never in league with Pharisees. Matthew, however, frequently groups the two together (Matt 3:7; 16:1,6,11,12; see also 22:34). The first gospel also has Pharisees and chief priests together in two passages: in

Matt 21:45 the two groups perceive that the parable of the vintner (21:33–46) was directed against them; and in 27:62 they present to Pilate a plan to prevent the spread of a rumor about Jesus' resurrection. These observations suggest that Matthew does not view the Jewish leaders in the same way that Luke does. It is significant for Luke that Pharisees and chief priests form two distinct groups, but in Matthew the distinctions between them are blurred. In this connection Mark and Luke are closer together than are Matthew and Luke.

The distinction between the Pharisaic block and the chief priestly block is, in Luke, underlined by the geographical separation between them. In Luke's gospel Pharisees are not mentioned after Jesus comes into the Jerusalem temple. From that point on, Jesus' controversies are altogether with the priestly block of opponents. In Matthew, however, no such separation occurs. After Jesus' entry into Jerusalem in Matt 21:10, there is explicit Pharisaic opposition to him in 21:45 and 22:15; and there are controversies between Jesus and Pharisees in 22:34–40,41–46. The cooperation between Pharisees and chief priests in Matt 27:62 has already been mentioned. In contrast to Luke, Matthew identifies Jerusalem as the scene of Jesus' attacks on Pharisees (cf. Matt 23:13,15,23,25,26,27,29). After he narrates Jesus' entry into Jerusalem (11:11), Mark has Pharisees in opposition to Jesus in only one passage and that one in parallel with Matthew (Mark 12:13; cf. Matt 22:15). This suggests that Matthew and, to a lesser extent, Mark do not identify Pharisaic opposition to Jesus exclusively with territory outside Jerusalem.

On the other hand, both Matthew and Mark confine chief priests to Jerusalem. The only times they are mentioned prior to Jesus' entry into Jerusalem are in the passion predictions, which anticipate the opposition of chief priests in Jerusalem (Matt 16:21; 20:18; Mark 8:31; 10:33).[2] This is precisely the same situation that we observed in Luke.

The issues in controversy between Jesus and the Pharisees are nearly the same in all three gospels. Indeed, many of the same pericopes appear in substantially the same form in all three, or sometimes in two, of the gospels. In Luke 5:27–32; Mark 2:13–17; Matt 9:9–13 there is controversy over Jesus' practice of eating with tax collectors and sinners. In Luke 5:33–35 and its parallels (Mark

2:18–20; Matt 9:14–15) questions are asked about fasting. In Luke 6:1–5; Mark 2:23–28; Matt 12:1–8 there is controversy over preparing and eating grain on the sabbath. In Luke 6:6–11; Mark 3:1–6; Matt 12:9–14 Jesus' practice of healing on the sabbath is at issue.

Not all of the pericopes in Luke that treat interchanges between Jesus and the Pharisees have parallels in Matthew or Mark (see Luke 14:1–6; 17:20–21). Moreover, Matthew and Mark have some materials for which Luke has no counterpart or has only a fragmentary parallel. In these pericopes, however, the issues are fundamentally the same. For example, in Matt 15:1–20; Mark 7:1–23 the issue involves the washing of hands before meals, an issue not unlike those involving Pharisees in Luke (cf. Luke 11:37–41). Pharisees question Jesus about divorce in Matt 19:3; Mark 10:2, a passage for which Luke has no parallel. Although not represented in Luke, these pericopes do not seem to depart from the general thrust of Luke's passages in which the issues between Jesus and the Pharisees involve matters of Torah observance.

Although both Luke and Matthew record Jesus' attacks on Pharisees, Matthew has more of them, and the rhetorical device that he uses in chapter 23 amplifies the hostile tone. The frequent repetition of the phrase "Woe to you, scribes and Pharisees, hypocrites" (cf. Matt 23:13,15,23,25,27,29), gives a vivid picture of Jesus as leading a vigorous and aggressive attack on his opponents. Matthew also has a unique passage in 5:20, where Jesus says to his audience, "For I tell you, unless your righteousness exceeds that of the scribes and Pharisees, you will never enter the kingdom of heaven." There are also some places where either Matthew or Mark or both have Pharisees making charges against Jesus or challenging him. Luke either omits these words or puts them in the mouths of others. In Matt 9:34 Pharisees charge that Jesus "casts out demons by the prince of demons." In a similar verse, Matt 12:24, Pharisees charge that Jesus uses the power of Beelzebul to cast out demons. In the parallels Mark 3:22 says that it was scribes who made this accusation, and Luke 11:15 is indefinite. In Matt 12:38 Pharisees and scribes request a sign from Jesus, and in 16:1 Pharisees and Sadducees do the same. Mark 8:11, which mentions only Pharisees, is probably parallel to Matt 12:38, but Luke 11:16

is indefinite: "while others, to test him, sought from him a sign from heaven."

In contrast to Luke, Matthew and Mark once indicate that the Pharisees have a direct connection with the death of Jesus. All three gospels have the narrative about Jesus' healing of a man with a withered hand on the sabbath (Matt 12:9–14; Mark 3:1–6; Luke 6:6–11). All three report that Jesus' opponents watched him closely in order to find some evidence for an accusation against him. All three note the hostility of these opponents. And in Matt 12:14; Mark 3:6 the Pharisees begin to devise a way to kill (*apollumi*) Jesus.[3] But in the Lukan parallel (Luke 6:11) the objectives of the scribes and Pharisees are less definite: "they discussed with one another what they might do to Jesus." As we saw earlier, Luke 6:7,11 is the closest Luke gets to defining the intentions of the Pharisaic block in regard to Jesus; but, especially in comparison with the other synoptic gospels, those intentions remain vague in Luke, and they do not include execution.

Despite the similarity among the three gospels in the treatment of the Pharisees, there nevertheless appears to be a significant difference. The difference is to be seen mainly in several passages in Luke's gospel that have unique settings. On three occasions Jesus dines in the home of a Pharisee (Luke 7:36–50; 11:37–41; 14:1–24). Luke uses all three occasions to relate controversies between Jesus and Pharisees, some of which are also found in Matthew and Mark. But neither of the other gospels pictures Jesus as dining with a Pharisee. Moreover, Luke has a pericope in which Pharisees warn Jesus about Herod Antipas (Luke 13:31–33). Luke's inclusion of these settings and passages tends to soften his presentation of Pharisees as opponents of Jesus. Without them, as in Matthew and Mark, the reader finds the opposition between Pharisees and Jesus to be unrelieved. The only statement in the other synoptic gospels that appears to be favorable to the Pharisees is in Matt 23:2–3. Here the Matthean Jesus advises his listeners to do what the scribes and Pharisees require them to do, because "the scribes and the Pharisees sit on Moses' seat." In context, however, the positive aspect of the saying is diminished, since it serves as an introduction to the several sayings in which Jesus condemns Pharisees and scribes.

When we compare the controversies between Jesus and the priestly block of opponents, we find substantial similarity among the three synoptic gospels. The chief priests intend to kill Jesus but fear the people (Luke 19:47–48; Mark 11:18–19). They question Jesus about his authority but are unable to answer his counterquestion about John the Baptist (Luke 20:1–8; Mark 11:27–33; Matt 21:23–27). Their caution about the people is mentioned in Luke 20:6; Mark 11:32; Matt 21:26. After Jesus tells the parable of the vintner, the scribes and chief priests perceive that it was directed at them, but they are afraid of the people (Luke 20:19). Matt 21:45 is similar, but it is the chief priests and Pharisees who respond to the parable. In the Markan version the subject is indefinite (Mark 12:12), but the probable reference is to chief priests, scribes, and elders (see Mark 11:27). Once again, in 22:1–2, Luke states that the chief priests and scribes sought to kill Jesus but feared the people. In the parallel in Mark 14:1–2 the same groups intend to kill Jesus but agree that it should not be done during Passover. Matt 26:1–5 is similar to Mark, except that the opponents are the chief priests and elders. All three gospels indicate that the chief priests were behind the arrest of Jesus (Matt 26:47; Mark 14:43; Luke 22:52), but only Luke indicates that they were actually present at the scene. All three agree in including the hearing before the Sanhedrin and in including the chief priests among those present (Matt 27:1; Mark 15:1; Luke 22:66). Finally, they agree in showing that the chief priests were among those who brought charges against Jesus in the trial before Pilate (Matt 27:12; Mark 15:3; Luke 23:1–2) and led the crowd to insist on his execution (Matt 27:20; Mark 15:11; Luke 23:18, cf. 23:13).

This comparison of the evangelists' treatment of the Jewish leaders has shown that there is substantial similarity among them. In all three gospels the Pharisees and chief priests form two blocks of opponents, and in all three gospels the chief priests are more closely connected with the death of Jesus than are the Pharisees. The issues around which controversy occurs are fundamentally the same in the three gospels. The issues that involve the Pharisees relate largely to Torah observance, while the issues that involve the chief priests relate to Jesus' authority.

There are, however, significant elements that point to a distinctive approach on Luke's part. Luke and Mark are more sensitive than Matthew to the distinct roles of Pharisees and chief priests and to the separation of Pharisees from Jerusalem. Luke has a more ambivalent attitude toward the Pharisees than either of the other two. He has passages that show them acting in less hostile ways, and he includes no passages that might tend to make the reader connect them with the death of Jesus. In this connection we should be reminded of the positive attitude toward the Pharisees that is exhibited in Acts.

In regard to the chief priests, Luke agrees with Matthew and Mark that their opposition was grounded in their refusal to accept Jesus' authority. But Luke seems more consistent than Matthew or Mark in associating Jesus' authority with the temple.

JERUSALEM AND THE TEMPLE

Our holistic approach to Luke–Acts has shown that the evangelist had an ambivalent attitude toward Jerusalem and the temple. On the one side, he identified the city as the place of the apostles and associated the temple with religious piety and peace. On the other side, the city was identified with the death of Jesus and was doomed to destruction, and the temple was a source of conflict.

No such ambivalent attitude is to be found in Matthew or Mark, because the more positive images of the city and the temple are missing in these gospels. Neither gospel has the pietistic tone that pervades the opening chapters of Luke, and neither gospel locates postresurrection appearances of Jesus in Jerusalem. Of course, neither gospel has anything like the opening chapters of Acts. Thus, in contrast to the ambivalent attitude toward the temple and the city in Luke–Acts, only a negative attitude is to be found in Matthew and Mark.

Negative images of Jerusalem and the temple abound in Matthew and Mark. Indeed, many of Luke's pericopes that contain these negative images have parallels in Matthew or Mark or both. Jesus' lament over Jerusalem in Luke 13:34–35 is almost identical to the saying in Matt 23:37–39. The passion prediction in Luke

18:31–34, including the reference to Jerusalem as the scene of Jesus' death, is paralleled in Matt 20:17–19 and Mark 10:32–34. Jesus' saying about the destruction of the temple in Luke 21:6 is also found in Matt 24:2 and Mark 13:2.

Although all three gospels contain apocalyptic words of Jesus about the destruction of the city of Jerusalem, there are significant verbal differences that set Luke apart from the other two. Luke 21:20–24 is a more detailed statement about the circumstances of the destruction than those in Matt 24:15–22 and Mark 13:14–20. Indeed, the greater detail in Luke's prediction is frequently cited as evidence for the later date of the third gospel. The Lukan Jesus speaks of Jerusalem surrounded by foot soldiers, the evacuation of the city, the captivity and dispersion of its citizens, and the domination of the fallen city by Gentiles, "until the times of the Gentiles are fulfilled" (Luke 21:24). It is also notable that neither Matthew nor Mark explicitly mentions the destruction of the city of Jerusalem. These two accounts, which exhibit a high degree of verbal similarity, focus attention on the "abomination of desolation" (Matt 24:15; Mark 13:14) as constituting a signal for the flight of the inhabitants of Judea to the mountains. Although Luke has nothing about the abomination of desolation, he includes the oracle about the flight to the mountains (Luke 21:21). Only in this gospel, however, does Jesus explicitly predict and describe the destruction of Jerusalem and the exile of its citizens.

The differences between Luke's account of Jesus' arrival in Jerusalem and the accounts in Matthew and Mark were noted in chapter 4. The major distinction is that Luke never explicitly states that Jesus entered Jerusalem, although he pictures him as teaching in the temple. In reading Luke's account at this point, we gained the impression that, as Conzelmann observed, Luke thinks of Jerusalem and the temple as different places.[4] This conception seems due to Luke's literary or theological interests rather than to any lack of topographical information. Matthew and Mark, on the other hand, demonstrate no hesitancy about having Jesus enter the city. Despite the significant differences between Matthew and Mark in their description of Jesus' triumphal entry, differences which need not deter us here, both gospels clearly state that Jesus entered Jerusalem (Matt 21:10; Mark 11:11).

Some of the passages that exhibit a negative image of Jerusalem are unique to Luke. These include Luke 9:31, the statement that Jesus will have his *exodos* in Jerusalem, and several statements in the section on Jesus in transit, notes that remind the reader that Jesus is headed for the city (Luke 9:51,53; 13:22; 17:11; 19:11). In addition, Luke 13:33, "for it cannot be that a prophet should perish away from Jerusalem," is unique to the third gospel. The same goes for the poignant saying about the city in 19:41–44.

Although it is loosely structured, Luke's central section is a narrative of Jesus' trip to Jerusalem. In reading through it we are frequently reminded of the fate that awaits him in the city. Matthew and Mark have one or two notes about Jesus' trip to Jerusalem (Mark 10:17,32; Matt 20:17), but neither has a travel narrative that compares with Luke's.

The most significant aspect of the literary function of the temple in the synoptic gospels is to be found in the fact that all three include a long section of Jesus' teaching in the temple (Matt 21:23–24:1; Mark 11:27–13:1; Luke 20:1–21:38). The agreement between Luke and the other two gospels is not, however, as extensive as it appears at first sight. For one thing, Luke's section of temple teaching is substantially longer than is the comparable section in either of the other two gospels, since only Luke locates the apocalyptic discourse of Jesus in the temple. At Matt 24:1; Mark 13:1 Jesus leaves the temple and goes to the Mount of Olives (cf. Matt 24:3; Mark 13:3), where he delivers the apocalyptic discourse (Matt 24:3–44; Mark 13:3–37). Thus the significant parallel between Matthew, Mark, and Luke at this point is confined to Matt 21:23–23:39; Mark 11:27–12:44; Luke 20:1–21:4. Although Luke 21:5–38 has parallels with Matthew 24 and Mark 13, the shift in location from the temple constitutes an important area of difference. Moreover, it is notable that while in Luke the temple teaching immediately follows the cleansing of the temple, in Matthew and Mark there are intervening pericopes that, in Matthew, include Jesus' healings in the temple (Matt 21:14–16, a pericope unique to Matthew) and, in both Matthew and Mark, the story of the cursing of the fig tree (Matt 21:18–22; Mark 11:20–24).[5] In the remaining material (Luke 20:1–21:4; Mark 11:27–12:44) Luke and Mark are substantially parallel. Mark has all the material that Luke has here and in almost exactly the same order. The only difference is that Mark has an additional pericope, the question about the great commandment (Mark 12:28–31), which Luke locates at 10:25–28. Aside from this one divergence, Luke and Mark have exactly the same pericopes in exactly the same order and with substantial verbal agreements between them. The table that follows, which treats Mark as the base, shows the similarities between the two gospels.[6]

TABLE I

	Mark	Luke	Verbal Agreements
The Question about Authority	11:27–33	20:1–8	66%
The Parable of the Vintner	12:1–12	20:9–19	54%
The Question about Taxes	12:13–17	20:20–26	53%
The Question about Resurrection	12:18–27	20:27–38	63%
The Great Commandment	12:28–31	10:25–28	41%
The Scribe's Response[7]	12:32–34	20:39–40	13%
David's Son	12:35–37	20:41–44	66%
"Beware of the Scribes"	12:38–40	20:45–47	85%
The Widow's Coin	12:41–44	21:1–4	51%

By contrast, Matthew and Luke have substantially less agreement at this point. In the section that tells of Jesus' temple teaching, Matthew has a great deal of material that Luke includes elsewhere, particularly the condemnations of the Pharisees and scribes in Matthew 23. Table II shows where Matthew and Luke agree and disagree. Matthew is treated as the base in this table.[8]

TABLE II

	Matthew	Luke	Verbal Agreements
The Question about Authority	21:23–27	20:1–8	68%
The Parable of the Two Sons[9]	21:28–32		
The Parable of the Vintner	21:33–46	20:9–19	39%
The Great Supper	22:1–14	14:15–24	12%
The Question about Taxes	22:15–22	20:20–26	42%
The Question about Resurrection	22:23–33	20:27–38	53%
The Great Commandment	22:34–40	10:25–28	45%
The Scribe's Response		20:39–40	
David's Son	22:41–46	20:41–44	46%

TABLE II (continued)

	Matthew	Luke	Verbal Agreements
Against Pharisees: Pretensions	23:1–12		
"Beware of the Scribes"[10]		20:45–47	
Against Pharisees: Exclusion	23:13	11:52	28%
Against Pharisees: Proselytism	23:15		
On Oaths	23:16–22		
Against Pharisees: Tithing	23:23–24	11:42	51%
Against Pharisees: Cleanliness	23:25–26	11:37–41	38%
Whitewashed Tombs	23:27–28	11:44	8%
Murdering the Prophets	23:29–36	11:47–51	28%
Jesus' Lament over Jerusalem	23:37–39	13:34–35	92%

These data have not been cited in order to clarify the literary relationships among the synoptic gospels, but in order to get a grasp on the question of Luke's distinctiveness. In the attempt to understand Luke's treatment of Jerusalem and the temple, it seemed important that he had devoted significant attention to Jesus' teaching in the temple and his confrontation with the chief priests over the question of authority. The question now is: Given the fact that all three gospels have a section in which Jesus teaches in the temple, how distinctive is Luke's version?

The similarity between Mark and Luke at this point clearly casts doubt on any distinctiveness that might have been attributed to Luke. Table I indicates that in the section from Luke 20:1 through 21:4 all eight of the pericopes that make up this section are also found in Mark, in the same order, and with a high degree of verbal agreement. The pericopes which raise the question of authority in acute ways, Luke 20:1–8,9–19, are among those found in both gospels. The most significant difference is that Luke locates the apocalyptic discourse in the temple, while Mark has it on the Mount of Olives.

The comparison between Luke and Matthew in Table II shows a very different picture. In the section between Luke 20:1 and 21:4 five of Luke's eight pericopes are also found in Matthew (the question about authority, the parable of the vintner, the question about taxes, the question about resurrection, and David's son). The five pericopes are in the same relative order, but with intervening material in Matthew. The verbal agreement between Luke and Matthew in the parallel material is impressive, but not so high as the agreement between Luke and Mark. Moreover, Matthew's inclusion of Jesus' attacks on the Pharisees in chapter 23 gives to his temple section a very different character from that found in Luke or Mark. Although Matthew contains the pericopes that raise the question of Jesus' authority in acute ways (Matt 21:23–27, the question about authority; and 21:33–46, the parable of the vintner), his temple section as a whole fundamentally differs from Luke's. Matthew does not consistently present Jesus in opposition to the chief priests or the temple as a battleground or object of conflict.

In comparing the synoptic gospels in regard to their treatment of the chief priests, we observed that the three agreed that the issues in controversy between the chief priests and Jesus related to the question of Jesus' authority. In comparing them on the literary function of the temple, however, it appears that there is a significant distinction. Luke seems more consistent than Matthew or Mark in associating Jesus' authority with the temple. The difference can be seen in a comparative study of the three versions of that highly significant pericope, the parable of the vintner (Matt 21:33–46; Mark 12:1–12; Luke 20:9–19). Matthew's version of the parable is similar to Luke's. In both, the owner of the vineyard has been unable to collect his rents from the tenants. But in Matthew the parable is directed against the Pharisees and the chief priests (Matt 21:45–46). By implication they are identified as the wicked tenants. In Luke it is the chief priests and scribes who seem to play the role of the tenants (Luke 20:19). This change constitutes a major difference. If the tenants are chief priests and their allies, then it would seem appropriate to identify the vineyard as the temple. If, however, the tenants are both chief priests and Pharisees, the temple is a less appropriate interpretation of the vineyard, since Matthew does not connect the two groups equally with the temple. The vineyard in Matthew must be the nation Israel, and Matthew must think of the Pharisees and chief priests as the appointed guardians of the nation, who have acted irresponsibly. Mark's version of the parable may be closer to Luke's. Although in his version those who respond to the parable are indefinite (Mark 12:12), we are probably to understand them to be chief priests, scribes, and elders, the last groups previously mentioned (Mark 11:27). In this respect Mark and Luke both seem to emphasize the temple as a place of dispute, while Matthew diffuses the point.

One unique verse in Luke tends to add emphasis to his treatment of the Jewish temple. This is 23:5, where the chief priests and their supporters charge that Jesus has taught not only in Galilee and Judea, but also in this place, i.e. the temple. It is not simply that this verse appears in Luke and not in the other gospels. It is that its appearance in Luke at this particular point tends to tie together a number of indications about issues that relate to the temple. We need only recall Jesus' teaching in the temple and the various scenes in the early chapters of Acts that were set in the temple and that pictured it as the location as well as the source of conflict between the apostles and the chief priests.

It appears necessary to conclude that although there are significant parallels between Luke and the other two synoptic gospels, Luke's distinctiveness is demonstrated in his ambivalent attitude toward Jerusalem and the temple and in his treatment of the temple as a place of conflict involving Jesus and a source of conflict over the question of Jesus' authority. Indeed, it is only Luke who alludes to the temple as constituting an issue related to the death of Jesus.

THE TRIAL OF JESUS

The most distinctive aspects of the Lukan approach to Jesus' death are to be found in the sections that deal with the trial. The differences between Luke's version of the trial of Jesus and those in the other synoptic gospels have frequently been observed. Indeed, many scholars who subscribe to the view that Luke used Mark are convinced that the third evangelist also had access to an account of the trial that was independent of Mark. In 1920 Alfred M. Perry argued that Luke's entire passion narrative (19:1–24:53) was based on a non-Markan source.[11] Sir John Hawkins had earlier shown that Luke's verbal resemblances to Mark were of a very low degree in the passion narrative and in two previous sections, 6:20–8:3 and 9:51–18:14.[12] B. H. Streeter took up Hawkins' calculations and came to the conclusion that Luke had access to a non-Markan source composed of Q and L.[13] Streeter referred to this document as proto-Luke, and he believed that Luke treated it as the basis of his gospel and interpolated Markan material at points that seemed appropriate to him. The proto-Luke theory was also accepted by Vincent Taylor and other scholars.[14] Some scholars who do not accept the theory of a non-Markan document such as Streeter described nevertheless find grounds for believing that Luke had independent access to a source for the trial of Jesus.[15]

Matthew (26:47–27:31) and Mark (14:43–15:20) are nearly identical in their reports of the various elements in the trial sequence. Matthew has only three narratives that are not in Mark: the death of Judas (27:3–10), the warning of Pilate's wife (27:19), and Pilate's washing of his hands (27:24–25).[16] Mark has one unique pericope about the flight of the naked young man (14:51–52). Luke, however, departs from both of the other synoptic gospels at several points and includes quite a bit of unique material. Table III demonstrates this point.

TABLE III

	Matthew	Mark	Luke
The Arrest of Jesus	26:47–56	14:43–50	22:47–53
The Naked Young Man		14:51–52	
The High Priest's House	26:57–58	14:53–54	22:54–55
The Sanhedrin Session	26:59–66	14:55–64	22:66–71
The Mockery of Jesus	26:67–68	14:65	22:63–65
Peter's Denial	26:69–75	14:66–72	22:56–62
Jesus Delivered to Pilate	27:1–2	15:1	23:1
The Death of Judas	27:3–10		
The Session Before Pilate	27:11–14	15:2–5	23:2–5
The Session Before Herod			23:6–12
The Second Session Before Pilate			23:13–16
The Passsover Amnesty	27:15–23	15:6–14	23:18–23
Jesus Sentenced to Die	27:24–26	15:15	23:24–25
Soldiers Mock Jesus	27:27–31	15:16–20	

Table III shows that Matthew and Mark are in substantial agreement in respect to the order of the various pericopes and hence the course of events at Jesus' trial. It also shows that Luke varies from the other two at significant points. First, he connects the mockery of Jesus with the events at the high priest's house on the evening of Jesus' arrest, whereas Matthew and Mark make it a part of the Sanhedrin session. Second, Luke sets the story of Peter's denial on the

evening of the arrest, while Matthew and Mark put it after the Sanhedrin session. Third, Luke has two sessions before Pilate, while
the others have one. Fourth, Luke alone has a session before Herod.
Fifth, Luke has no account of Roman soldiers mocking Jesus.

The differences in the arrangement of material and the inclusion
or exclusion of the various incidents tell only part of the story. Even
in the sections where Luke may be regarded as having material that
is parallel to Matthew and Mark, there are significant differences.
We shall examine the most important of these.

*The Sanhedrin Session (Matt 26:59–66; Mark 14:55–64; Luke
22:66–71).* Luke's account has both formal and verbal similarities
with the parallels in Matthew and Mark. In all three gospels Jesus is
asked if he is the Christ; in all three he refers to the Son of man seated
at the right hand of power; and in all three there is the rhetorical
question that ends the session, "What further testimony do we
need?" But there the resemblance ends. In Luke the Sanhedrin session takes place on the morning after the arrest, while in Matthew
and Mark it is on the night of the arrest. Matthew and Mark report
an attempt to secure false witnesses against Jesus, but Luke does
not. In Matthew and Mark there is testimony that Jesus threatened
to destroy and rebuild the temple, but not in Luke.[17] In Matthew
and Mark the high priest is portrayed as the prosecutor and presiding judge, but in Luke no definite role is assigned to him. In Matthew and Mark, Jesus refers to the Son of man coming on the
clouds, but not in Luke. Luke is also different from the other two in
not mentioning the detail about the high priest tearing his clothing
and in omitting any mention of blasphemy or a death penalty. In
Luke the high priest does not ask the other members for their verdicts, as he does in Matthew and Mark.

In comparison with the narratives about the Sanhedrin session in
Matthew and Mark, Luke's seems to deemphasize the legal aspects.
The absence of witnesses, charges, and convictions turns the ses-
sion into something other than a judicial proceeding. While it is
plausible to talk about two trials in Matthew and Mark, the first
Jewish and the second Roman, it is technically incorrect to speak of
Luke's narrative in this way. The session before the Sanhedrin in
Luke is a hearing in which the Jewish leaders officially reject Jesus

and then agree to deliver him to Pilate. In Matthew and Mark it is a trial in which Jesus is convicted of blasphemy.

The Session Before Pilate (Matt 27:11–14; Mark 15:2–5, Luke 23:2–5). Again, there are formal and verbal similarities among all three of the synoptic gospels. Pilate asks Jesus if he is king of the Jews, and Jesus answers, "You say" (*su legeis,* Matt 27:11; Mark 15:2; Luke 23:3). But Luke's account differs from the other two in including the statement of charges in 23:2,5 and Pilate's first declaration of Jesus' innocence in 23:4.

The importance of Luke's unique material cannot be overstressed. In comparison with the narratives in Matthew and Mark, Luke's appears to be a carefully crafted account which largely gives expression to the concepts that Jesus was wrongfully charged with certain political crimes and that the Roman judge who presided in his case declared him innocent.

The Passover Amnesty (Matt 27:15–23; Mark 15:6–14; Luke 23:18–23). Despite the phrase we are using here, Luke actually does not mention a Passover amnesty. Both Matthew and Mark describe the usual practice, and Mark explains that Barabbas was imprisoned for murder and insurrection. (Matthew also inserts here the about Pilate's wife's dream, 27:19). Under the influence of the chief priests the crowd calls for the release of Barabbas and the crucifixion of Jesus. In Luke the incident involving Barabbas is told without any explanation of a Passover amnesty. In all three gospels, however, it is the insistent demands of the chief priests and the crowd that prevail over Pilate's declarations of innocence. All three have a statement about Pilate's capitulation. Matt 27:26 and Mark 15:15 record that he released Barabbas, punished Jesus, and delivered him up to crucifixion. Mark adds that he did this to please the crowd. Luke 23:24–25 reads more like a judicial verdict. Pilate gave sentence (*epekrinen*) to release "the man who had been thrown into prison for insurrection and murder, whom they asked for; but Jesus he delivered up to their will."

At this point it should be observed that Luke is far more intent on showing that Pilate declared Jesus innocent than are the other synoptic evangelists. In Matthew the Roman governor does not explicitly make a declaration but rather washes his hands in order to symbolize his own innocence (27:24). He responds to the advice sent to him from his wife to "have nothing to do with that righteous man" (27:19), but he does not in fact declare him innocent. Pilate comes closer to making such a declaration in Mark 15:14, where he asks Jesus' accusers, "Why, what evil has he done?" In Luke, however, the Roman governor quite clearly declares Jesus innocent and does so not once, but three times (23:4,15,22). In addition, Luke notes that Herod also declared Jesus innocent (23:15), as did the Roman centurion (23:47; cf. Matt 27:54; Mark 15:39).

Moreover, the motif of the innocence of Jesus comes through clearly in the pericopes that Luke employs to show the falsity of the charges that he records in 23:2. All the evangelists were surely convinced of the innocence of Jesus, but Luke converts that conviction into a literary theme that dominates his narrative of the trial.

Despite the many details on which Luke differs from Matthew and Mark, there are some fundamental areas on which all the evangelists agree. Luke's emphasis on the opposition of the chief priests and the changed attitude of the crowd is paralleled in the other gospels. Matthew and Mark share Luke's concern to show that the legal procedures used in Jesus' case were irregular. The synoptic gospels are unanimous in stressing the guilt of the Jewish leaders in putting Jesus to death.

From a literary perspective, however, Luke's presentation of the trial of Jesus is distinctive. Although we may point to certain parallel pericopes and to similar concepts that appear to lie behind the work of all three evangelists, the ways in which Luke orders the trial are not the same as the ways used in the other two gospels. He includes incidents that the others do not have, such as the hearing before Herod and the record of charges. He totally transforms the Sanhedrin session, so that it cannot be conceived along judicial lines. He arranges his materials so as to have four components to Jesus' trial, as he also does with Paul's trial in Acts.

Ironically, the comparison of Luke's trial narrative with the others suggests something about Luke that was not noticed when we examined his account separately. In both of the other synoptic gospels the Sanhedrin session is presented as a judicial hearing, even a trial. Witnesses are present, charges are made, testimony is given, interrogation is pursued, and a final conviction is recorded. In Luke, however, there is none of this kind of judicial formality. The result of this change is to focus attention on the Roman trial as the one that counts legally. It is here that charges are made and verdicts are given. One might therefore be tempted to conclude that Luke had a greater tendency to blame the Romans for the death of Jesus than did the other evangelists. That is not the case, however, for Luke makes it clear that it was only under the constant pressure of the chief priests and the crowd that Pilate capitulated. Luke's emphasis on Pilate's declarations of innocence is not to be discounted.

In this connection it should be observed that Luke has in fact tied his narrative together in a more convincing way than has Matthew or Mark. In both of the other synoptic gospels the Sanhedrin convicted Jesus of blasphemy and then went before Pilate, where the assumed charge was that he claimed to be king of the Jews (Matt 27:11; Mark 15:2). Neither author sought to explain the connection between these charges. With Luke, however, since there is no mention of blasphemy, this particular problem evaporates. But Luke also connects the hearing before the Sanhedrin with the trial before Pilate by recording the charge that Jesus' teaching has come to the temple (23:5). This charge reminds the reader that, in the parable of the vintner, Jesus had claimed authority over the temple because of his status as Son of God (Luke 20:9–19) and that the chief priests had rejected this claim during the hearing (Luke 22:70–71). The reader of Luke knows that Jesus died because the chief priests rejected him and falsely charged him with political crimes.

A comparison of Luke with Matthew and Mark may suggest that Luke presents a trial narrative that is not quite so harsh on the Jews as are the others. The basis for this judgment lies in the fact that Luke omits any formal trial before a Jewish body. Our study shows, however, that this judgment will not hold up. The most that can be said is that the Jews did not have a legal responsibility for Jesus' death, according to Luke. But the moral responsibility of the chief priests and their allies is in no way mitigated by Luke. To be sure, he does not have those brutal words that Matthew records in 27:25, "And all the people answered, 'His blood be on us and on our children!' " Luke does not finally indicate that the blame for Jesus' death should rest on the people, and certainly not on their descendants. But he does blame the leaders—i.e., the chief priests and their allies—and he does his best to exonerate Pilate and Herod, as he does in the case of all those in positions of secular political power.

CONCLUSION

If we are able to talk about the distinctiveness of Luke's literary composition so far as the death of Jesus is concerned, it will be necessary to distill from that composition certain concepts that appear to have guided the author. Although some of the concepts may have guided Matthew or Mark or both at some points, the combination of them describes Luke alone. Since the concepts have been discussed with reasonable fullness in this and the preceding chapters, a brief list should now suffice.

(1) The theme of initial acceptance and final rejection, found in fragmentary form in Matthew and Mark, is a prominent aspect of Luke–Acts.

(2) The distinction between Pharisaic opposition and the opposition of chief priests is more sharply made in Luke and Mark than in Matthew, and Luke has an ambivalent attitude toward Pharisees that is not shared by the other evangelists.

(3) The identification of the chief priests as the Jewish leaders who opposed Jesus to the death is found in all three synoptic gospels; in Luke it is only the chief priests and their allies who are finally responsible for Jesus' death.

(4) All three gospels display a negative attitude toward Jerusalem and the temple, but only Luke balances the negative with more positive images.

(5) The concept that Jesus was opposed by the chief priests because he claimed to have authority in the temple is more clearly represented in Luke than in the other synoptic gospels.

(6) Luke has a distinctive approach to the trial of Jesus, one that emphasizes his innocence of political charges, his rejection by the Jewish leaders and the crowd, and the declarations of innocence by the political authorities.

NOTES

1. Note, however, the textual variants to Mark 6:3.

2. Matt 2:4 is technically an exception. Here chief priests and scribes are questioned by Herod the Great about the birthplace of the Messiah. The inquiry takes place in Jerusalem, but it is only indirectly related to the opposition of the chief priests to Jesus.

3. In Mark 3:6 Herodians and Pharisees are included in the plot.

4. Hans Conzelmann, *The Theology of St. Luke,* trans. Geoffrey Buswell (New York: Harper and Bros., 1960), p. 75.

5. Matthew tells the story of the cursing of the fig tree as a continuous narrative (21:18–22). Mark, however, splits the narrative so that the actual cursing occurs before the cleansing of the temple (11:12–14) and the discovery of the withered tree comes after the cleansing (11:20–24). Luke has no parallel to the cursing of the tree, although he has the parable of the barren fig tree in 13:6–9.

6. In Tables I and II the percentages of verbal agreement are based on calculations in Joseph B. Tyson and Thomas R. W. Longstaff, *Synoptic Abstract,* The Computer Bible, Vol. 15 (Wooster, Ohio: Biblical Research Associates, 1978). The figures here include agreements of continuity, identity, and equivalency, as defined in *Synoptic Abstract.* Since Mark is used as the base gospel in Table I, the verbal agreements are based on the Markan text; that is, the percentage of verbal agreements is a function of the number of words in Mark that agree with words in Luke, compared with the total number of words in Mark. In the pericope on the question of authority, for example, 66 percent of the words in Mark 11:27–33 agree with words in Luke 20:1–8, either in terms of continuity, identity, or equivalency. The percentages are roughly the same in parallel pericopes of approximately the same number of words. If we were to use Luke as the base gospel for the pericope on the question of authority, the percentage of verbal agreement would be 70 percent, since Luke has slightly fewer words in this pericope (118) than does Mark (125). Greater variances appear in parallel pericopes of different lengths. For example, in the pericope on the scribe's response (Mark 12:32–34; Luke 20:39–40) Mark has 75 words, and Luke has only 15. Thus, the percentage of agreement using Mark as the base is about 13 percent (10/75), and that using Luke as the base is about 67 percent (10/15). Because of these variances it is important to specify the gospel that is being used as the base for all such comparisons.

7. The pericope on the scribe's response is only a verbal parallel in Mark and Luke, since the contexts in the two gospels are not the same. In Mark the response forms an integral part of the saying on the great commandment (12:28–31), while in Luke it is the conclusion to the pericope on the resurrection (20:27–38). But the verbal parallels are impressive, especially from Luke's side. Furthermore, it is interesting that in the Lukan pericope the question about the resurrection is asked by Sadducees (20:27) and the response to Jesus' answer is given by scribes (20:39). Note also that one scribe is involved in Mark, while in Luke the response comes from "some of the scribes."

8. See note 6 above.

9. Luke 7:29–30 has some slight verbal similarities with Matt 21:32, but the parable itself does not appear in Luke.

10. Note, however, the significant parallel between Matt 23:6–7 and Luke 20:46.

11. Alfred M. Perry, *The Sources of Luke's Passion-Narrative* (Chicago: University of Chicago Press, 1920).

12. John C. Hawkins, "Three Limitations to St. Luke's Use of St. Mark," in *Studies in the Synoptic Problem,* ed. William Sanday (Oxford: Clarendon Press, 1911), pp. 29–94.

13. B. H. Streeter, *The Four Gospels* (London: Macmillan and Co., 1924), pp. 199–222. The symbol Q is used to designate the source for material that is found in Matthew and Luke but not Mark. The letter L is used to designate material found only in Luke. Thus, proto-Luke is thought of as consisting of these two strands of non-Markan material.

14. E.g., Vincent Taylor, *Behind the Third Gospel* (Oxford: Clarendon Press, 1926); *The Passion Narrative of St. Luke,* ed. O. E. Evans (Cambridge: Cambridge University Press, 1972).

15. E.g., C. H. Dodd, *History and the Gospel* (New York: Charles Scribner's Sons, 1938), p. 80, n. 1; Paul Winter, *On the Trial of Jesus* (Berlin: Walter de Gruyter, 1961), pp. 20–30; David R. Catchpole, *The Trial of Jesus* (Leiden: E. J. Brill, 1971), pp. 153–220; Gerard S. Sloyan, *Jesus on Trial* (Philadelphia: Fortress Press, 1973), pp. 89–109.

16. Neither Mark nor Luke has a parallel to any of these pericopes.

17. A charge that Jesus threatened to destroy the temple is reflected in Acts 6:14.

CONCLUSION

Our concern in this book has been to investigate the ways in which Jesus' death was portrayed in Luke–Acts. The investigation has focused attention on the opponents of the Lukan Jesus and the circumstances that led to his death. It remains now to summarize the results of our study, to raise some questions about the consistency of Luke's approach, and to suggest some implications about the author and his community.

Throughout our study it has been a central contention that it is possible to achieve a valid understanding of Luke's literary work and his perspective on the death of Jesus by using a holistic approach to his writing. This means that comparisons with related gospels are at best secondary. The fact that there are parallels between Luke and the other gospels is important for source criticism and probably for historical studies. But the particular literary themes, patterns, and characterizations that we have found to be a part of Luke–Acts are no less important because they may have parallels in the other gospels. The existence of parallels means that Luke made use of source material and at some points was affected by the themes and characterizations that he found in that material. But once he made use of material from some other source, that material played its role in Luke's overall composition. Although this author's perspective may at points have been affected by material he took over from his sources, it is nevertheless his own perspective that comes through in the final shaping of the book.

Our study has shown that Luke was aware of the ways of writing narrative and made use of major literary techniques. He used the theme of conflict throughout his narrative and governed his entire writing by the use of certain overarching literary patterns. One of his favorite devices was the motif of transposition. Although he did not produce a traditional Greek tragedy, he nevertheless made use of certain elements drawn from this genre.

He clearly had a keen interest in the death of Jesus. His interest did not exclude the theological dimension but was not limited to it. Indeed, he seems to be deeply concerned to tell the reader about the circumstances that led to Jesus' death and to identify the opponents and the issues. For him the opponents were certain groups of Jewish leaders—most importantly, the Pharisees and the chief priests. We have seen that although Luke does not shy away from narrating incidents in which Jesus is in conflict with Pharisees, he avoids any implication that this conflict was related to Jesus' death. The Lukan Jesus confronts Pharisees on a number of Torah-related issues, and he attacks them for some aspects of their life styles. Apparently Luke wants the reader to be well informed about the differences between the teachings of Jesus and those of the Pharisees. But he also lets it be known that on fundamental points, especially the belief in resurrection, Pharisees and Christian believers stand shoulder to shoulder. There are no lasting conflicts between the two groups. Indeed, the Lukan Paul is the prime example of one who is both a Pharisee and a Christian believer.

The situation with the chief priests, however, is totally different. Their hostility toward Jesus is unrelieved, and it is they who orchestrate his execution. The issues between Jesus and the priestly block of opponents are related to the temple, and they involve the priestly rejection of Jesus as Lord of the temple. Correlatively, the issues also involve opposition to Jesus' successors and their attempts to teach in the temple.

The place of the Jewish public is complex, but in the final analysis it is to be located with Jesus' most hostile opponents. The people join the chief priests in presenting charges against him and demanding his crucifixion. They insist that Paul should not be allowed to live. The issues at this point are only allusively treated in Luke–Acts, but they seem to involve the Christian mission to the Gentiles.

Luke apparently wants the reader to understand that the break between the Christian believers and the Jews was the result of Jewish
rejection, not of Christian exclusivism. It is more difficult to tell
why, according to Luke, the Jews rejected the message of Jesus and
the apostles, but the reasons seem to have something to do with
problems that accompanied efforts to achieve community between
Jews and Gentiles. Although the gospel of Luke offers little help
here, Acts gives the impression that such matters as dietary regulations and circumcision were paramount issues.

In telling the story of the trial of Jesus, Luke emphasizes the legal
innocence of Jesus. Not only does he take special pains to show that
Jesus did not do what the chief priests claimed that he did, but he
also goes to great lengths to show that the legally constituted judges
repeatedly declared him innocent. In order to bring this off, Luke
was obliged to alter his characterization of both Herod and Pilate.
But as a result he succeeded in writing a trial narrative that consistently lays the blame on the chief priests, their allies, and the crowd
for the death of Jesus and suggests that temple-related issues were
behind the charges that were presented to Pilate. As he does
throughout Acts, Luke presents Roman authorities as judicious
and sympathetic.

Luke's portrayal of the circumstances surrounding the death of
Jesus is dominated by the conviction that it was a matter of divine
necessity. This conception, together with the clearly elevated role
of the hero, brings Luke into line with the tradition of Greek tragedy. The Lukan Jesus affirms that his passion is necessary, and he
goes to Jerusalem in order to fulfill the scriptures about himself.
After the resurrection he reminds his disciples that it was necessary
to fulfill the scriptures, and the apostles likewise proclaim this necessity. The conviction of divine necessity constitutes Luke's main
contribution to the theological discussion of Jesus' death. But he
seems uninterested in piercing through to an understanding of the
theological reason for the death or in analyzing what it was intended
to accomplish.[1] The benefits of forgiveness of sins and the Spirit are
more closely connected with the resurrection than the death. The
parallels between the career of Jesus and that of Paul indicate that
Jesus' successors may expect the same fate as the master. They have
been called to be witnesses to the death and resurrection of Jesus,

which means not only that they proclaim it but that they also imitate it in becoming Christian martyrs.

Although it is possible to point to a single dominating conception that lies back of Luke's narrative, it still is necessary to ask if his treatment of the death of Jesus has internal consistency. At one level it seems necessary to answer this question in the negative. There are, after all, certain reversals in roles and changes of characterization. The Jewish public does not consistently play the same role throughout the narrative, but rather fulfills a literary pattern of initial acceptance and final rejection. The portrayal of Herod and Pilate includes a rather drastic change in character. Moreover, the first opponents the reader confronts turn out not to be the ones who finally bring about the death of the hero. The issues they raise do not seem to be relevant to the death of Jesus, and they are not alluded to in the trial narratives. Finally, the ambivalent treatment of Jerusalem and the temple would seem to exhibit a lack of consistency.

But there is a fundamental consistency in the ways in which Luke has focused attention on the chief priests as the ones who engineered the death of Jesus and in his depiction of the temple as the source of conflict between them and him. As a result, Luke's trial narrative has fewer internal problems than do those in the other synoptic gospels. There is something plausible about a narrative in which the hero attempts to take control of a religious institution and comes up against the powerful protectors of that institution. No one would claim that Luke is simplistically consistent, but that only makes his narrative more intriguing.

It is tempting at this point to subject Luke's treatment of the death of Jesus to a historical analysis. Is Luke drawing, in part at least, on a tradition that has historical plausibility? More directly, is it a historical "fact" that Jesus died, not because the Romans suspected him of treason, but because the powerful Jewish priests opposed him, rejected him, and demanded his execution? Is it the case that Jesus' attempt to take over the temple was behind the crucifixion? It is not possible to answer these questions with certainty, and any attempt to do so would require the use of critical methods that are quite different from those used here. On the other hand, our study of Luke–Acts has shown that there was a person who at one time was convinced about the way things had been.

To determine why Luke believed as he did is probably an impossible task. It is, however, possible to say something about the kind of person he must have been. Moreover, unless we are to think that Luke was acting alone, it is reasonable to think that he was associated with a community that may be described as Christian, anti-priestly, and pro-Roman. It would be a community that regretted the Christian break with Judaism but blamed the Jews for it. It would be a community that appreciated its past and perhaps regretted that the happy beginning in Jerusalem and in the precincts of the temple did not continue on into the present. But it would be a community that saw its devotion to Christ as opposed to any supposed claims of a Jewish priesthood. It would be a community that believed that the destruction of the city of Jerusalem and its temple was not only a punishment for the death of Jesus and not only a fulfillment of his apocalyptic words. These cataclysmic events also constituted God's rejection of the wicked priests, who had not submitted to the demands of God and his Son and had made of the temple a den of thieves. Above all, it would be a community that saw its own future as one associated with Gentiles rather than Jews. This community, and Luke himself, probably saw in the events of 70 C.E. a symbol for the church's own future. To Luke the historic tie between the church and Judaism had become as dead as the temple and Jerusalem, "until the times of the Gentiles are fulfilled" (Luke 21:24). In 70 C.E. the Romans demonstrated that the future belonged to Gentiles, and Luke, likewise, saw something similar for the church. As the Lukan Paul said in his last words in Acts, "Let it be known to you then that this salvation of God has been sent to the Gentiles; they will listen" (28:28). It is no accident that Paul delivers these words in Rome.

NOTE

1. Luke 22:20, accepted in the United Bible Societies' *Greek New Testament,* 3rd ed., points toward a concept of vicarious suffering or possibly substitutionary atonement. The textually difficult verse Acts 20:28 seems to suggest that the church was established through blood, but Luke has little of such language.

BIBLIOGRAPHY

Arndt, W. F., and F. W. Gingrich. *A Greek-English Lexicon of the New Testament.* 2nd ed. Chicago: University of Chicago Press, 1979.

Auerbach, Erich. *Mimesis: The Representation of Reality in Western Literature.* Translated by Willard R. Trask. Princeton: Princeton University Press, 1953.

Bachmann, Michael. *Jerusalem und der Tempel: Die geographisch-theologischen Elementen in der lukanischen Sicht des jüdischen Kultzentrums.* Stuttgart: W. Kohlhammer, 1980.

Bailey, Kenneth E. *Poet and Peasant and Through Peasant Eyes.* Grand Rapids: Eerdmans, 1976, 1980.

Baltzer, K. "The Meaning of the Temple in the Lukan Writings." *Harvard Theological Review* 58 (1965): 263–77.

Bammel, Ernst, ed. *The Trial of Jesus.* Naperville, Ill.: Allenson, 1970.

Barrett, C. K. *Luke the Historian in Recent Study.* London: Epworth Press, 1961.

Beardslee, William. *Literary Criticism of the New Testament.* Philadelphia: Fortress Press, 1970.

Beardsley, Monroe C. "Textual Meaning and Authorial Meaning." *Genre* 1 (1968): 169–81.

Bilezikian, Gilbert G. *The Liberated Gospel: A Comparison of the Gospel of Mark and Greek Tragedy.* Grand Rapids: Baker Book House, 1977.

Booth, Wayne C. *The Rhetoric of Fiction.* Chicago: University of Chicago Press, 1961.

Boucher, Madeleine. *The Mysterious Parable: A Literary Study.* Washington: Catholic Biblical Association, 1977.

Bowker, John. *Jesus and the Pharisees.* Cambridge: Cambridge University Press, 1973.

Brandon, S. G. F. *The Trial of Jesus of Nazareth.* New York: Stein and Day, 1968.

Brodie, L.T. "A New Temple and a New Law." *Journal for the Study of the New Testament* 5 (1979): 21–45.

Brown, Raymond E. *The Birth of the Messiah: A Commentary on the Infancy Narratives in Matthew and Luke.* Garden City, N.Y.: Doubleday, 1977.

Brown, Schuyler. *Apostasy and Perseverance in the Theology of Luke.* Rome: Pontifical Biblical Institute, 1969.

Buchanan, George W. "Has the Griesbach Hypothesis Been Falsified?" *Journal of Biblical Literature* 93 (1974): 550–72.

Büchele, Anton. *Der Tod Jesu im Lukasevangelium: Eine redaktionsgeschichtliche Untersuchung zu Lk 23.* Frankfurt am Main: Josef Knecht, 1978.

Bultmann, Rudolf. *The History of the Synoptic Tradition.* Translated by John Marsh. New York: Harper and Row, 1963.

173

_____. "The Gospels (Form)." Translated by R. A. Wilson. In *Twentieth Century Theology in the Making,* Vol. 1. Edited by Jaroslav Pelikan. New York: Harper and Row, 1969, pp. 86–92.

Burkill, T. A. "The Competence of the Sanhedrin." *Vigiliae christianae* 10 (1956): 80–96.

_____. "The Trial of Jesus." *Vigiliae christianae* 12 (1958): 1–18.

Butler, B. C. *The Originality of St. Matthew.* Cambridge: Cambridge University Press, 1951.

Cadbury, Henry J. *The Style and Literary Method of Luke.* Cambridge, Mass.: Harvard University Press, 1920.

_____. *The Making of Luke–Acts.* 2nd ed. London: SPCK, 1958.

Cartlidge, David R., and David L. Dungan. *Documents for the Study of the Gospels.* Philadelphia: Fortress Press, 1980.

Cassidy, R. J., and P. J. Scharper, eds. *Political Issues in Luke–Acts.* Maryknoll, N.Y.: Orbis Books, 1983.

Catchpole, David R. *The Trial of Jesus.* Leiden: E. J. Brill, 1971.

_____. "The Answer of Jesus to Caiaphas (Matt. XXVI. 64)." *New Testament Studies* 17 (1970–71): 213–26.

Cohn, Haim. *The Trial and Death of Jesus.* New York: Harper and Row, 1967.

_____. *Jewish Law in Ancient and Modern Israel.* New York: Ktav, 1971.

Conzelmann, Hans. *The Theology of St. Luke.* Translated by Geoffrey Buswell. New York: Harper and Bros., 1960.

_____. *Die Apostelgeschichte.* Tübingen: J. C. B. Mohr (Paul Siebeck), 1963.

Cook, Michael J. "Jesus and the Pharisees—The Problem as It Stands Today." *Journal of Ecumenical Studies* 15 (1978): 441–60.

_____. *Mark's Treatment of the Jewish Leaders.* Leiden: E. J. Brill, 1978.

Creed, John M. *The Gospel According to St. Luke.* London: Macmillan and Co., 1930.

Dahl, Nils A. "A People for His Name (Acts xv. 14)." *New Testament Studies* 4 (1958): 319–27.

Daiches, David. *Critical Approaches to Literature.* Englewood Cliffs, N.J.: Prentice-Hall, 1956.

Detweiler, Robert. *Story, Sign, and Self.* Philadelphia: Fortress Press, 1978.

Dewey, Joanna. *Markan Public Debate.* Chico, Calif.: Scholars Press, 1980.

Dibelius, Martin. *From Tradition to Gospel.* Translated by Bertram L. Woolf. New York: Charles Scribner's Sons, 1935.

_____. *Studies in the Acts of the Apostles.* Edited by Heinrich Greeven. Translated by M. Ling. New York: Charles Scribner's Sons, 1956.

Dodd, C. H. *History and the Gospel.* New York: Charles Scribner's Sons, 1938.

Drury, John. *Tradition and Design in Luke's Gospel.* Atlanta: John Knox Press, 1976.

Ellis, John M. *The Theory of Literary Criticism.* Berkeley: University of California Press, 1974.

Farmer, William R. *The Synoptic Problem.* 2nd ed. Macon, Ga.: Mercer University Press, 1976.

_____. "Modern Developments of Griesbach's Hypothesis." *New Testament Studies* 23 (1977): 275–95.

_____, ed. *New Synoptic Studies: The Cambridge Gospel Conference and Beyond.* Macon, Ga.: Mercer University Press, 1983.

Fish, Stanley. *Is There a Text in This Class?* Cambridge, Mass.: Harvard University Press, 1980.

Fitzmyer, Joseph A. *The Gospel According to Luke (I-IX).* Garden City, N.Y.: Doubleday, 1981.

Flender, Helmut. *St. Luke: Theologian of Redemptive History.* Translated by R. H. and Ilse Fuller. Philadelphia: Fortress Press, 1967.

Foakes-Jackson, F. J., and Kirsopp Lake. *The Acts of the Apostles.* 5 vols. Reprint. Grand Rapids: Baker Book House, 1979.

Franklin, Eric. *Christ the Lord: A Study in the Purpose and Theology of Luke–Acts.* Philadelphia: Westminster Press, 1975.

Frye, Northrop. *Anatomy of Criticism.* Princeton: Princeton University Press, 1957.

_____. *Creation and Recreation.* Toronto: University of Toronto Press, 1980.

_____. *The Great Code: The Bible and Literature.* New York: Harcourt Brace Jovanovich, 1981.

Frye, Roland M. "On the Historical-Critical Method in New Testament Studies." *Perspective* 14 (1973): 28–33.

Fuller, Reginald H., E. P. Sanders, and Thomas R. W. Longstaff. "The Synoptic Problem: After Ten Years." *Perkins Journal* 28 (1975): 63–74.

Gasque, Ward. *A History of the Criticism of the Acts of the Apostles.* Tübingen: J. C. B. Mohr, 1975.

George, Augustin. "Israel dans l'oeuvre de Luc." *Revue biblique* 75 (1968): 481–525.

Goulder, Michael D. *Type and History in Acts.* London: SPCK, 1964.

Gros Louis, K. R. R., et al., eds. *Literary Interpretations of Biblical Narratives.* 2 vols. Nashville: Abingdon Press, 1974, 1982.

Guthke, Karl. *Modern Tragicomedy.* New York: Random House, 1966.

Haaker, K. "Dibelius und Cornelius: Ein Beispiel formgeschichtlicher Überlieferungskritik." *Biblische Zeitschrift* 24 (1980): 234–51.

Hadas, Moses. *A History of Greek Literature.* New York: Columbia University Press, 1950.

_____, and Morton Smith. *Heroes and Gods.* New York: Harper and Row, 1965.

Haenchen, Ernst. "Judentum und Christentum in der Apostelgeschichte." *Zeitschrift für die neutestamentliche Wissenschaft* 54 (1963): 155–87.

_____. *Der Weg Jesu: Eine Erklärung des Markus-Evangeliums und der kanonischen Parallelen.* 2nd ed. Berlin: Walter de Gruyter, 1968.

_____. *The Acts of the Apostles: A Commentary.* Translated by Bernard Noble et al. Oxford: Basil Blackwell, 1971.

Harvey, A. E. *Jesus on Trial: A Study in the Fourth Gospel.* Atlanta: John Knox Press, 1976.

Hengel, Martin. *Acts and the History of Earliest Christianity.* Translated by John Bowden. Philadelphia: Fortress Press, 1980.

Hill, David. "The Rejection of Jesus at Nazareth." *Novum Testamentum* 13 (1971): 161–80.

Hirsch, E. D., Jr. *Validity in Interpretation.* New Haven: Yale University Press, 1967.

Hopper, Stanley R., and David L. Miller, eds. *Interpretation: The Poetry of Meaning.* New York: Harcourt, Brace and World, 1967.

Hultgren, Arland J. *Jesus and His Adversaries: The Form and Function of the Conflict Stories in the Synoptic Tradition.* Minneapolis: Augsburg Publishing House, 1979.

_____. "Interpreting the Gospel of Luke." In *Interpreting the Gospels.* Edited by James L. Mays. Philadelphia: Fortress Press, 1981, pp. 183–96.

Huntley, John. "A Practical Look at E. D. Hirsch's *Validity in Interpretation.*" *Genre* 1 (1968): 242–55.

Ingarden, Roman. *The Literary Work of Art.* Translated by George G. Grabowicz. Evanston: Northwestern University Press, 1973.

Jervell, Jacob. *Luke and the People of God.* Minneapolis: Augsburg Publishing House, 1972.

_____. *The Unknown Paul.* Minneapolis: Augsburg Publishing House, 1984.

Johnson, Luke T. *The Literary Function of Possessions in Luke–Acts.* Missoula, Mont.: Scholars Press, 1977.

Juel, Donald. *Messiah and Temple.* Missoula, Mont.: Scholars Press, 1977.

_____. *Luke–Acts: The Promise of History.* Atlanta: John Knox Press, 1983.

Kähler, Martin. *The So-Called Historical Jesus and the Historic Biblical Christ.* Translated by Carl E. Braaten. Philadelphia: Fortress Press, 1964.

Karris, Robert J. *Luke: Artist and Theologian: Luke's Passion Account as Literature.* New York: Paulist Press, 1985.

Keck, Leander E., and J. Louis Martyn, eds. *Studies in Luke–Acts.* Nashville: Abingdon Press, 1966.

Kee, Howard C. "Aretalogy and Gospel." *Journal of Biblical Literature* 92 (1973): 402–22.

Kelber, Werner H., ed. *The Passion in Mark.* Philadelphia: Fortress Press, 1976.

Kermode, Frank. *The Genesis of Secrecy: On the Interpretation of Narrative.* Cambridge, Mass.: Harvard University Press, 1979.

Kingsbury, Jack Dean. *Matthew: Structure, Christology, Kingdom.* Philadelphia: Fortress Press, 1975.

Klijn, A. F. J. "Scribes, Pharisees, Highpriests, and Elders in the New Testament." *Novum Testamentum* 3 (1959): 259–67.

Knox, John. *Marcion and the New Testament: An Essay in the Early History of the Canon.* Chicago: University of Chicago Press, 1942.

Kodell, J. "Luke's Use of *Laos,* 'People,' Especially in the Jerusalem Narrative (Lk 19:28–24:53)." *Catholic Biblical Quarterly* 31 (1969): 327–43.

Koester, Helmut. "One Jesus and Four Primitive Gospels." In *Trajectories Through Early Christianity.* Edited by James M. Robinson and Helmut Koester. Philadelphia: Fortress Press, 1971, pp. 158–204.

Krieger, Murray. *A Window to Criticism.* Princeton: Princeton University Press, 1964.

Kurz, William S. "Hellenistic Rhetoric in the Christological Proof of Luke–Acts." *Catholic Biblical Quarterly* 42 (1980): 171–95.

Linnemann, Eta. *Studien zur Passiongeschichte.* Göttingen: Vandenhoeck und Ruprecht, 1970.

Lohmeyer, Ernst. *Galiläa und Jerusalem.* Göttingen: Vandenhoeck und Ruprecht, 1936.

Maddox, Robert. *The Purpose of Luke–Acts.* Edinburgh: T. and T. Clark, 1982.

Marshall, I. Howard. *The Gospel of Luke: A Commentary on the Greek Text.* Grand Rapids: Eerdmans, 1978.

Mattill, Andrew J. "The Jesus–Paul Parallels and the Purpose of Luke–Acts: H. H. Evans Reconsidered." *Novum Testamentum* 17 (1975): 15–46.

_____. *Luke and the Last Things.* Dillsboro: Western North Carolina Press, 1979.

_____, and Mary B. Mattill. *A Classified Bibliography of Literature on the Acts of the Apostles.* Leiden: E. J. Brill, 1966.

Metzger, Bruce M. *A Textual Commentary on the Greek New Testament.* London and New York: United Bible Societies, 1971.

Minear, Paul S. *To Heal and to Reveal: The Prophetic Vocation According to Luke.* New York: Seabury Press, 1976.

Moessner, David P. *Lord of the Banquet: The Prophet Like Moses of the Lukan Travel Narrative.* University of Basel Dissertation, 1982.

_____. "Luke 9:1–50: Luke's Preview of the Journey of the Prophet Like Moses of Deuteronomy." *Journal of Biblical Literature* 102 (1983): 575–605.

Momigliano, Arnaldo. *The Development of Greek Biography.* Cambridge, Mass.: Harvard University Press, 1971.

Neyrey, Jerome H. "Jesus' Address to the Women of Jerusalem (Lk. 23:27–31)—A Prophetic Judgment Oracle." *New Testament Studies* 29 (1983): 74–86.

Oliver, H. H. "The Lucan Birth Stories and the Purpose of Luke–Acts." *New Testament Studies* 10 (1964): 202–26.

O'Neill, J. C. *The Theology of Acts in Its Historical Setting.* London: SPCK, 1961.

Orchard, Bernard. *Matthew, Luke and Mark.* Manchester, Eng.: Koinonia Press, 1976.

_____, ed. *A Synopsis of the Four Gospels in a New Translation Arranged According to the Two-Gospel Hypothesis.* Macon, Ga.: Mercer University Press, 1982.

O'Toole, Robert F. *The Christological Climax of Paul's Defense.* Rome: Biblical Institute Press, 1978.

_____. *The Unity of Luke's Theology.* Wilmington, Del.: Michael Glazier, 1984.

Patte, Daniel. *What Is Structural Exegesis?* Philadelphia: Fortress Press, 1976.

_____, and Aline Patte. *Structural Exegesis: From Theory to Practice.* Philadelphia: Fortress Press, 1978.

Perrin, Norman. "The Literary *Gattung* 'Gospel'—Some Observations." *Expository Times* 82 (1970): 4–7.

Perry, Alfred M. *The Sources of Luke's Passion-Narrative.* Chicago: University of Chicago Press, 1920.

Petersen, Norman R. *Literary Criticism for New Testament Critics.* Philadelphia: Fortress Press, 1978.

Pilgrim, W. E. *Good News to the Poor: Wealth and Poverty in Luke–Acts.* Minneapolis: Augsburg Publishing House, 1981.

Plümacher, Eckhard. *Lukas als hellenistischer Schriftsteller.* Göttingen: Vandenhoeck und Ruprecht, 1972.

Propp, Vladimir. *Morphology of the Folk Tale.* Translated by Laurence Scott. *International Journal of American Linguistics* 24 (1958), Part 3.

Rehkopf, Friedrich. *Die lukanische Sonderquelle: Ihr Umfang und Sprachgebrauch.* Tübingen: J. C. B. Mohr (Paul Siebeck), 1959.

Rese, Martin. "Neuere Lukas-Arbeiten: Bemerkungen zur gegenwärtigen Forschungslage." *Theologische Literaturzeitung* 106 (1981): 225–37.

_____. "Die Aussagen über Jesu Tod und Auferstehung in der Apostelgeschichte—ältestes Kerygma oder lukanische Theologumena?" *New Testament Studies* 30 (1984): 335–53.

Rhoads, David, and Donald Mitchie. *Mark as Story.* Philadelphia: Fortress Press, 1982.

Richard, Earl. *Acts 6:1–8:4: The Author's Method of Composition.* Missoula, Mont.: Scholars Press, 1978.

_____. "Luke—Writer, Theologian, Historian: Research and Orientation of the 1970's." *Biblical Theology Bulletin* 13 (1983): 3–15.

Richards, I. A. *Principles of Literary Criticism.* New York: Harcourt, Brace and Co., 1924.

Ricoeur, Paul. "What Is a Text?" Explanation and Interpretation." In *Mythic-Symbolic Language and Philosophical Anthropology.* Edited by David M. Rasmussen. The Hague: Martinus Nijhoff, 1971, pp. 135–50.

Riddle, Donald W. "The Occasion of Luke–Acts." *Journal of Religion* 10 (1930): 545–62.

Rivkin, Ellis. "Beth Din, Boulé, Sanhedrin: A Tragedy of Errors." *Hebrew Union College Annual* 46 (1975): 181–99.

_____. "Scribes, Pharisees, Lawyers, Hypocrites: A Study in Synonymity." *Hebrew Union College Annual* 49 (1978): 135–42.

_____. *A Hidden Revolution.* Nashville: Abingdon Press, 1978.

Robinson, B. P. "The Place of the Emmaus Story in Luke–Acts." *New Testament Studies* 30 (1984): 481–97.

Robinson, Charles A., Jr., ed. *An Anthology of Greek Drama.* 1st series. New York: Holt, Rinehart and Winston, 1949.

Robinson, William C. *Der Weg des Herrn: Studien zur Geschichte und Eschatologie im Lukas-Evangelium.* Hamburg: Herbert Reich, 1964.

Roloff, Jürgen. *Die Apostelgeschichte.* Göttingen: Vandenhoeck und Ruprecht, 1981.

Sanday, William, ed. *Studies in the Synoptic Problem.* Oxford: Clarendon Press, 1911.

Sanders, Jack T. "The Pharisees in Luke–Acts." In *The Living Text: Essays in Honor of Ernest W. Saunders.* Edited by Dennis E. Groh and Robert Jewett. Lanham, Md.: University Press of America, 1985, pp. 141–88.

Schierling, S. P., and M. J. Schierling. "The Influence of the Ancient Romances on Acts of the Apostles." *Classical Bulletin* 54 (1978): 81–88.

Schmidt, Karl Ludwig. *Der Rahmen der Geschichte Jesu.* Berlin: Trowitzsch und Sohn, 1919.

———. "Die Stellung der Evangelien in der allgemeinen Literaturgeschichte." In *Eucharisterion.* Edited by Hans Schmidt. Göttingen: Vandenhoeck und Ruprecht, 1923. Part 2, pp. 50–134.

Schneider, Gerhard. *Verleugnung, Verspottung und Verhör Jesu nach Lukas 22, 54–71.* Munich: Kösel-Verlag, 1969.

———. *Die Passion Jesu nach den drei älteren Evangelien.* Munich: Kösel Verlag, 1973.

———. *Die Apostelgeschichte.* Freiburg: Herder, 1980.

Schneider, Johannes. "Zur Analyse des lukanischen Reiseberichtes." In *Synoptische Studien: Alfred Wikenhauser zum siebzigsten Geburtstag.* Munich: Karl Zink, 1953, pp. 207–29.

Scholes, Robert, and Robert Kellogg. *The Nature of Narrative.* London: Oxford University Press, 1966.

Schonfield, Hugh J. *The Passover Plot.* New York: Bernard Geis, 1965.

Schubert, Paul. "The Structure and Significance of Luke 24." In *Neutestamentliche Studien für Rudolf Bultmann.* Edited by Walter Eltester. Berlin: Töpelmann, 1957, pp. 165–86.

Schürmann, Heinz. *Der Paschamahlbericht Lk 22, (7–14.) 15–18.* Münster: Aschendorff, 1953.

Scott, Wilbur S. *Five Approaches of Literary Criticism.* New York: Collier Books, 1962.

Shuler, Philip L. *A Genre for the Gospels: The Biographical Character of Matthew.* Philadelphia: Fortress Press, 1982.

Simon, Marcel. *St. Stephen and the Hellenists in the Primitive Church.* London: Longmans, Green and Co., 1958.

Sloyan, Gerard S. *Jesus on Trial.* Philadelphia: Fortress Press, 1973.

Streeter, B. H. *The Four Gospels: A Study of Origins.* London: Macmillan and Co., 1924.

Suggs, M. Jack. "Gospel, Genre." *Interpreter's Dictionary of the Bible.* Supplementary Volume. Nashville: Abingdon Press, 1976, pp. 370–72.

Talbert, Charles H. *Luke and the Gnostics.* Nashville: Abingdon Press, 1966.

———. *Literary Patterns, Theological Themes and the Genre of Luke–Acts.* Missoula, Mont.: Scholars Press, 1974.

———. *What Is a Gospel? The Genre of the Canonical Gospels.* Philadelphia: Fortress Press, 1977.

———, ed. *Perspectives on Luke–Acts.* Macon, Ga.: Mercer University Press, 1978.

_____. *Reading Luke: A Literary and Theological Commentary on the Third Gospel.* New York: Crossroad Books, 1982.

_____, ed. *Luke–Acts: New Perspectives from the Society of Biblical Literature Seminar.* New York: Crossroad Books, 1984.

_____, and Edgar V. McKnight, "Can the Griesbach Hypothesis Be Falsified?" *Journal of Biblical Literature* 91 (1972): 338–68.

Tannehill, Robert C. "The Mission of Jesus According to Luke IV: 16–30." In *Jesus in Nazareth.* Edited by E. Grässer et al. Berlin: Walter de Gruyter, 1972, pp. 51–75.

_____. *The Sword of His Mouth.* Philadelphia: Fortress Press, 1975.

Taylor, Vincent. *Behind the Third Gospel.* Oxford: Clarendon Press, 1926.

_____. *The Formation of the Gospel Tradition.* 2nd ed. London: Macmillan and Co., 1935.

_____. *The Passion Narrative of St. Luke.* Edited by Owen E. Evans. Cambridge: Cambridge University Press, 1972.

Tiede, David L. *Prophecy and History in Luke–Acts.* Philadelphia: Fortress Press, 1980.

Tyson, Joseph B. "The Opposition to Jesus in the Gospel of Luke," *Perspectives in Religious Studies* 5 (1978): 144–50.

_____. "Acts 6:1–7 and Dietary Regulations in Early Christianity." *Perspectives in Religious Studies* 10 (1983): 145–61.

_____. "The Jewish Public in Luke–Acts." *New Testament Studies* 30 (1984): 574–83.

_____, and Thomas R. W. Longstaff. *Synoptic Abstract.* The Computer Bible, Volume 15. Wooster, Ohio: Biblical Research Associates, 1978.

Van Unnik, W. C., "Once More St. Luke's Prologue," *Neotestamentica* 7 (1973): 7–26.

Via, Dan O., Jr. *The Parables.* Philadelphia: Fortress Press, 1967.

_____. *Kerygma and Comedy in the New Testament.* Philadelphia: Fortress Press, 1975.

Votaw, Clyde W. "The Gospels and Contemporary Biographies," *American Journal of Theology* 19 (1915): 45–73, 217–49.

Walaskay, Paul W. *'And So We Came to Rome': The Political Perspective of St. Luke.* Cambridge: Cambridge University Press, 1983.

Weinert, F. D. "The Meaning of the Temple in Luke–Acts." *Biblical Theology Bulletin* 11 (1981): 85–89.

Wellek, René. *Concepts of Criticism.* New Haven: Yale University Press, 1963.

_____, and Austin Warren. *Theory of Literature.* New York: Harcourt, Brace, and Co., 1949.

Wilckens, Ulrich. *Die Missionsreden der Apostelgeschichte.* Neukirchen kreis Moers: Neukirchener Verlag, 1961.

Wilder, Amos N. *Early Christian Rhetoric: The Language of the Gospels.* London: Student Christian Movement Press, 1964.

Wilson, S. G. *Luke and the Law.* Cambridge: Cambridge University Press, 1983.

Wimsatt, W. K., Jr., and M. C. Beardsley. "The Intentional Fallacy." In *The Verbal Icon*. Edited by W. K. Wimsatt, Jr. Lexington: University of Kentucky Press, 1954, pp. 3–18.

Winter, Paul. *On the Trial of Jesus*. Berlin: Walter de Gruyter, 1961.

Zeitlin, Solomon. *Who Crucified Jesus?* New York: Harper and Brothers, 1942.

_____. "The Political Synedrion and the Religious Synedrion." *Jewish Quarterly Review* 36 (1945): 109–40.

Ziesler, J. A. "Luke and the Pharisees." *New Testament Studies* 25 (1979): 146–57.

INDEX

MODERN AUTHORS

183

SCRIPTURE

The death of Jesus is of central importance in all four New Testament gospels. For centuries much attention and scholarship have been devoted to both the historical and theological aspects of this event. Recent years, however, have witnessed an amazing methodological proliferation in New Testament studies. New ways of studying these texts have been vigorously and actively pursued. Among the most interesting and most promising of these developments has been the application of literary-critical methods to New Testament works.

In *The Death of Jesus in Luke–Acts*, Joseph B. Tyson applies literary-critical methods to the two New Testament writings attributed to Luke. Since it is generally accepted that the Gospel of Luke and the Book of Acts were written by the same author and were intended to be read consecutively, Tyson departs from tradition and treats them as a literary whole. His focus is on the death of Jesus which is, of course, the most dramatic segment of Luke and the central event in Acts. Tyson's clear treatment of Luke's view of the growing opposition to Jesus (from both the Jewish public and the Jewish leadership) and his discussion of the circumstances that ultimately led to Jesus's crucifixion provide us a deeper understanding of these two important texts. His careful analysis of the ways in which Luke differs from Matthew and Mark helps us to recognize Luke's uniqueness as a literary chronicler of events.